LaunchPad
macmillan learning
launchpadworks.com

A Pocket Guide to Public Speaking

SIXTH EDITION

Dan O'Hair

University of Kentucky

Hannah Rubenstein

Rob Stewart

Texas Tech University

bedford/st.martin's

Macmillan Learning

Boston | New York

For Bedford/St. Martin's

Vice President, Editorial, Macmillan Learning Humanities: Edwin Hill
Senior Program Director for Communication: Erika Gutierrez
Marketing Manager: Amy Haines
Director of Content Development: Jane Knetzger
Development Editor: Will Stonefield
Senior Media Editor: Tom Kane
Assistant Editor: Kimberly Roberts
Content Project Manager: Pamela Lawson
Senior Workflow Project Supervisor: Joe Ford
Production Supervisor: Robin Besofsky
Media Project Manager: Emily Brower
Manager of Publishing Services: Andrea Cava
Project Management: Lumina Datamatics, Inc.
Composition: Lumina Datamatics, Inc.
Photo Permissions Editor: Angela Boehler
Permissions Manager: Kalina Ingham
Design Director, Content Management: Diana Blume
Text Design: Kall Design
Cover Design: William Boardman
Printing and Binding: RR Donnelley

ISBN 978-1-319-10278-4

Printed in China.

2 3 4 5 6   23 22 21 20

For *information, write:* Bedford/St. Martin's, 75 Arlington Street, Boston, MA 02116

Acknowledgments

Joe Ayres and Tim S. Hopf. "Visualization: Is It More than Extra-Attention?" From *Communication Education,* Volume 38 (1989), pp. 1–5. © National Communication Association, reprinted by permission of Taylor & Francis Ltd, www.tandfonline.com on behalf of the National Communication Association.

2017 University of Southern California Commencement Address. Reproduced with permission of Will Ferrell.

At the time of publication all Internet URLs published in this text were found to accurately link to their intended website. If you do find a broken link, please forward the information to will.stonefield@macmillan.com so that it can be corrected for the next printing.

Coverage in *A Pocket Guide to Public Speaking*, Sixth Edition, Correlated with NCA's Learning Outcomes in Communication.

Note: This table aligns with the 2018 learning outcomes of the National Communication Association (NCA).

NCA Outcome Correlation Grid	
NCA Outcome	Relevant coverage in *A Pocket Guide to Public Speaking*
LOC #1: Describe the communication discipline and its central questions	Coverage of foundational communication concepts begins in Chapter 1, with an overview of the four main categories of human communication and an exploration of the transactional model of communication. Subsequent chapters address core communication competencies, including responsible listening, ethical speech, intercultural awareness, and argument construction.
LOC #2: Employ communication theories, perspectives, principles, and concepts	The text is grounded in current communication theories and scholarship. Each chapter helps students understand and employ key scholarly concepts. These include *rhetorical situation* (Ch. 1), *oral style* (Ch. 1), *cognitive restructuring* (Ch. 3), *dialogic communication* (Ch. 4), *selective perception* (Ch. 5), *source credibility* (Ch. 10), *classical rhetorical proofs* (Ch. 23), the *elaboration likelihood model of persuasion* (Ch. 23), and *initial, derived, and terminal credibility* (Ch. 23), among many others.
LOC #3: Engage in communication inquiry	The book discusses many critical and scholarly approaches to communication, from the classical canons of rhetoric and classical proofs (Ch. 1) to modern treatments of speech anxiety (Ch. 3), development of source credibility (Chs. 4 and 29), speech organization (Chs. 11–13), and models and means of persuasion (Chs. 23–25). LaunchPad also includes a robust video assessment program that lets students comment on their own speech videos and on professional speech videos from external sources, which further helps students engage in critical inquiry.

(continued)

NCA Outcome	Relevant coverage in *A Pocket Guide to Public Speaking*
LOC #4: Create messages appropriate to the audience, purpose, and context	Chapter 4 introduces students to ethical considerations of audience, topic, and purpose. Chapter 6 explains how to tailor a speech message to an audience, including assessing such psychological and demographic factors as gender, socioeconomic status, ethnicity, culture, and group membership. Chapter 7 explains how to identify appropriate topics, and Chapter 25 offers strategies for adapting a speech to specific audience types.
LOC #5: Critically analyze messages	Chapter 9 offers advice for critically assessing speech sources and includes an extended discussion of the differences between *information, propaganda, misinformation,* and *disinformation.* In LaunchPad, the new video assessment program provides ample opportunity for critical analysis: students and instructors can pull video of speeches from anywhere on the web and then engage in conversation.
LOC #6: Demonstrate the ability to accomplish communicative goals (self-efficacy)	Chapter 3 discusses barriers that often impede communication self-efficacy and provides step-by-step guidance for overcoming those barriers, from pinpointing the onset of speech anxiety to visualizing success. In LaunchPad, new "before and after" speech videos show a speaker improving from a rough first attempt to a polished, final speech; students can watch this progression, which helps them achieve their own communication goals.
LOC #7: Apply ethical communication principles and practices	Chapter 4 enables students to reflect on and actively engage their own values when considering the role of ethics in the speechmaking process. Included are guidelines for avoiding plagiarism and using one's right to free speech responsibly. The discussion includes other core ethical concepts, such as responsibility, integrity, and respecting the audience's values.
LOC #8: Utilize communication to embrace difference	Chapter 6 explains how to speak to diverse audiences while respecting their values. The chapter includes guidelines for speaking to people from different cultures.
LOC #9: Influence public discourse	Chapter 1 discusses the potential of public speaking to promote civic engagement and influence public discourse (p. 3). Chapter 4 explains how to engage in positive public discourse while avoiding invective, slander, and outright hate speech. Chapters 23 and 24 explain how public speaking can sway listeners' opinions and change the public conversation.

How to Use the Book and Digital Resources ● ● ● ● ●

A Pocket Guide to Public Speaking, Sixth Edition, is designed to provide quick, clear answers to your questions about public speaking—whether you're in a public speaking class, in a course in your major, on the job, or in your community. Here you will find the tools you need to help you prepare and deliver a wide range of speeches and presentations.

In Parts 1 through 5 you will find chapters that cover all the steps necessary to create a speech—from planning, research, and development to organization, practice, and delivery. Part 6 includes three chapters about presentation aids and how to use them effectively. Chapters in Part 7 contain guidelines for creating three of the most commonly assigned speeches in public speaking classes: *informative, persuasive,* and *special occasion.* For specific guidelines on preparing online presentations, communicating and speaking in small groups, and speaking on the job, see Part 8. Part 9 contains advice on speaking in other college courses, from science and math to engineering, education, and nursing and allied health.

◉ Finding What You Need in the Book

TABLES OF CONTENTS. Browsing through the brief table of contents inside the front cover will usually guide you to the information you need. If not, consult the more detailed table of contents included inside the back cover.

INDEX. If you can't locate what you need in either set of contents, consult the index at the back of the book, beginning on page 307. This can be especially useful if you're looking for something specific and you know the term for it. For example, if you need to prepare a sales proposal for a business course, you could simply look under "sales proposal" (or "sales pitch") in the index and then go to the designated pages.

LISTS OF FEATURES. On pages 316–18 (just before the end of the book), you'll find a quick guide to some of the most consulted parts of this book: the *Quick Tips, Sample Speeches, Visual Guides* (illustrated explanations of key points), and *Checklists.*

SPEAKING BEYOND THE SPEECH CLASSROOM. In Part 8, "Online, Group, and Business Contexts," you'll find useful information on preparing online presentations, communicating and speaking in groups, and interacting in the workplace. In Part 9, "Speaking in Other College Courses," you'll find detailed directions for speaking in a range of college classes including courses in the social sciences, arts and humanities, education, science and mathematics, engineering and architecture, and nursing and allied health.

GLOSSARY. For definitions of key terms highlighted in the book, see pages 273–94.

Quick Speech Preparation

If you have to prepare a speech quickly (for example, giving a first speech early in the semester), consult Chapters 1–3 in *A Pocket Guide:*

- Chapter 1, "Becoming a Public Speaker," provides a brief discussion of public speaking basics.
- Chapter 2, "From A to Z: Overview of a Speech," offers quick guidance on each step in the speechmaking process, from selecting a topic to delivery.
- Chapter 3, "Managing Speech Anxiety," provides techniques that will help you overcome any fears of public speaking you may have.

For more on specific types of speeches, consult Chapters 22–25 in Part 7 on informative, persuasive, and special occasion speeches, or the appropriate chapter in Part 8 or Part 9.

Other Useful Tools

CITATION GUIDELINES. Appendix A (pp. 252–65) contains guidelines for documenting sources in the following styles: *Chicago*, American Psychological Association (APA), Modern Language Association (MLA), Council of Science Editors (CSE), and Institute of Electrical and Electronics Engineers (IEEE).

TIPS FOR NON-NATIVE SPEAKERS OF ENGLISH. Appendix D (pp. 269–72) addresses the most common ESL challenges, including pronunciation of certain words and challenges in being understood.

LaunchPad
macmillan learning

launchpadworks.com

LaunchPad is an easy-to-use platform that offers digital tools to support the speechmaking process. It contains the e-book plus high-quality multimedia content and ready-made assessment options, including LearningCurve adaptive quizzing that will give you a leg up on learning key concepts and a new video assessment program that allows immediate, responsive feedback on video assignments. Your book may have come with an access card to LaunchPad at your instructor's request. If not, access can be purchased online from the URL listed above.

☑ LearningCurve

LearningCurve is an online learning tool that adapts to what you already know and helps you learn the topics that you need to practice. LearningCurve ensures that you receive as much targeted practice as you need in order to master the material.

◉ Video

LaunchPad for *A Pocket Guide to Public Speaking* provides access to more than 120 video clips from student speeches. **Video** icons appear near sample speeches, indicating that you can watch the video of the speech in LaunchPad.

New video assessment program

This new video assessment program in LaunchPad helps students and instructors record and provide immediate feedback. Students can record speeches directly into their assignment via the Macmillan Mobile Video iOS/Android apps, and instructors and peers can assess the speech live while the student is delivering it. Afterward, students can watch their video paired with feedback to help them start preparing for their next speech. Online students can live-stream a speech while the instructor and classmates give feedback in real time, providing an experience similar to delivering a live speech.

⒠ E-readings

E-readings offer additional online content, including a complete tutorial on how to create presentation aids using Microsoft PowerPoint, Prezi, and Apple Keynote.

Preface ● ● ● ●

The Sixth Edition of *A Pocket Guide to Public Speaking* reflects our continuing mission to provide students with a truly effective speech resource that is comprehensive yet brief, affordable, and student friendly, based on solid scholarship and the rhetorical tradition. We designed this guide to be useful in the widest possible range of situations, from the traditional speech classroom and courses across the curriculum, to the workplace, and in the community.

Our primary goal in writing *A Pocket Guide* has always been to meet the needs of speech instructors who find mainstream, full-size introductory speech texts either too overwhelming, too prescriptive, or too costly for their classes. We also aim to adapt to the changing realities of technology in the discipline by providing helpful guidance on online research and online presentations as well as digital options for reading and studying with *A Pocket Guide* that students can access easily on a number of devices.

A Pocket Guide to Public Speaking has been a popular choice for instructors and students since the first edition was published in 2003. More than 350,000 instructors and students across the academic spectrum—from courses in speech and the humanities to education, engineering, and business—have embraced the book, making it the most successful pocket-size speech text available. We have used their helpful feedback to create this sixth edition.

◉ Features

A Pocket Guide to Public Speaking addresses all of the topics and skills typically covered in an introductory speech text. And because the book is meant to be used throughout students' academic careers and in a wide variety of classroom settings and beyond, examples are drawn from a broad range of speech situations and disciplines. Speech excerpts, sample outlines, and full-length visually annotated sample speeches provide useful models that help students see how speech fundamentals can be applied effectively.

Throughout the text, users will find many tools to help them focus on key public speaking concepts: charts and tables that summarize salient points; *Checklists* that reinforce critical content; insightful *Quick Tips* that offer succinct and practical advice; *Visual Guides* that illustrate the steps for accomplishing challenging speech tasks; and *Appendices* that offer citation guidelines, help with question-and-answer sessions and preparing for TV and radio communication, and support for non-native speakers of English.

◉ New to This Edition

As with previous editions, we have focused this revision on what instructors say are the greatest challenges of teaching and learning public and presentational speaking. The new edition is designed to help students master basic skills while also addressing the challenges that digital technology brings to public speaking.

LaunchPad offers powerful content and exciting assessment tools.

- **LaunchPad for *A Pocket Guide to Public Speaking*, Sixth Edition, now delivers a comprehensive, easily assignable media package.** In response to feedback from instructors, this edition of LaunchPad contains the full e-book, along with new auto-scored chapter quizzes that help students master course material. LaunchPad also includes a wealth of assessment and activities—from LearningCurve adaptive quizzing to new iClicker questions—to help students overcome core public speaking challenges. LaunchPad can be purchased on its own or packaged with the text.

- **A powerful new video assessment program makes it easy for instructors and peers to provide immediate feedback.** Video can be recorded, uploaded, or streamed directly into an assignment via computer or from the Macmillan Mobile Video apps for iOS and Android devices. Instructors and classmates can provide a wealth of real-time feedback during the speech from comments, to markers, to audio and even video suggestions tagged to a specific times in the video. Additionally, rubric functionality is available for instructor, peer, and self-assessment. Students can use this feedback to improve their public speaking skills from speech to speech.

- **New video scenarios at the beginning of each Part are a fun way to preview upcoming steps in the speech making process.** The text directs students to LaunchPad to watch a sometimes humorous video scenario related to a key concept, like delivery or preparation. After watching each video in LaunchPad, students answer a series of critical thinking questions, increasing their understanding of foundational public speaking concepts. This new feature is great for discussion and helps students understand and tackle common challenges in the public speaking course.

New speeches on contemporary topics, paired with video in LaunchPad, engage students and serve as models.

- **A new informative speech,** accompanied by questions in LaunchPad, shows how student speakers can polish their organization and delivery. The speech, titled "Going Carbon Neutral on Campus," appears in Chapter 22 in the book with margin annotations explaining the speaker's effective use of rhetorical techniques. The speech also appears as a new, professionally shot video in Launch-Pad, available with electronic transcripts and closed captioning. A "needs improvement" version of the speech video is available, allowing students to see how the speaker progressed from a rough first attempt to a final speech with strong delivery.

- **A new special occasion speech by actor and comedian Will Ferrell.** Ferrell explains his own experiences with speech anxiety in a moving and inspirational address to the 2017 graduating class of the University of Southern California. The speech includes margin annotations explaining Ferrell's effective use of rhetorical devices, such as anecdotes and emotional appeals.

A wealth of new research gives students the tools they need to succeed. As in previous editions, new peer-reviewed studies focus on the common challenges that students face in the course. The sixth edition introduces new studies about audience demographics, speaking to culturally diverse audiences, and using body language to make one's speech memorable, among many others.

The new edition continues to give students the tools they need to prepare and deliver successful speeches.

- **A new visual guide on using effective body language provides speakers with best practices they can apply.** The guide reinforces key skills discussed in Chapter 18, including eye contact with the audience and effective gestures. The feature helps students put speech concepts from the text into action.

- **A new detailed table on organizational patterns maps out each pattern using the same topic.** Students and instructors say that organizational patterns are among the most difficult concepts to master. This new visual chart brings clarity and helps students confidently choose the best organizational pattern for their speech purpose.

Current examples help students engage with course material. New in-text examples include Emma Watson's powerful United Nations speech about the HeForShe gender equality campaign; and the students from Marjory Stoneman Douglas High School, who use public speaking to influence civic discourse about gun violence.

Digital and Print Formats

For more information on formats and packaging options, please visit the online catalog at **macmillanlearning.com/pocketspeak6e**.

- To get the most out of the book, package the print book with LaunchPad. This dynamic course platform includes a new video assessment program that allows custom video assignments with real-time commenting by students and instructors; LearningCurve adaptive quizzing; and exclusive e-pages that expand on key concepts from the print book, including an in-depth tutorial on creating presentations using Microsoft PowerPoint, Apple Keynote, and Prezi. LaunchPad is available packaged at a significant discount with the text. Use ISBN 978-1-319-22441-7.
- **E-books.** *A Pocket Guide to Public Speaking* is available as an e-book for use on computers, tablets, and e-readers. See **macmillanlearning.com/ebooks** to learn more.
- **Customize *A Pocket Guide to Public Speaking*** using Bedford Select for Communication. Create the ideal textbook for your course with only the chapters you need. You can rearrange chapters, delete unnecessary chapters, and add your own original content to create just the book you're looking for. With Bedford Select, students pay only for material that will be assigned in the course, and nothing more. For more information, visit **macmillanlearning.com/selectcomm**.
- **Macmillan Learning Student Store.** You want to give your students affordable rental, packaging, and e-book options. So do we. Learn more at **store.macmillanlearning.com**.

Student Resources

For more information on student resources or to learn about package options, please visit the Macmillan online catalog at **macmillanlearning.com/pocketspeak6e**.

- *The Essential Guides.* These brief yet comprehensive and affordable print booklets focus on a range of topics and are designed to supplement a main text in a public speaking course. These guides are available to be packaged with *A Pocket Guide to Public Speaking,* Sixth Edition, for a very low price. Versions include *The Essential Guide to Rhetoric,* Second Edition, by Christian O. Lundberg and William M. Keith; *The Essential Guide to Presentation Software*, Second Edition, by Allison Joy Bailey and Rob Patterson; *The Essential Guide to Interpersonal Communication,* Third Edition, by Steven McCornack and Kelly Morrison; *The Essential Guide to Group Communication,* Third Edition, by Dan O'Hair, Mary O. Wiemann, and Andrea M. Davis; and *The Essential Guide to Intercultural Communication* by Jennifer Willis-Rivera.

Instructor Resources

For more information or to download instructor resources, please visit the online catalog at **macmillanlearning.com/pocketspeak6e**. The Instructor's Manual and Test Bank are also available in LaunchPad for *A Pocket Guide to Public Speaking*, Sixth Edition.

- ***Instructor's Resource Manual.*** The online instructor's manual was prepared by Karin Becker, *University of North Dakota*; Paula Baldwin, *George Mason University*; Elaine Wittenberg-Lyles, *University of North Texas*; and Melinda M. Villagran, *George Mason University*. This comprehensive manual offers useful guidance for new and experienced instructors, and outlines and activities for every chapter in the main text. The Instructor's Resource Manual has been updated with new guidance on online instruction and using the video assessment program in LaunchPad.

- ***Computerized Test Bank.*** The Computerized Test Bank was prepared by Diana Rehling, *St. Cloud State University*; Paula K. Baldwin, *George Mason University*; Elaine Wittenberg-Lyles, *University of North Texas*; and Merry Buchanan, *University of Central Oklahoma*. The Computerized Test Bank contains more than 1500 true/false, multiple-choice, fill-in-the-blank, and essay/short answer questions that have been carefully crafted to test students' specific knowledge of the text. The questions appear in easy-to-use software that allows instructors to add, edit, resequence, and print questions and answers. Instructors can also export the questions into a variety of course management systems. The Computerized Test Bank can be downloaded from the Instructor Resources tab of the book's catalog page, andthe content is loaded into LaunchPad.

- ***Lecture Slides.*** These downloadable presentation slides have been revised and redesigned for the sixth edition and are ready to use in your public speaking classroom. Each chapter has a set of slides that include key terms, key concepts, figures, and charts from the chapter. The slides can be downloaded from the Instructor Resources tab of the book's catalog page, and the content is loaded into LaunchPad.

- *iClicker Questions.* If you use iClicker in your classroom, don't miss the brand-new suite of iClicker questions for *A Pocket Guide to Public Speaking,* Sixth Edition. These questions test students' knowledge of foundational concepts in each chapter, making it easy for you to assess your students' understanding and progress. The questions come preloaded into LaunchPad.

- *Communication in the Classroom: A Collection of G.I.F.T.S.* This new resource was prepared by John S. Seiter, Jennifer Peeples, and Matthew L. Sanders of *Utah State University,* who have collected over 100 powerful ideas for classroom activities. Many activities are designed specifically for the public speaking course, and all activities have been submitted by real instructors who have tested and perfected them in real classrooms. Each activity includes a detailed explanation and debrief, drawing on the instructors' experiences.

- *ESL Students in the Public Speaking Classroom: A Guide for Instructors,* **Second Edition.** This resource was prepared by Robbin D. Crabtree, *Loyola Marymount University;* and David Alan Sapp, *Fairfield University.* The guide addresses specific challenges ESL students may experience in the public speaking course and offers instructors valuable advice for helping students overcome obstacles.

- *Coordinating the Communication Course: A Guidebook.* This resource was written by leading scholars and course coordinators Deanna Fassett, *San José State University;* and John T. Warren, late of *Southern Illinois University Carbondale.* The guidebook offers practical advice on every topic central to the course coordinator role. Starting with establishing a clear program vision, the text continues on with thoughtful guidance, tips, and best practices on crucial topics like creating continuity across multiple sections, orchestrating meaningful assessment, hiring and training instructors, and advocating for promotion, and for the course and program itself.

- **The Macmillan Learning Communication COMMunity** is our new online space for instructor development and engagement. Find such resources to support your teaching as class activities, video assignments, and invitations to conferences and webinars. Connect with our team, our authors, and other instructors through online discussions and blog posts at **community.macmillan .com/community/communication**.

◉ Acknowledgments

We would like to thank all our colleagues at Bedford/St. Martin's: Vice President of Editorial for the Humanities Edwin Hill, Senior Program Director for Communication Erika Gutierrez, Senior Development Manager Susan McLaughlin, Marketing Manager Amy Haines, Senior Workflow Project Supervisor Joe Ford, hardworking and careful Content Project Manager Pamela Lawson, Production Supervisor Robin Besofsky, lightning-quick and helpful Assistant Editor Kimberly Roberts, and Senior Media Editor Tom Kane—we are truly grateful for your knowledge, creativity, expertise, and hard work throughout this process. We are especially grateful to Development Editor Will Stonefield for his enthusiastic, thoughtful developmental editing and tireless stewarding of this text through every stage of this revision and to market.

Thanks to all the instructors who participated in reviews for the sixth edition: Monique Bourdage, *Finlandia University*; Ayanna Bridges, *Metropolitan Community College Maple Woods*; Constance Hudspeth, *Seminole State College of Florida*; Carlton Hughes, *Southeast Kentucky Community and Technical College*; Melissa Johnson, *Valencia College*; James McNamara, *Alverno College*; Elizabeth Monske, *Northern Michigan University*; Emily Paramonova, *Pierce College*; Todd Parker, *California State University, Northridge*; Shawn Queeney, *Bucks County Community College*; Nicolas Rangel, *Houston Community College*; Ann Reading, *Thaddeus Stevens College of Technology*; Michelle Rush, *Ivy Tech Community College Valparaiso Campus*; Kevin Rushing, *Valencia College*; Meagan Sovine, *Houston Community College*; Summer Wagner, *Golden West College*; Elyse Warford-Spearman, *Pierce College*; Eric Warner, *College of Central Florida*; Crystal Whitaker, *Howard Community College*; and Andrew Winckles, *Adrian College*.

part

(1)

Getting
Started

VIDEO ACTIVITY
Go to LaunchPad to watch students Melissa and Cecily talk about the importance of the public speaking course. Visit **launchpadworks.com**

LaunchPad includes:

☑ **LearningCurve** adaptive quizzing

▶ A curated collection of video clips and full-length speeches

Additional resources, such as presentation software tutorials and documentation help.

CHAPTER 1 ●●●●

Becoming a Public Speaker

The ability to speak confidently and convincingly in front of others is a crucial skill for anyone who wants to take an active role in life. This pocket guide offers the tools you need to create and deliver effective speeches, from presentations to fellow students to speeches delivered in virtually any setting—including those presented online. Here you will find the basic components of any good speech and acquire the skills to deliver presentations in a variety of specialized contexts—from the college classroom to the civic, business, and professional arenas. You'll also find proven techniques to build your confidence by overcoming the anxiety associated with public speaking.

◉ Gain a Vital Life Skill

Public speaking provides a sense of empowerment and satisfaction rarely found elsewhere. More than ever, it has become both a vital life skill and a potent weapon in career development. Business magnate Warren Buffett passionately extols the role that public speaking has played in his success:

> Be sure to do it, whether you like it or not . . . do it until you get comfortable with it. . . . Public speaking is an asset that will last you 50 or 60 years, and it's a necessary skill; and if you don't like doing it, that will also last you 50 or 60 years. . . . Once you tackle the fear and master the skill, you can run the world. You can walk into rooms, command people, and get them to listen to you and your great ideas.[1]

Advance Your Professional Goals

Skill in public speaking will give you an unmistakable edge professionally. Employers of new college graduates consistently reveal that ability in oral and written communication is among the most important skills they look for in new

SKILLS EMPLOYERS RATE AS MOST IMPORTANT

1. Ability to work in a team
2. Problem-solving skills
3. Communication skills (written)
4. Strong work ethic
5. **Communication skills (verbal)**
6. Leadership
7. Initiative
8. Analytical/quantitative skills
9. Flexibility/adaptability
10. Detail-oriented
11. Interpersonal skills (relates well to others)
12. Technical skills

Source: National Association of Colleges and Employers, *Job Outlook 2017*, **www.naceweb.org/about-us/press/2017/ employers-seek-teamwork-problem-solving-skills-on-resumes/**

hires—more so even than leadership, quantitative, technical, or interpersonal skills. Survey after survey confirms the value of skill in oral communication, making the public speaking course potentially the most valuable one you can take during your undergraduate career.

Enhance Your Career as a Student

Preparing speeches calls upon numerous skills that you will need in other college courses. As in the speech class, many courses also require that you research and write about topics, analyze audiences, outline and organize ideas, and support claims. These and other skill sets covered in this pocket guide, including working with presentation media and controlling voice and body during delivery, are valuable in any course that includes an oral-presentation component, from English composition to engineering. Guidelines for speaking across the curriculum—including speaking in science and mathematics, technical, social science, arts and humanities, education, nursing and allied health, and business courses—are the focus of Part 9.

Find New Opportunities for Civic Engagement

Public speaking also offers you ways to enter the public conversation about social concerns and become a more engaged citizen. Public speaking gives you a voice that can be heard and can be counted.

Climate change, immigration reform, gun violence—such large civic issues require our considered judgment and action. Yet today too many of us leave it up to politicians, journalists, and other "experts" to make decisions about critical issues such as these. Voter turnout in the United States is much lower than in most established democracies, with only about 50 percent of young persons ages 18–29 voting in the 2016 presidential election.[2] This same age group barely shows up at the polls at all for congressional, state, and local elections. When we as citizens speak up in sufficient numbers, democracy functions better and change that truly reflects the will of the people occurs. For example, the students who survived the 2018 school shooting in Parkland, Florida, have emerged as powerful voices in favor of gun control. Speaking passionately at rallies and in public forums, the Parkland students have made a real impact on civic discourse: they helped pressure state lawmakers into passing new restrictions on gun purchases.

As you study public speaking, you will have the opportunity to research topics that are meaningful to you, consider alternate viewpoints, and choose a course of action.[3] You will learn to distinguish between argument that advances constructive goals and uncivil speech that serves merely to inflame and demean others. You will learn, in short, the "rules of engagement" for effective public discourse.[4] As you do, you will gain confidence in your ability to join your voice with others in pursuit of issues you care about.

The Classical Roots of Public Speaking

Originally, the practice of giving speeches was known as **rhetoric** or **oratory**. Rhetoric flourished in the Greek city-state of Athens in the fifth century B.C.E. and referred to making effective speeches, particularly those of a persuasive nature.

Athens was the site of the world's first direct democracy, and public speaking was the vehicle that allowed it to succeed. Meeting in a public square called the **agora**, Athenians routinely spoke with great skill on the issues of public policy; and their belief that citizenship demands active participation in public affairs endures in modern democracies to this day.

Greek, and later Roman, teachers divided the process of preparing a speech into five parts—*invention, arrangement, style, memory,* and *delivery*—called the **canons of rhetoric**. These parts correspond to the order in which these teachers believed a speech should be put together.

- *Invention* refers to discovering the types of evidence and arguments you will use to make your case (see Chapter 24).
- *Arrangement* is organizing the evidence and arguments in ways best suited to the topic and audience (see Chapter 12).

- *Style* is the way the speaker uses language to express the speech ideas (see Chapter 15).
- *Memory* is the practice of the speech until it can be delivered artfully (see Chapter 16).
- *Delivery* is the vocal and nonverbal behavior you use when speaking (see Chapters 17 and 18).

Although founding scholars such as the great Greek rhetorician Aristotle (384–322 B.C.E.) and the Roman statesman and orator Cicero (106–43 B.C.E.) surely did not anticipate the ever-present PowerPoint or Prezi slideshow that accompanies contemporary speeches, the speechmaking structure they bequeathed to us as the canons of rhetoric remains remarkably intact. Often identified by terms other than the original, these canons nonetheless continue to be taught in current books on public speaking, including this pocket guide.

QUICK TIP

Voice Your Ideas in a Public Forum

The Greeks called it the *agora;* the Romans, the *forum.* Today, the term **public forum** denotes a variety of venues for the discussion of issues of public interest, including traditional physical spaces such as town halls as well as virtual forums streamed to listeners online. Participation in any of these forums offers an excellent opportunity to pose questions and deliver brief comments, thereby providing you with exposure to an audience and building confidence. To find a forum in your area, check with your school or local town government, or online at the National Issues Forums Institute (**www.nifi.org**).

Learning to Speak in Public

None of us is born knowing how to deliver a successful speech. Rather, public speaking is an acquired skill that improves with practice. It is also a skill that shares many features with other familiar activities, such as conversing and writing, and it can be much less daunting when you realize that you can draw on expertise you already have.

Draw on Conversational Skills

In several respects, planning and delivering a speech resembles engaging in a particularly important conversation. When speaking with a friend, you automatically check to make certain you are understood and adjust your meaning accordingly. You also discuss issues that are appropriate to the circumstances. When a stranger is involved, however, you try to get to know his or her interests and attitudes before revealing any strong opinions. These instinctive adjustments to *audience*, *topic*, and *occasion* represent critical steps in creating a speech. Although public speaking requires more planning, both the conversationalist and the public speaker try to uncover the audience's interests and needs before speaking.

Draw on Skills in Composition

Preparing a speech also has much in common with writing. Both depend on having a focused sense of who the audience is.[5] Both speaking and writing often require that you research a topic, offer credible evidence, employ effective transitions, and devise persuasive appeals. The principles of organizing a speech parallel those of organizing an essay, including offering a compelling introduction, a clear thesis statement, supporting ideas, and a thoughtful conclusion.

Develop an Effective Oral Style

Although public speaking has much in common with everyday conversation and with writing, a speech is a unique form of communication characterized by an oral style of language. Language as used in a speech is simpler, more rhythmic, more repetitious, and more interactive than either conversation or writing.[6] Effective speakers use familiar words, easy-to-follow sentences, and frequent repetition to emphasize ideas and help listeners follow along.

Language in a speech also is often more interactive and inclusive of the audience than written language. Audience members want to know what the speaker thinks and feels and that he or she recognizes them and relates the message to them. Speakers accomplish this by making specific references to themselves and to the audience. Yet in contrast to conversation, in order to develop an effective oral style you must practice the words you will say and the way you will say them.

Effective public speakers, engaging conversationalists, and compelling writers share an important quality: They keep their focus on offering something of value to their audience.

Demonstrate Respect for Difference

Every audience member wants to feel that the speaker has his or her particular needs and interests at heart, and to feel recognized and included in the message. To create this sense of inclusion, a public speaker must be able to address diverse audiences with sensitivity, demonstrating respect for differences in culture and identity. Striving for inclusion and adopting an audience-centered perspective will bring you closer to the goal of every public speaker—establishing a genuine connection with the audience.

Public Speaking as a Form of Communication

Public speaking is one of four categories of human communication: dyadic, small group, mass, and public speaking.

- **Dyadic communication** happens between two people, as in a conversation.
- **Small group communication** involves a small number of people who can see and speak directly with one another.
- **Mass communication** occurs between a speaker and a large audience of unknown people who usually are not present with the speaker, or who are part of such an immense crowd that there can be little or no interaction between speaker and listener.
- In **public speaking**, a speaker delivers a message with a specific purpose to an audience of people who are present during the delivery of the speech. Public speaking always includes a speaker who has a reason for speaking, an audience that gives the speaker its attention, and a message that is meant to accomplish a specific purpose. Public speakers address audiences largely without interruption and take responsibility for the words and ideas being expressed.

Public Speaking as an Interactive Communication Process

In any communication event, several elements are present. These include the source, the receiver, the message, the channel, and shared meaning (see Figure 1.1).

The **source**, or sender, creates a message. Creating, organizing, and producing the message is called **encoding**—the process of converting thoughts into words. The recipient of the source's message is the **receiver**, or audience; interpreting the message is called **decoding**. Audience members decode the meaning of the message selectively, based on their own experiences and attitudes.

Feedback, the audience's response to a message, can be conveyed both verbally and nonverbally. The **message** is the content of the communication process: thoughts and ideas put into meaningful expressions, expressed verbally and nonverbally.

The medium through which the speaker sends a message is the **channel**. If a speaker delivers a message in front of a live audience, the channel is the air through which sound waves travel. Among other channels are phones, televisions, and the internet. **Noise** is any interference with the message. Noise can disrupt the communication process through physical sounds such as cell phones ringing and people talking or

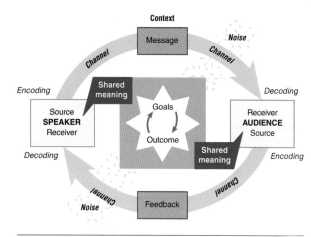

FIGURE 1.1 The Communication Process

texting, through psychological distractions such as heated emotions, or through environmental interference such as a too-cold room or the presence of unexpected people.

Shared meaning is the mutual understanding of a message between speaker and audience. The lowest level of shared meaning exists when the speaker has merely caught the audience's attention. As the message develops, a higher degree of shared meaning is possible. Thus listener and speaker together truly make a speech a speech—they "co-create" its meaning.

Two other factors are critical to consider when preparing and delivering a speech—context and goals. *Context* includes anything that influences the speaker, the audience, or the occasion—and thus, ultimately, the speech. In classroom speeches, the context would include (among other things) the physical setting, the order and timing of speeches, and the cultural orientations of audience members. Part of the context of any speech is the situation that created the need for the speech in the first place. All speeches are delivered in response to a specific **rhetorical situation**, or a circumstance calling for a public response.[7] Is the speech in response to a recent event affecting the audience? Bearing the rhetorical situation in mind ensures that you maintain an **audience-centered perspective**—that is, that you keep the needs, values, attitudes, and wants of your listeners firmly in focus.

A final prerequisite for any effective speech is a clearly defined **specific speech purpose** or goal—what you want the audience to learn or do as a result of the speech. Establishing a specific speech purpose early on will help you proceed through speech preparation and delivery with a clear focus in mind (see pp. 51–52).

CHAPTER 2

From A to Z: Overview of a Speech

Public speaking is an applied art, and every speaking opportunity, including that provided by the classroom, offers you valuable hands-on experience. To help you get started quickly, this chapter previews the steps involved in putting together any speech or presentation. Subsequent chapters expand on these steps. Figure 2.1 illustrates the process of preparing for a speech.

◎ Analyze the Audience

The first step in preparing any speech is to consider the audience—how their interests, needs, and opinions will influence their responses toward a given topic, speaker, and occasion. *Audience analysis* is a process of learning about audience members' attributes and motivations using tools such as interviews and questionnaires (see Chapter 6). For a brief first speech, however, especially one delivered in the classroom, start with your own powers of observation. Consider some simple demographic characteristics: ratio of males to females, age ranges, and apparent cultural and socioeconomic backgrounds. Take these characteristics into account as you select a topic and draft the speech, focusing on ways you can relate it meaningfully to this particular audience.

◎ Select a Topic

Unless the topic is assigned, the next step is to decide what you want to speak about. First, consider the speech occasion and reason for speaking. What topics will be suitable to your audience's needs and wants in these circumstances? Using

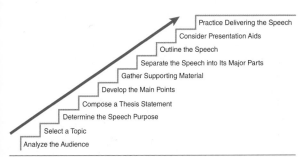

FIGURE 2.1 Steps in the Speechmaking Process

these parameters, let your interests and expertise guide you in selecting something to speak about (see Chapter 7 on selecting a topic and purpose).

◉ Determine the Speech Purpose

A speech without a purpose is like a car without fuel—it won't get you anywhere. Actually, a speech requires that you fix *two* purposes in your mind. First, for any given topic, you should direct your speech toward one of three general speech purposes—to *inform*, to *persuade*, or to *mark a special occasion*. Thus you need to decide whether your goal is simply to give your audience information about the topic, to persuade them to accept one position to the exclusion of other positions, or to help them memorialize an occasion such as a wedding, a funeral, or an awards event.

You should also mentally formulate a specific speech purpose—a statement of what you want the audience to learn, agree with, or perhaps act upon as a result of your speech. For example, if your general purpose is to inform, your specific purpose might be "to inform my audience about how self-driving cars will impact insurance policies." If your general purpose is to persuade, the specific purpose might be "to persuade my audience that they should support tighter regulations on insuring self-driving vehicles."

◉ Compose a Thesis Statement

Next, compose a thesis statement that clearly expresses the central idea of your speech. While the specific purpose focuses your attention on the outcome you want to achieve with the speech, the thesis statement concisely identifies, in a single sentence, what the speech is about:

General Purpose:	To inform
Specific Purpose:	To inform my audience about three critical steps we can take to combat identity theft
Thesis Statement:	The best ways to combat identity theft are to review your monthly financial statements, periodically check your credit report, and secure your personal information in both digital and print form.

From this point forward in the development of your speech, refer to the thesis statement often to make sure that you are on track to illustrate or prove it.

QUICK TIP

Speak with Purpose

To ensure that the audience learns or does what you want them to as a result of your speech, keep your thesis and speech goals in sight. Write your thesis statement and general and specific speech purposes on a sticky note and place it on the edge of your computer screen. It will be an important guide in developing your speech.

◉ Develop the Main Points

Organize your speech around two or three main points. These are the primary pieces of knowledge (in an informative speech) or the key claims (in a persuasive speech). If you create a clear thesis for your speech, the main points will be easily identifiable.

Thesis: The best ways to combat identity theft are to review your monthly financial statements, periodically check your credit report, and secure your personal information in both digital and print form.

    I. Review your monthly bank statements, credit card bills, and similar financial records to be aware of all transactions.

    II. Check your consumer credit report at least twice a year.

    III. Keep your personal identifying digital and print information highly secure.

◉ Gather Supporting Materials

Use supporting material to illustrate or prove your main points. Supporting material potentially includes the entire world of information available to you—from personal experiences to every conceivable kind of credible source. Plan to research your topic to provide evidence for your assertions and lend credibility to your message (see Chapter 9).

◉ Arrange the Speech into Its Major Parts

Every speech will have an introduction, a body, and a conclusion. Develop each part separately, then bring them together using transition statements (see Chapter 11). The

---

DEVELOPING SPEECH PARTS

Introduction
- Pique the audience's interest with a quotation, short story, example, or other means of gaining their attention described in Chapter 14.
- Introduce yourself and your topic.
- Preview the thesis and main points.

(Use a transition statement to signal the start of the speech body.)

Body
- Develop the main points and illustrate each one with relevant supporting material.
- Organize your ideas and evidence in a structure that suits the topic, audience, and occasion.

(Use transitions to move between main points and to the conclusion.)

Conclusion
- Review the thesis and reiterate how the main points confirm it.
- Leave the audience with something to think about.

---

introduction serves to draw the audience's interest to the topic, speaker, and thesis. The speech body contains the speech's main points and subpoints. The conclusion restates the speech thesis and reiterates how the main points confirm it (see Chapter 14 on the introduction and conclusion).

◉ Outline the Speech

An outline is a plan for arranging the elements of your speech in support of your thesis. Outlines are based on the principle of coordination and subordination—the logical placement of ideas relative to their importance to one another. Coordinate points are of equal importance and are indicated by their parallel alignment. Subordinate points are given less weight than the points they support and are placed to the right of them. (For a full discussion of outlining, see Chapter 13.)

Coordinate Points	I. Main Point 1
	II. Main Point 2
	A. Subpoint 1
	B. Subpoint 2

Subordinate
Points

I. Main Point 1
 A. First level of subordination
  1. Second level of subordination
  2. Second level of subordination
   a. Third level of subordination
   b. Third level of subordination

As your speeches become more detailed, you will need to select an appropriate **organizational pattern** (see Chapters 12 and 24). You will also need to familiarize yourself with developing both working and speaking outlines (see Chapter 13). To allow for the full development of your ideas, a working outline generally contains points stated in close-to-complete sentences. A speaking outline is far briefer and uses either short phrases or key words.

◎ Consider Presentation Aids

As you prepare your speech, consider whether using visual, audio, or a combination of different presentation aids will help the audience understand points. (See Chapters 19–21.)

◎ Practice Delivering the Speech

Preparation and practice are necessary for the success of even your first speech in class. You will want to feel and appear natural to your listeners, an effect best achieved by rehearsing both the verbal and nonverbal **delivery** of your speech (see Chapters 17 and 18). So practice your speech at least six times. For a four- to six-minute speech, that's only about one-half hour of actual practice time.

QUICK TIP

Be Aware of Your Nonverbal Delivery

Audiences are highly attuned to a speaker's facial expressions, gestures, and general body movement. As you rehearse, practice smiling and otherwise animating your face in ways that feel natural to you. Audiences want to feel that you care about what you are saying, so avoid a dead-pan, or blank, expression. Make eye contact with your practice audience. Doing so will make audience members feel that you recognize and respect them. Practice gestures that feel natural to you, steering clear of exaggerated movements.

CHAPTER 3

Managing Speech Anxiety

Contrary to what most of us think, feeling nervous about giving a speech is not only normal but desirable. Channeled properly, nervousness (or more specifically, the adrenaline that accompanies it) can actually boost performance. The key is knowing how to make this state work *for* rather than *against* us. This chapter introduces specific anxiety-reducing techniques that speakers use to minimize their tension and maximize their speaking experience.

> I focus on the information rather than being graded. I also practice my speech a ton to really make sure I do not speak too quickly. I time myself so that I can develop an average time. This makes me more confident [in dealing] with time requirements. And, because I know that I am well prepared, I really try to just relax.
>
> —*Kristen Obracay, student*

◉ Identify What Makes You Anxious

Anxiety is a state of uneasiness brought on by uncertainty and fear about the outcome of an event. Lacking positive public-speaking experience, feeling different from members of the audience, or feeling uneasy about being the center of attention—each of these factors can lead to the onset of **public-speaking anxiety** (PSA), a situation-specific social anxiety that arises from anticipating giving an oral presentation.[1] Fortunately, we can learn techniques to tame this anxiety in each of these situations and make it work for us. An important first step is to identify what makes us anxious.

Lack of Positive Experience

If you are new to public speaking or have had unpleasant experiences, anxiety about what to expect is only natural. Without positive experiences to draw on, it's hard to put this anxiety into perspective. It's a bit of a vicious circle. Some people react by deciding to avoid speeches altogether, yet gaining more experience is key to overcoming speech anxiety.

Feeling Different

The prospect of being in front of an audience makes many of us extra-sensitive to our perceived personal shortcomings, such as a less-than-perfect haircut or an accent. We may believe that no one could be interested in anything we have to say.

As inexperienced speakers, we become anxious because we assume that being different somehow means being inferior. Actually, each of us is different from everyone else.

However, nearly everyone experiences nervousness about giving a speech.

> I control my anxiety by mentally viewing myself as being 100 percent equal to my classmates.
>
> —*Lee Morris, student*

Being the Center of Attention

Certain audience behaviors—such as chatting with a neighbor or checking text messages—can cause us as speakers to think we've lost the audience's attention by doing something wrong; we wonder about our mistakes and whether others noticed these supposed flaws. Left unchecked, this kind of thinking can distract us from the speech itself, with all our attention now focused on "me." Our self-consciousness makes us feel even more conspicuous and sensitive to even the smallest faults, which increases our anxiety! Actually, an audience rarely notices anything about us that we don't want to reveal.

> It's always scary to speak in front of others, but you just have to remember that everyone is human. . . . Nobody wants you to fail; they're not waiting on you to mess up.
>
> —*Mary Parrish, student*

◉ Pinpoint the Onset of Anxiety

Different people become anxious at different times during the speechmaking process.[2] Depending on when anxiety strikes, the consequences can include everything from procrastination to poor speech performance. But by pinpointing the onset of speech anxiety, you can manage it promptly with specific anxiety-reducing techniques.

Pre-Preparation Anxiety

Some people feel anxious the minute they know they will be giving a speech. **Pre-preparation anxiety** can be a problem when we delay planning for the speech, or when it so preoccupies us that we miss vital information needed to fulfill the speech assignment. If this form of anxiety affects you, start very early using the stress-reducing techniques described later in this chapter.

Preparation Anxiety

For a few people, anxiety arises only when they actually begin to prepare for the speech. These individuals might feel overwhelmed by the time and planning required or hit a roadblock that puts them behind schedule. Preparation pressures produce a cycle of stress, procrastination, and outright avoidance, all of which contribute to **preparation anxiety**. If you find yourself feeling anxious during this stage, immerse yourself in the speech's preparation but calm your nerves by taking short, relaxing breaks to regain your confidence and focus.

Pre-Performance Anxiety

Some people experience anxiety as they rehearse their speech. This is when the reality of the situation sets in: They worry that the audience will be watching and listening only to them, feel that their ideas aren't expressed ideally, or sense that time is short. If this **pre-performance anxiety** is strong enough, some may even decide to stop rehearsing. If you experience heightened anxiety at this point, practice **positive self-talk**, turning negative thoughts to positive ones (see "Modify Thought and Attitudes" below).

> I experience anxiety before, during, and after the speech. My "before speech" anxiety begins the night before my speech, but then I begin to look over my notecards, and I start to realize that I am ready for this speech. I practice one more time and I tell myself I am going to be fine.
>
> —*Paige Mease, student*

Performance Anxiety

For most people, anxiety is highest just as a speech begins.[3] **Performance anxiety** usually is most pronounced during the introduction of the speech when we are most aware of the audience's attention. Audiences we perceive as negative usually cause us to feel more anxious than those we sense are positive or neutral.[4] But experienced speakers agree that by controlling their nervousness during the introduction, the rest of the speech goes quite smoothly.

Regardless of when anxiety about a speech strikes, the important thing to remember is that you can manage the anxiety and not let it manage you—by harming your motivation or by causing you to avoid investing the time and energy required to deliver a successful speech.

◉ Use Proven Strategies to Build Your Confidence

A number of proven strategies exist to help you rein in your fears about public speaking, from positive self-talk and visualization to various relaxation techniques. The first step in taming speech anxiety is to have a thorough plan for each presentation.

Prepare and Practice

If you know your material and have adequately rehearsed your delivery, you're far more likely to feel confident. Once you have prepared the speech, be sure to rehearse it several times.

> Knowing your material is crucial! The worst anxiety comes when you feel unprepared. You just can't help but be nervous, at least a little. If you are confident about what you're speaking, the anxiety fades and you'll feel more comfortable.
>
> —*Shea Michelle Allen, student*

Modify Thoughts and Attitudes

Negative thoughts about speechmaking increase speech anxiety, but positive thoughts reduce it.[5] A positive attitude actually results in lowered heart rate and reduced anxiety during the delivery of the speech.[6] As you prepare for and deliver your speech, envision it as a valuable, worthwhile, and challenging activity. Use these steps to challenge negative beliefs and encourage positive self-talk:

1. Identify your negative self-talk.
2. Examine the beliefs underlying the negative thoughts.
3. Replace negative self-talk and beliefs with positive statements and mental images.
4. Continue practicing these steps until you feel confident about your speech.

QUICK TIP

Envision Your Speech as a Conversation

Rather than thinking of your speech as a formal performance where you will be judged and critiqued, try thinking of it as a kind of ordinary conversation. In this way, you will feel less threatened and more relaxed about the process. Here's what Virgin airlines founder and entrepreneur Richard Branson recommends:

> Close your mind to the fact that you're on a stage with hundreds of people watching you and instead imagine yourself in a situation where you'd be comfortable speaking to a group . . . in your dining room at home, telling a story to friends over dinner. . . . This trick has certainly removed some of the anxiety for me.[7]
>
> —*Richard Branson, entrepreneur*

Visualize Success

Visualization—the practice of summoning feelings and actions consistent with successful performance—is a highly effective method of reducing speech anxiety.[8]

Like positive self-talk, visualization is a form of **cognitive restructuring**—training your mind to think in a more positive way about something that makes you anxious. It requires you to close your eyes and visualize a series of positive feelings and actions that will occur on the day of your speech.

⚓ **LaunchPad**   Visit LaunchPad to listen to an audio file that guides you through a series of techniques that encourage self-confidence through positive visualization. Go to launchpadworks.com

> Close your eyes and allow your body to get comfortable in the chair in which you are sitting. Take a deep, comfortable breath and hold it . . . now slowly release it through your nose. Now take another deep breath and make certain that you are breathing from the diaphragm . . . hold it . . . now slowly release it and note how you feel while doing this. Now one more deep breath . . . hold it . . . and release it slowly . . . and begin your normal breathing pattern.
>
> Now begin to visualize the beginning of a day in which you are going to give an informative speech. See yourself getting up in the morning, full of energy, full of confidence, looking forward to the day's challenges. As you dress, think about how the clothes you choose make you look and feel good about yourself. As you are drive, ride, or walk to the speech setting, note how clear and confident you feel. You feel thoroughly prepared for the topic you will be presenting today.
>
> Now you see yourself standing or sitting in the room where you will present your speech, talking very comfortably and confidently with others in the room. The people to whom you will be presenting your speech appear to be quite friendly and are very cordial in their greetings and conversations prior to the presentation. You feel absolutely sure of your material and of your ability to present the information in a forceful, convincing, positive manner.
>
> Now you see yourself approaching the area from which you will present. You are feeling very good about this presentation and see yourself move eagerly forward. All of your audiovisual materials are well organized, well planned, and clearly aid your presentation.[9]

◉ Activate the Relaxation Response

Before, during, and sometimes after a speech you may experience rapid heart rate and breathing, dry mouth, faintness, freezing-up, or other uncomfortable sensations. These physiological reactions result from the **"fight-or-flight" response**—the body's automatic response to threatening or fear-inducing events. Research shows that you can counteract these sensations by activating a *relaxation response*[10] using techniques such as meditation and controlled breathing.

Briefly Meditate

You can calm yourself considerably before a presentation with this brief meditation exercise:

1. Sit comfortably in a quiet space.
2. Relax your muscles, moving from neck to shoulders to arms to back to legs.
3. Choose a word, phrase, or prayer (e.g., "*Namaste*," "*Om*," "Hail Mary, full of grace"). Breathe slowly and say it until you become calm (about ten to twenty minutes).

QUICK TIP

Stretch Away Stress

You can significantly lessen pre-speech jitters by stretching. A half-hour to one-hour session of whole-body stretches and simple yoga poses, combined with deep breathing, will help discharge nervous energy and sharpen mental focus.

Use Stress-Control Breathing

When you feel stressed, the center of your breathing tends to move from the abdomen to the upper chest, leaving you with a reduced supply of air. The chest and shoulders rise, and you feel out of breath. *Stress-control breathing* gives you more movement in the stomach than in the chest.[11] Try it in two stages.

STAGE ONE   Inhale air and let your abdomen go out. Exhale air and let your abdomen go in. Do this for a while until you get into the rhythm of it.

STAGE TWO   As you inhale, use a soothing word such as *calm* or *relax*, or use a personal mantra like this: "Inhale *calm*, abdomen out, exhale *calm*, abdomen in." Go slowly, taking about three to five seconds with each inhalation and exhalation.

Begin stress-control breathing *several days* before a speech. Then, once the occasion arrives, perform it while awaiting your turn at the podium and just before you start your speech.

> I have two ways to cope with my nervousness before I'm about to speak. I take a couple of deep breaths from my

stomach; I breathe in through my nose and out through my mouth. This allows more oxygen to the brain so you can think clearly. I also calm myself down by saying, "Everything will be okay, and the world is not going to crumble before me if I mess up."

—*Jenna Sanford, student*

◎ Use Movement to Minimize Anxiety

During delivery, you can use controlled movements with your hands and body to release nervousness (see Chapter 18):

- Practice natural gestures, such as holding up your index finger when stating your first main point. Think about what you want to say as you do this, instead of thinking about how you look or feel.
- Move as you speak. You don't have to stand perfectly still behind the podium when you deliver a speech. Walk around as you make some of your points. Movement relieves tension and helps hold the audience's attention.

QUICK TIP

Enjoy the Occasion

Most people ultimately find that giving speeches can indeed be fun. It's satisfying and empowering to influence people, and a good speech is a sure way to do this. Think of giving a speech in this way, and chances are you will find much pleasure in it.

◎ Learn from Feedback

Speech evaluations help to identify ways to improve what you do. You can learn a lot through self-evaluation, but self-perceptions can be distorted,[12] so objective evaluations by others often are more helpful. Ultimately, all speakers rely on audience feedback to evaluate the effectiveness of their speeches.

✓ CHECKLIST

Steps in Gaining Confidence

- ❑ Prepare and practice, early and often.
- ❑ Modify thoughts and attitudes—practice positive self-talk.
- ❑ Practice visualization.
- ❑ Use stress-control breathing, meditation, and other relaxation techniques.
- ❑ Incorporate natural, controlled movements.
- ❑ Learn from the experience of public speaking and enjoy it.

CHAPTER 4

Ethical Public Speaking

When we have an audience's attention, we are in the unusual position of being able to influence or persuade listeners and, at times, to move them to act—for better or worse. With this power to affect the minds and hearts of others comes *responsibility*—"a moral obligation to behave correctly towards or in respect of a person or thing."[1] Taking responsibility for your words lies at the heart of being an ethical speaker.

Ethics is the study of moral conduct. Applied to public speaking, **communication ethics** addresses our responsibilities when seeking influence over other people and for which there are positive and negative, or "right" and "wrong," choices of action.[2] For example, should you show a gory photograph without warning to convince audience members to support animal rights? Should you bother to check the credibility of a suspect source before offering it to the audience? Is it ethical to present only one side of an argument?

◉ Demonstrate Competence and Character

Ethics is derived from the Greek word **ethos**, meaning "character." As Aristotle first noted, the foremost duty speakers have toward their audience is to demonstrate *positive ethos*, or good character. Speakers in ancient Greece were regarded positively when they displayed the "virtues" of *competence*, *good moral character*, and *goodwill*. Today, surprisingly little has changed. Modern research on source credibility (a contemporary term for ethos) reveals that people place their greatest trust in speakers who

- Have a solid grasp of the subject (Aristotle's *competence*).
- Are honest and straightforward (*good moral character*).
- Are genuinely respectful of and interested in the welfare of their listeners[3] (*goodwill*).

◉ Respect Your Listeners' Values

Our sense of ethics, of right and wrong actions, is reflected in our **values**—our most enduring judgments or standards of what's good and bad in life and of what's important to us. Values shape how we see the world and form the basis on which we judge the actions of others.[4]

Because values are so central to who we are, consideration of the audience's values is an important aspect of preparing an ethical speech. No member of an audience wants his or her values attacked, treated without respect, or even merely unacknowledged. Yet conflicting values lie at the heart of many controversies that today's public speakers might address, making it difficult to speak about certain topics without challenging cherished beliefs. The United States is a country of immigrants, for example, but a sizable minority (34 percent) of the population views newcomers as a threat to American customs and values. Attitudes vary considerably by age—68 percent of young adults ages 18–29 believe immigrants strengthen the country—and by education, race, religion, and other variables.[5] As you plan speeches on controversial topics, anticipate that audience members will hold a range of values that will differ not only from your own, but from each other's. Audience analysis is key to discovering and planning for these differences (see Chapter 6).

Contribute to Positive Public Discourse

An important measure of ethical speaking is whether it contributes something positive to **public discourse**—speech involving issues of importance to the larger community, such as race relations or immigration reform.

Perhaps the most important contribution you can make to public debates of this nature is the advancement of constructive goals. An ethical speech appeals to the greater good rather than to narrow self-interest. It steers clear of **invective**, or verbal attacks, designed to discredit and belittle those with whom you disagree. Ethical speakers avoid arguments that target a person instead of the issue at hand (*ad hominem* attack) or that are built upon other fallacies of reasoning (see Chapter 23).

Use Your Rights of Free Speech Responsibly

The United States vigorously protects **free speech**—defined as the right to be free from unreasonable constraints on expression[6]—thereby assuring protection both to speakers who treat the truth with respect and to those whose words are inflammatory and offensive. But while offensive speech is often legally protected under the **First Amendment**, racist, sexist, or ageist slurs, gay-bashing, and other forms of negative or hate speech clearly are unethical. **Hate speech** is any offensive communication—verbal or nonverbal—directed against people's race, ethnicity, national origin, gender, religion, sexual orientation, disability, and the like.

Be aware that even under the First Amendment, certain types of speech are not only unethical but actually illegal:

- Speech that incites people to imminent violence, or so-called **"fighting words."**
- Speech that expresses blackmail, perjury, child pornography, or obscenity.[7]
- Speech that can be proved to be defamatory or potentially harmful to an individual's reputation at work or in the community, called **slander.**

If you are talking about public figures or matters of public concern, you will not be legally liable for defamation unless it can be shown that you spoke with a **reckless disregard for the truth**—that is, if you knew that what you were saying was false but said it anyway. If your comments refer to private persons, it will be easier for them to assert a claim against you. You will have the burden of proving that what you said was true.

QUICK TIP

Beware the Heckler's Veto

Drowning out a speaker's message with which you disagree—called a **heckler's veto**—demonstrates disrespect both to the speaker and to fellow listeners. It robs audience members of the ability to make up their own minds about an issue and silences the free expression of ideas. Tolerance for opposing viewpoints is a necessary ingredient of an ethical—and democratic—society. How is your school community doing on this score?

◉ Observe Ethical Ground Rules

Ethical speech rests on a foundation of dignity and integrity. **Dignity** refers to bearing and conduct that is respectful to self and others. **Integrity** signals the speaker's incorruptibility—that he or she will avoid compromising the truth for the sake of personal expediency.[8] Speaking ethically also requires that we adhere to certain moral ground rules, or "pillars of character," including being *trustworthy, respectful, responsible, fair,* and *civic-minded.*[9]

Be Trustworthy

Trustworthiness is a combination of honesty and dependability. Speakers demonstrate their trustworthiness by supporting their points truthfully and by not presenting misleading or false information.

Demonstrate Respect

Speakers demonstrate **respect** by treating audience members with civility and courtesy.[10] Respectful speakers address listeners as unique human beings and avoid **ethnocentrism** and **stereotyping** (see Chapter 15). They refrain from any form of personal attack, and focus on issues rather than on personalities.

Make Responsible Speech Choices

Responsibility means being accountable for what you say. Ask yourself: Will learning about my topic in some way benefit my listeners? Do I use sound evidence and reasoning? (See Chapter 24.) Do I make emotional appeals because they are appropriate, rather than to shore up otherwise weak arguments? (See Chapter 23.)

Demonstrate Fairness

Fairness refers to making a genuine effort to see all sides of an issue and acknowledging the information listeners need in order to make informed decisions.[11] Bear in mind that most subjects are complicated and multifaceted; rarely is there only one right or wrong way to view a topic.

Be Civic-Minded

Being **civic-minded** means caring about your community, as expressed in your speeches and your deeds. At the broadest level, being civic-minded is essential to the democratic process because democracy depends on our participation.

◎ Avoid Plagiarism

Crediting sources is a crucial aspect of any speech. **Plagiarism**—the use of other people's ideas or words without acknowledging the source—is unethical. You are obviously plagiarizing when you simply "cut and paste" material from sources into your speech and represent as your own. But it is also plagiarism to copy material into your speech draft from a source (such as a magazine article or website) and then change and rearrange words and sentence structure here and there to make it appear as if it were your own.

Orally Acknowledge Your Sources

The rule for avoiding plagiarism as a public speaker is straightforward: *Any source that requires credit in written form should be acknowledged in oral form.* These sources include direct quotations, as well as paraphrased and summarized information—any facts and statistics, ideas, opinions, or theories gathered and reported by others (see Chapter 10). More than any other single action, acknowledging sources lets listeners know you are trustworthy and will represent both fact and opinion fairly and responsibly.

Citing Quotations, Paraphrases, and Summaries

When citing other people's ideas, you can present them in one of three ways:

- **Direct quotations** are verbatim—or word for word— presentations of statements made by someone else. Direct quotes should always be acknowledged in a speech.
- A **paraphrase** is a restatement of someone else's ideas, opinions, or theories in the speaker's own words. Because paraphrases alter the *form* but not the *substance* of another person's ideas, you must acknowledge the original source.
- A **summary** is a brief overview of someone else's ideas, opinions, or theories. While a paraphrase contains approximately the same number of words as the original source material stated in the speaker's own words, a summary condenses the same material, distilling only its essence.

Note how a speaker could paraphrase and summarize, *with credit*, the following excerpt from an article published in the *New Yorker* titled "Strange Fruit: The Rise and Fall of Açaí," by John Colapinto.

Original Version:	Açai was virtually unknown outside Brazil until 10 years ago, when Ryan and Jeremy Black, two brothers from Southern California, and their friend Edmund Nichols began exporting it to the United States. Since then, the fruit has followed a cycle of popularity befitting a teenage pop singer: a Miley Cyrus–like trajectory from obscurity to hype, critical backlash, and eventual ubiquity. Embraced as a "superfruit"—a potent combination of cholesterol-reducing fats and anti-aging antioxidants—açai became one of the fastest-growing foods in history. . . ."

Compare the original version of the excerpt to how it could be properly quoted, paraphrased, or summarized in a speech. Oral citation language is bolded for easy identification.

Direct Quotation:	**As John Colapinto states in an article titled "Strange Fruit: The Rise and Fall of Açai," published in the May 30, 2011, issue of the *New Yorker*,** "The fruit has followed a cycle of popularity befitting a teenage pop singer: a Miley Cyrus–like trajectory from obscurity to hype, critical backlash, and eventual ubiquity."
Oral Paraphrase:	**In an article titled "Strange Fruit: The Rise and Fall of Açai," published in the May 30, 2011, issue of the *New Yorker*, John Colapinto explains that** until two brothers from Southern California named Ryan and Jeremy Black, along with their friend Edmund Nichols, began exporting açai to the United States ten years ago, it was unknown here. Now, says Colapinto, açai is seen as a "superfruit" that can help with everything from lowering cholesterol to fighting aging through its antioxidant properties.
Oral Summary:	**In an article titled "Strange Fruit: The Rise and Fall of Açai," published in the May 30, 2011, issue of the *New Yorker*, John Colapinto says that** açai, a fruit grown in Brazil that was unknown in this country until ten years ago, is now marketed as a "superfruit" that has powerful health benefits.

For detailed directions on crediting sources in your speech, see Chapter 10, "Citing Sources in Your Speech."

✔ CHECKLIST

Correctly Quote, Paraphrase, and Summarize Information

- ❑ If *directly* quoting a source, repeat the source word for word and acknowledge whose words you are using.
- ❑ If *paraphrasing* someone else's ideas, restate the ideas in your own words and acknowledge the source.
- ❑ If *summarizing* someone else's ideas, briefly describe their essence and acknowledge the source.

Fair Use, Copyright, and Ethical Speaking

Copyright is a legal protection afforded the creators of original literary and artistic works.[12] When including copyrighted materials in your speeches—such as reproductions of graphs or photographs, a video or sound clip—you must determine when and if you need permission to use such works.

When a work is copyrighted, you may not reproduce, distribute, or display it without the permission of the copyright holder. For any work created from 1978 to the present, a copyright is good during the author's lifetime plus fifty years. After that, unless extended, the work falls into the **public domain**, which means anyone may reproduce it. Not subject to copyright are federal (but *not* state or local) government publications, common knowledge, and select other categories.

An exception to the prohibitions of copyright is the doctrine of fair use, which permits the limited use of copyrighted works without permission for the purposes of scholarship, criticism, comment, news reporting, teaching, or research.[13] This means that when preparing speeches for the classroom, you have much more latitude to use other people's creative work without seeking permission, but *with* credit in all cases, including display of the copyright symbol (©) on any copyrighted handouts or presentation aids you include in your speech. (For more information, see **www.copyright.gov**.)

Creative Commons is an organization that allows creators of works to decide how they want other people to use their copyrighted works. It offers creators six types of licenses, three of which are perhaps most relevant to students in the classroom: *attribution* (lets you use the work if you give credit the way the author requests); *noncommercial* (lets you use the work for *noncommercial purposes* only); and *no derivative works* (lets you use only verbatim—exact—versions of the work).

The rules of fair use apply equally to works licensed under Creative Commons and the laws of copyright. Student speakers may search the Creative Commons website for suitable materials for their speech at **creativecommons.org**.

CHAPTER 5

Listeners and Speakers

Imagine giving a speech that no one heard. Merely considering such a circumstance points to the central role of the listener in a speech. In fact, all successful communication is two-way, including that of public speaking.

Connecting with a speaker takes effort and commitment. We can bring our full attention and critical faculties to bear on the speech event, tune out, or automatically reject the message. For the speaker, connecting with audience members also entails work, requiring that we learn about, or listen to, their concerns—by analyzing the audience before delivering the speech (see Chapter 6) and by being responsive to listeners during it. Thus it is listener and speaker together who truly make a speech possible.

◉ Recognize the Centrality of Listening

More than any other single communication act, we listen—to *gain understanding,* to *evaluate and act on information*, and to *provide support*.[1] Many of us assume that these and other listening acts come naturally, but listening is an intentional act. While **hearing** is the physiological, largely involuntary process of perceiving sound, **listening** is the conscious act of receiving, constructing meaning from, and responding to spoken and nonverbal messages.[2] Listening involves consciously *selecting* what you will listen to, *giving it your attention, processing* and *understanding* it, *remembering* the information, and *responding* to it—either verbally, nonverbally, or through both channels.[3]

QUICK TIP

Succeed by Listening

College students in the United States spend more time listening (about 24 percent) than they do on any other communication activity, such as speaking (20 percent), using the internet (13 percent), writing (9 percent), or reading (8 percent).[4] Listening is also the number one activity employees do during the work day.[5] Managers overwhelmingly associate listening skills with competence, efficiency, and leadership potential, and they promote employees who display those skills and hire new entrants who possess them.[6] In both college and work arenas, skill in listening leads to success.

Recognize That We Listen Selectively

In any given situation, no two audience members will process the information in exactly the same way. The reason lies in **selective perception**—people pay attention selectively to certain messages while ignoring others.[7] Two major factors influence what we listen to and what we ignore:

1. We pay attention to what we hold to be important.
2. We pay attention to information that touches our beliefs and expectations and we ignore, downplay, or even belittle messages that contradict them.

To a certain extent, selective perception is simple human nature, but both as listener and speaker, there are steps you can take to counter it.

- As a *listener*, evaluate the speaker's message without prejudgment and avoid screening out parts of the message that don't immediately align with your views.
- As a *speaker*, give the audience good reasons to care about your message. Demonstrate the topic's relevance to them, and anticipate and address audience attitudes and beliefs.

Anticipate Obstacles to Listening

Selective perception is hardly our only obstacle to listening. Numerous distractions keep us from listening in a way that is focused and purposeful. In any listening situation, including that of listening to speeches, try to identify and overcome common obstacles, whether stemming from the environment or our own behavior.

Minimize External and Internal Distractions

A **listening distraction** is anything that competes for the attention we are trying to give to something else. *External distractions* can originate outside of us, in the environment, while *internal distractions* arise from our own thoughts and feelings.

External listening distractions, such as the din of jackhammers or competing conversations, can significantly interfere with our ability to listen, so try to anticipate and plan for them. If you struggle to see or hear over noise or at a distance, arrive early and sit in the front. To reduce internal listening distractions, avoid daydreaming, be well rested, monitor yourself for lapses in attention, and consciously focus on listening.

✓ CHECKLIST

Dealing with Distractions While Delivering a Speech

❑ *Problem:* Passing distractions (chatting, entry of latecomers)
Solution: Pause until distraction recedes

❑ *Problem:* Ongoing noise (construction)
Solution: Raise speaking volume

❑ *Problem:* Sudden distraction (collapsing chair, falling object)
Solution: Minimize response and proceed

❑ *Problem:* Audience interruption (raised hand, prolonged comment)
Solution: Acknowledge audience reaction and either follow up or defer response to conclusion of speech

---

Refrain from Multitasking

You cannot actively listen well while multitasking. Activities such as checking a cell phone or calendar, finishing an assignment, or responding to a text divert our attention from the message and reduce our ability to interpret it accurately.

Guard against Scriptwriting and Defensive Listening

When we, as listeners, engage in *scriptwriting*, we focus on what we, rather than the speaker, will say next.[8] Similarly, people who engage in **defensive listening** decide either that they won't like what the speaker is going to say or that they know better. Remind yourself that effective listening precedes effective rebuttal. Try waiting for the speaker to finish before devising your own arguments.

Beware of Laziness and Overconfidence

Laziness and overconfidence can manifest themselves in several ways: We may expect too little from speakers, ignore important information, or display an arrogant attitude. Later, we discover we missed important information.

Work to Overcome Cultural Barriers

Differences in dialects or accents, nonverbal cues, word choices, and even physical appearance can serve as barriers to listening, but they need not if you keep your focus on the message rather than the messenger. Refrain from judging a speaker on the basis of his or her accent, appearance, or demeanor; focus instead on what is actually being said. Whenever possible, reveal your needs to him or her by asking questions.

QUICK TIP

Listening Styles and Cultural Differences

Research suggests a link between our listening styles and a culture's predominant communication style.[9] A study of young adults in the United States, Germany, and Israel found distinct listening style preferences that mirrored key value preferences, or preferred states of being, of each culture. Germans tended toward action-oriented listening, Israelis displayed a content-oriented style, and Americans exhibited both people- and time-oriented styles. While preliminary in nature and not valid as a means of stereotyping a given culture's group behavior, these findings confirm the cultural component of all forms of communication, including listening. They also point to the need to focus on intercultural understanding as you learn about your audience.

◉ Practice Active Listening

Active listening—listening that is focused and purposeful—is a skill you can cultivate. Setting listening goals, listening for main ideas, watching for nonverbal cues (see Chapter 18), and using critical thinking strategies will help you become a more adept listener.

Set Listening Goals

Determine ahead of time what you need and expect from the listening situation.

1. **Identify your listening needs:** "I must know my classmate's central idea, purpose in speaking, main points, and organizational pattern in order to complete a required written evaluation."

2. **Identify why listening will help you:** "I will get a better grade on the evaluation if I am able to identify and evaluate the major components of Sara's speech."

3. **Make an action statement (goal):** "I will minimize distractions, practice the active listening steps during the speech, take notes, and ask questions about anything I do not understand."

4. **Assess goal achievement:** "I did identify the components of the speech I decided to focus upon and wrote about them in class."

Listen for Main Ideas

To ensure that you retain the speaker's key points, try these strategies:

- Listen for introductions, transitions, and conclusions to alert you to the main points. Most speakers preview their main points in the introduction. Transitions often alert you to an upcoming point. Conclusions often recap main points.
- Take notes on the speaker's main points. Several different methods of note taking—bullet, column, and outline—can be helpful.

QUICK TIP

Listen Responsibly

As listeners, we are ethically bound to refrain from disruptive and intimidating tactics—such as heckling, name-calling, interrupting out of turn, and other breaches of civility—as a means of silencing those with whom we disagree. The ability to dissent is a hallmark of a free society, but to preserve that freedom, we must refrain from using disruptive and intimidating tactics in place of civil dialogue.

◉ Strive for the Open and Respectful Exchange of Ideas

In contrast to *monologue*, in which we try merely to impose what we think on another person or group of people, **dialogic communication** is the open sharing of ideas in an atmosphere of respect.[10] True dialogue encourages both listener and speaker to reach conclusions together. For listeners, this means maintaining an open mind and listening with empathy.[11] For the speaker, this means approaching a speech not as an argument that must be "won," but as an opportunity to achieve understanding with audience members.

◉ Evaluate Evidence and Reasoning

Purposeful, focused listening and **critical thinking**—the ability to evaluate claims on the basis of well-supported reasons—go hand in hand. As you listen to speeches, use your critical faculties to do the following:

- *Evaluate the speaker's evidence.* Is it accurate? Are the sources credible and can they be located?
- *Analyze the speaker's assumptions and biases.* What lies behind the assertions? Does the evidence support them?
- *Assess the speaker's reasoning.* Does it betray faulty logic? Does it rely on fallacies in reasoning? (See pp. 185–187.)
- *Consider multiple perspectives.* Is there another way to view the argument? How do other viewpoints compare with the speaker's?
- *Summarize and assess the relevant facts and evidence.* If the speaker asks for action (as in some persuasive speeches; see Chapter 23), decide how you will act on the basis of the evidence rather than acting just to "go along" with what other people do.

◉ Offer Constructive and Compassionate Feedback

Follow these guidelines when evaluating the speeches of others:

- *Be honest and fair in your evaluation of the speech.* Assess the speech as a whole and remain open to ideas and beliefs that differ from your own.
- *Adjust to the speaker's style.* Each of us has a unique communication style, a way of presenting ourselves through a mix of verbal and nonverbal signals. Don't judge the content of a speaker's message by his or her style.
- *Be compassionate in your criticism.* Always start by saying something positive, and focus on the speech, not the speaker.
- *Be selective in your criticism.* Make specific rather than global statements. Rather than statements such as, "I just couldn't get into your topic," give the speaker something he or she can learn from: "I wanted more on why the housing market is falling. . . ."

part

②

Development

VIDEO ACTIVITY
Go to LaunchPad to watch a video
in which an unfortunate professor fails
to analyze his audience. Visit
launchpadworks.com

LaunchPad includes:

✓ **LearningCurve** adaptive quizzing

▶ A curated collection of video clips and
full-length speeches

Additional resources, such as presentation
software tutorials and documentation help.

CHAPTER 6 ●●●●

Analyzing the Audience

Advertisers are shrewd analysts of people's needs and wants,
extensively researching our buying habits and lifestyle choices
to identify what motivates us. To engage your listeners and
sustain their involvement in your message, you too must
investigate your audience. **Audience analysis** is the process
of gathering and analyzing information about audience
members' attributes and motivations with the explicit aim of
preparing your speech in ways that will be meaningful to
them. This is the single most important aspect of preparing
for any speech.

Taking the measure of the audience is critical because
audience members, and people in general, tend to evaluate
information in terms of their own—rather than the speaker's—
point of view, at least until they are convinced to take a second
look.[1] You may want listeners to share your enthusiasm about
an issue, but unless you know something about their perspectives on the topic, you won't be able to appeal to them effectively. Thus, assuming an **audience-centered perspective**
throughout the speech preparation process—from selection
and treatment of the speech topic to making decisions about
how you will organize, word, and deliver it—will help you
prepare a presentation that your audience will want to hear.

◉ Adapt to Audience Psychology: Who Are Your Listeners?

To analyze an audience, speakers investigate both psychological and demographic factors. **Psychographics** focuses on
the audience's attitudes, beliefs, and values—their *feelings
and opinions,* including those related to the topic, speaker,
and occasion. (See p. 40 for *demographics*—the statistical

characteristics of an audience, such as age, ethnic or cultural background, and socioeconomic status.)

Attitudes, beliefs, and values, while intertwined, reflect distinct mental states that reveal a great deal about us. **Attitudes** are our general evaluations of people, ideas, objects, or events.[2] To evaluate something is to judge it as relatively good or bad, desirable or undesirable. People generally act in accordance with their attitudes (although the degree to which they do so depends on many factors).[3]

Attitudes are based on **beliefs**—the ways in which people perceive reality.[4] Beliefs are our feelings about what is true or real. The less faith listeners have that something exists—a UFO, for instance—the less open they are to hearing about it.

Both attitudes and beliefs are shaped by *values*—our most enduring judgments about what's good in life, as shaped by our culture and our unique experiences within it. We feel our values strongly and strive to realize them.

As a rule, audience members are more interested in and pay greater attention to topics toward which they have positive attitudes and that are in keeping with their values and beliefs. The less we know about something, the more indifferent we tend to be. It is easier (though not simple) to spark interest in an indifferent audience than it is to turn negative attitudes around.

"If the Value Fits, Use It"

Evoking some combination of the audience's values, attitudes, and beliefs in the speeches you deliver will make them more personally relevant and motivating. Many advocacy groups recognize the power of appealing to their constituents' values. For example, the Biodiversity Project, an organization that helps environmental groups raise public awareness, counsels speakers to appeal directly to the three foremost values their audience members hold about the environment (discovered in nationally representative surveys commissioned by the Project), offering the following as an example:

> You care about your family's health (value #1 as identified in survey) and you feel a responsibility to protect your loved ones' quality of life (value #2). The local wetland provides a sanctuary to many plants and animals. It helps clean our air and water and provides a space of beauty and serenity (value #3). All of this is about to be destroyed by irresponsible development.[5]

Gauge Listeners' Feelings toward the Topic

Consideration of the audience's attitudes (and beliefs and values) about a topic is key to offering a speech that will resonate with them. Is your topic one with which the audience is familiar, or is it new to them? Do listeners hold positive, negative, or neutral attitudes toward the topic? Once you have this information (using tools such as interviews and surveys; see pages 45 and 65), adjust the speech accordingly (see also the table on p. 39 for additional strategies for appealing to different audiences).

If the topic is *new* to listeners,

- Start by showing why the topic is relevant to them.
- Relate the topic to familiar issues and ideas about which they already hold positive attitudes.

If listeners know *relatively little* about the topic,

- Stick to the basics and include background information.
- Steer clear of jargon, and define unclear terms.
- Repeat important points, summarizing information often.

If listeners are *negatively disposed* toward the topic,

- Focus on establishing rapport and credibility.
- Don't directly challenge listeners' attitudes; instead begin with areas of agreement.
- Discover why they have a negative bias in order to tactfully introduce the other side of the argument.
- Offer solid evidence from sources they are likely to accept.
- Give good reasons for developing a positive attitude toward the topic.[6]

If listeners hold *positive attitudes* toward the topic,

- Stimulate the audience to feel even more strongly by emphasizing the side of the argument with which they already agree.
- Tell stories with vivid language that reinforce listeners' attitudes.[7]

If listeners are a *captive audience* (see p. 39),

- Motivate listeners to pay attention by stressing what is most relevant to them.
- Pay close attention to the length of your speech.

Gauge Listeners' Feelings toward You as the Speaker

How audience members feel about you will also have significant bearing on their responsiveness to the message. A speaker who is well liked can gain an initial hearing even when listeners are unsure what to expect from the message itself.

To create positive audience attitudes toward you, first display the characteristics of speaker credibility (*ethos*) described in Chapter 4. Listeners have a natural desire to identify with the speaker and to feel that he or she shares their perceptions,[8] so establish a feeling of commonality, or **identification**,

✓ CHECKLIST

Appeal to Audience Attitudes, Beliefs, and Values

Have you . . .

❏ Investigated audience members' attitudes, beliefs, and values toward your topic?

❏ Assessed the audience's level of knowledge about the topic?

❏ Considered strategies to address positive, negative, and neutral responses to your speech topic?

❏ Considered appealing directly to audience members' attitudes and values in your speech?

with them. Use eye contact and body movements to include the audience in your message. Share a personal story, emphasize a shared role, and otherwise stress mutual bonds. Word your speech with inclusive language such as the personal pronouns *we*, *you*, *I*, and *me* (see p. 120).

Gauge Listeners' Feelings toward the Occasion

Depending on the circumstances calling for the speech (the rhetorical situation), people will bring different sets of expectations and emotions to it. Members of a **captive audience**, who are required to hear the speaker, may be less positively disposed to the occasion than those of a **voluntary audience** who attend of their own free will. Whether planning a wedding toast or a business presentation, failure to anticipate and adjust for the audience's expectations risks alienating them.

QUICK TIP

Rise to the Top of the Applicant Pool with Audience Analysis

Audience analysis is a potent tool when preparing for job interviews. Discover how many people will meet with you, their roles in the organization, and their areas of expertise. Research the company's background and its culture. Visit the company's website, investigate employees' LinkedIn profiles, and research news articles on the company. During the interview, use inclusive language to put the focus on the company: "*Your* product saw tremendous growth this year…." Earn the interviewers' respect by gathering key details and anticipating what they will want and need to know from you.

◉ Adapt Your Message to Audience Demographics

Demographics are the statistical characteristics of a given population. At least eight characteristics are typically considered when analyzing speech audiences: *age, ethnic and cultural background, socioeconomic status* (including *income, occupation,* and *education*), *religious and political affiliations, gender and sexual orientation,* and *group affiliations.* Any number of other traits—for example, disability or place of residence—may be important to investigate as well. Knowing where audience members fall in relation to audience demographics will help you identify your **target audience**—those individuals within the broader audience whom you are most likely to influence in the direction you seek. You may not be able to please everyone, but you should be able to establish a connection with your target audience.

Age

Each age group has its own concerns, psychological drives, and motivations. Thus being aware of the **generational identity** of your audience—such as Generation Z (those born since 2000) or Generation Y (also called Millennials, those born between 1980 and 1999)—allows you to develop points that are relevant to the experiences and interests of the widest possible cross section of your listeners. The table below lists some of the prominent characteristics of today's generations.

Generational Identity and Today's Generations	
Generation	Characteristics
Traditional 1925–1945	Respect for authority and duty, disciplined, strong sense of right and wrong
Baby Boomer 1946–1964	Idealistic, devoted to career, self-actualizing, values health and wellness
Generation X 1965–1979	Seeks work-life balance, entrepreneurial, technically savvy, flexible, questions authority figures, skeptical
Generation Y/ Millennials 1980–1999	Technically savvy, optimistic, self-confident, appreciative of diversity, entrepreneurial
Generation Z 2000–	Comfortable with the highest level of technical connectivity, naturally inclined to collaborate online, boundless faith in power of technology to make things possible[9]

Ethnic and Cultural Background

An understanding of and sensitivity to the ethnic and cultural composition of your listeners are key factors in delivering a successful (and ethical) speech. Some audience members may have a great deal in common with you. Others may be fluent in a language other than yours and must struggle to understand you. Some members of the audience may belong to a distinct **co-culture**, or social community whose perspectives and style of communicating differ significantly from yours. All will want to feel recognized by the speaker. (See pp. 43–45 for guidelines on adapting to diverse audiences.)

Socioeconomic Status

Socioeconomic status (SES) includes income, occupation, and education. Knowing roughly where an audience falls in terms of these key variables can be critical in effectively targeting your message.

INCOME   *Income* determines people's experiences on many levels, from how they are housed, clothed, and fed, to what they can afford. Beyond this, income has a ripple effect, influencing many other aspects of life. Given how pervasively income affects people's life experiences, insight into this aspect of an audience's makeup can be quite important.

OCCUPATION   In many speech situations, the *occupation* of audience members can be an important demographic characteristic to know. Occupational interests often are tied to other areas of social concern, such as politics, the economy, education, and social reform. Personal attitudes, beliefs, and goals are also closely tied to occupational standing.

EDUCATION   Level of *education* strongly influences people's perspectives and range of abilities. Higher levels of education have been linked to greater flexibility of opinions and often lead to increased lifetime earnings, better health outcomes, and greater civic engagement;[10] such factors may be important

---

QUICK TIP

Addressing On-the-Job Audiences

On the job, presentations ranging from business reports to scientific talks are typically delivered to fellow workers, colleagues, managers, clients, or others. Audiences include the *expert or insider audience, colleagues within the field,* the *lay audience,* and the *mixed audience.* For guidance on analyzing and addressing audiences in the workplace, see Chapter 29.

to consider when preparing a speech. Depending upon audience members' level of education, your speech may treat topics at a higher or lower level of sophistication, with fewer or more clarifying examples.

Religion

Beliefs, practices, and sometimes social and political views vary among religious traditions, making religion another key demographic variable. At least a dozen major religious traditions coexist in the United States.[11] Not all members of the same religious tradition will agree on all religiously based issues. Catholics disagree on birth control and divorce, Jews disagree on whether to recognize same-sex unions, and so forth. Awareness of an audience's general religious orientation can be critical when your speech touches on controversial topics with religious implications, such as capital punishment, same-sex marriage, and teaching about the origins of humankind.

Political Affiliation

As with religion, beware of making unwarranted assumptions about the sensitive issue of an audience's political values and beliefs. Some people avoid anything that smacks of politics while others enjoy a lively debate. Conservative individuals hold certain views that liberals dispute, and the chasm between far right and far left is great indeed. If your topic involves politics, you'll need to obtain background information on the audience's views.

Gender and Sexual Orientation

Distinct from the fixed physical characteristics of biological sex, **gender** is our social and psychological sense of ourselves as males or females.[12] Making assumptions about the preferences, abilities, and behaviors of your audience members based on their presumed gender or sexual orientation (e.g., their romantic preferences) can seriously undermine their receptivity to your message. To ensure that you treat issues of gender and sexual orientation evenly, use language sensitive to them (e.g., "spouse or partner") and avoid gender stereotypes and sexist language (see p. 124).

Group Affiliations

The various groups to which audience members belong—whether social, civic, work-related, or religiously or politically affiliated—reflect their interests and values and so provide insight into what they care about. Investigating the audience members' group affiliations will help you craft a message that will appeal to them.

QUICK TIP

Be Sensitive to Disability When Analyzing an Audience

More than 19 percent of the population have some sort of physical, mental, or employment disability; more than half of these have a severe disability.[13] About 9 percent of undergraduates (not including veterans) are counted as disabled.[14] Disabilities range from sight and hearing impairments to constraints on physical mobility and employment. Keep *persons with disabilities (PWD)* in mind when you speak, and use language and examples that afford them respect and dignity.

Adapt to Diverse Audiences

In the United States, one-third of the population, or 116 million people, belong to a racial or an ethnic minority group,[15] and about 43 million people, or over 13 percent, are foreign born.[16] Nationwide, 21 percent of the population speaks a language other than English in the home; about two-thirds of these speak Spanish.[17] These figures suggest that audience members will hold different cultural perspectives and employ different styles of communicating that may or may not mesh with your own.

How might you prepare to speak in front of an ethnically and culturally diverse audience, including that of your classroom? In any speaking situation, your foremost concern should be to treat your listeners with dignity and to act with integrity (see Chapter 5). As described below, since values are central to who we are, identifying your listeners' values with respect to your topic can help you to avoid ethnocentrism (see p. 24) and deliver your message in a culturally sensitive manner.

Adapt to Cross-Cultural Values

People in every culture possess **cultural values** related to their personal relationships, religion, occupation, and so forth, and these values can significantly influence how audience members respond to a speaker's message. For example, while dominant cultural values in U.S. society include *achievement and success, equal opportunity, material comfort*, and *democracy*,[18] in Mexico, *famillismo (family loyalty)*, *respecto* (respect), and *fatalismo* (fatalism) are strongly held cultural values. Surveys of several Asian societies identify *a spirit of harmony, humility toward superiors, awe of nature*, and *desire for prosperity* as important values.[19] Becoming familiar with differences, as well as points of similarity, in cultural values can help you frame messages effectively and with sensitivity.

Individual audience analysis is always the first step when seeking to learn about an audience. But public speakers will also benefit by sensitizing themselves to broader national differences in cultural values, especially when time and opportunity constraints make it difficult to gather detailed information on an audience. Cultural researcher Geert Hofstede's wide-ranging research reveals six major "value dimensions," or "broad preferences for one state of affairs over another," as being significant across all cultures, but in widely varying degrees. To find out how eighty-six countries rank in terms of these values and to compare your home culture with another culture, see **www.hofstede-insights.com/product/compare-countries/**.

Several other global surveys can also be extremely useful for learning about cultural values, including the *Pew Global Attitudes Project* (**www.pewglobal.org**), *Gallup World Poll* (**worldview.gallup.com**), and the World Values Survey (**www.worldvaluessurvey.org**).

Focus on Universal Values

As much as possible, try to determine the attitudes, beliefs, and values of audience members. At the same time, you can focus on certain values that, if not universally shared, are probably universally aspired to in the human heart. These include love, truthfulness, fairness, freedom, unity, tolerance, responsibility, and respect for life.[20]

✓ CHECKLIST

Reviewing Your Speech in the Light of Audience Demographics

❑ Does your speech acknowledge potential differences in values and beliefs and address them sensitively?

❑ Have you reviewed your topic in light of the age range and generational identity of your listeners? Do you use examples they will recognize and find relevant?

❑ Have you tried to create a sense of identification between yourself and audience members?

❑ Are your explanations and examples at a level appropriate to the audience's sophistication and education?

❑ Do you make any unwarranted assumptions about the audience's political or religious values and beliefs?

❑ Does your topic carry religious or political overtones that are likely to stir your listeners' emotions in a negative way?

◉ Tools for Learning About Your Audience

You can discover information about your audience through personal interviews, surveys, and published sources. Often, it takes just a few questions to get some idea of audience members' opinions and demographic characteristics.

Conduct Interviews

Interviews, even brief ones, can reveal a lot about the audience's interests and needs. You can conduct interviews one-on-one or in a group, in person or by telephone or online. Consider interviewing a sampling of the audience, or even just one knowledgeable representative of the group that you will address. As with questionnaires (see "Survey the Audience," which follows), interviews usually consist of a mix of open- and closed-ended questions. (See pp. 66–67 for more on conducting interviews.)

Survey the Audience

Surveys can be as informal as a poll of several audience members or as formal as the pre-speech distribution of a written survey, or **questionnaire**—a series of fixed-alternative, scale, or open-ended questions. **Fixed-alternative questions** contain a limited choice of answers, such as "Yes," "No," or "For *x* years":

"Do you smoke cigarettes?"

Yes _____ No _____ I quit, but I smoked for _____ years.

Scale questions—also called *attitude scales*—measure the respondents' level of agreement or disagreement with specific positions or indicate how important listeners judge something to be:

"Flag burning should be outlawed."

Strongly Agree____ Agree____ Disagree____
Strongly Disagree____ Undecided____

"How important is religion in your life?"

Very Important____ Important____
Moderately Important____
Of Minor Importance____ Unimportant____

Open-ended questions (also called *unstructured questions*) begin with a *how, what, when, where,* or *why,* and they are particularly useful for probing beliefs and opinions. This style of question allows respondents to elaborate as much as they wish:

"How do you feel about using the results of DNA testing to prove innocence or guilt in criminal proceedings?"

Often, it takes just a few fixed-alternative and scale questions to draw a fairly clear picture of audience members' backgrounds and attitudes and where they fall in demographic categories. You may wish to use web-based survey software, such as SurveyMonkey or QuestionPro, to generate surveys electronically using premade templates and distribute them online.

Consult Published Sources

Organizations of all kinds publish information describing their missions, operations, and achievements. Sources include websites and related online articles, brochures, newspaper and magazine articles, and annual reports.

Although published opinion polls won't specifically reflect your particular listeners' responses, they too can provide valuable insight into how a representative state, national, or international sample feels about the issue in question. Consider consulting these and other polling organizations:

- National Opinion Research Center (NORC): **www.norc.uchicago.edu**
- Roper Center for Public Opinion Research: **ropercenter.cornell.edu**
- Gallup: **www.gallup.com**
- Pew Research Center U.S. Politics and Policy: **www.people-press.org**

◉ Analyze the Speech Setting and Context

As important as analyzing the audience is assessing (and then preparing for) the setting in which you will give your speech—size of audience; location; time; length of speech; and rhetorical situation (the particular circumstances or reasons why you are delivering the speech about this topic at this time), as seen in the following checklist.

✓ CHECKLIST
Analyzing the Speech Situation

- ❑ Where will the speech take place?
- ❑ How long am I expected to speak?
- ❑ What special events or circumstances of concern to my audience should I acknowledge?
- ❑ How many people will attend?
- ❑ Will I need a microphone?
- ❑ How will any projecting equipment I plan to use in my speech, such as an LCD projector, function in the space?
- ❑ Where will I stand or sit in relation to the audience?
- ❑ Will I be able to interact with listeners?

CHAPTER 7

Selecting a Topic and Purpose

Perhaps no folk saying was ever truer for the public speaker than this one: "You've got to know where you are going in order to get there." That is, unless you can clearly identify *what* you want to say and *why* you want to say it—your topic and purpose—you won't be able to get *there*—giving a speech that works. Figure 7.1 demonstrates the steps involved in selecting a topic and purpose and forming a thesis for your speech; this chapter explains these steps. Once they are completed, you will be ready to flesh out the speech with the supporting material described in Chapter 8.

◉ Explore Topics for Your Speech

A good topic must stir the audience's curiosity as well as your own. You must feel excited enough about it to devote the necessary time to research and organization, so allow yourself the space to discover topics to which you are genuinely drawn. Focus on topics about which you can speak competently and bring fresh information to your listeners. At the same time, consider each potential topic's appeal to the audience (based on audience analysis, including psychological and demographic information; see Chapter 6).

Identify Personal Interests

Personal interests run the gamut from favorite activities and hobbies to deeply held goals and values. You can translate personal experiences into powerful topics, especially if sharing them in some way benefits the audience. "What it's like" stories, for example, yield captivating topics: What is it like to be part of a medical mission team working in Uganda? What have you learned as a longtime practitioner of spinning, biking, hiking, or yoga? How have managed your health complications to live a full life?

Consider Current Events and Controversial Issues

Think about events and issues that most affect you and your audience, and see if you can make a difference. Black Lives Matter, opioid addiction, Confederate memorials, Cuba-U.S. relations, minimum wage laws, the DACA program—the list of pressing and controversial topics is long. Which ones matter to you and your audience?

FIGURE 7.1 Selecting a Topic and Purpose

Survey Grassroots Issues: Engage the Community

Audience members, including college students, respond enthusiastically to local issues that may affect them directly. Review your community's news, including your school's paper and press releases, and read news blogs for the local headlines. What social, environmental, health, political, or other issues are affecting your community?

Steer Clear of Overused and Trivial Topics

To avoid boring your classmates and instructor, stay away from tired issues, such as drunk driving and the health risks of cigarettes, as well as trite topics such as "how to change a tire." Instead, seek out subject matter that yields new information or different perspectives. For ideas, consult your favorite print or online publications. One way to find fresh topics is to check websites that provide information on search trends, hot topics, and ideas that are trending now, such as Google Trends (**www.google.com/trends**), Zeitgeist Minds (**www.zeitgeistminds.com**), Twitter Trends (**www.twitter.com**), and Facebook Trending (**www.facebook.com**).

Try Brainstorming to Generate Ideas

Brainstorming is a method of spontaneously generating ideas through word association, topic (mind) mapping, or internet browsing. Brainstorming works! It is a structured and effective way to identify topic ideas in a relatively brief period of time.

To brainstorm by **word association**, write down *one* topic that might interest you and your listeners. Then jot down the first thing that comes to mind related to it. Repeat the process until you have fifteen to twenty items. Narrow the list to two or three, and then select a final topic:

> energy → solar energy → solar panels → Elon Musk's SolarCity company

Topic (mind) mapping is a brainstorming technique in which you lay out words in diagram form to show categorical relationships among them. Put a potential topic in the middle of a piece of paper. As related ideas come to you, write them down, as shown in Figure 7.2.

Use Internet Tools

Yet other online means for finding (and narrowing) a topic are the databases available on a library's home page (see also p. 62). Consult *general databases* such as Academic OneFile

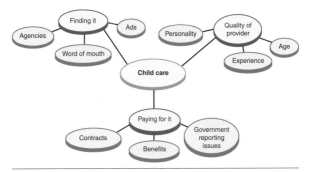

FIGURE 7.2 A Topic Map

(for browsing and starting the search process) and *subject-specific databases* such as Ethnic NewsWatch (for in-depth research on a topic). Popular internet search engines such as Google also offer a wealth of resources to discover and narrow topics. Each search engine offers options for specialized searches within books, news, blogs, images, and other sources. You can narrow topics by limiting searches to within a range of dates (e.g., 1900–1950), to a geographic region (e.g., Europe), or to a particular language.

QUICK TIP

Jump-Start Your Search Using Trusted Websites

Sites on your library's home page, such as *Opposing Viewpoints in Context* and *Issues and Controversies Online,* can help you select and narrow topics on vital issues. In addition, for trustworthy background information on pressing social, political, environmental, and regional issues, librarians often refer students to two related online publications—*CQ Researcher* (published weekly) and *CQ Global Researcher* (published monthly). Each topic entry includes an overview of the current situation, pro/con statements from opposing positions, and bibliographies of key sources. Ask your librarian about related resources.

◉ Identify the General Purpose of Your Speech

Once you have an idea for a topic, you'll need to refine and adapt it to your general speech purpose. The **general speech purpose** for any speech answers the question, "What is my objective in speaking on this topic to this audience on this occasion?" Public speakers typically accomplish one of three general purposes: to inform, to persuade, or to mark a special occasion.

- Do you aim primarily to educate or inform listeners about your topic? The general purpose of an **informative speech** is *to increase the audience's awareness and understanding of a topic by defining, describing, explaining, or demonstrating your knowledge of the subject.*

- Is your goal to influence listeners to accept your position on a topic and perhaps to take action (e.g., "only eat sustainably farmed beef")? The general purpose of the persuasive speech is *to effect some degree of change in the audience's attitudes, beliefs, or even specific behaviors.*

- Are you there to mark a special occasion, such as an awards ceremony, funeral, or wedding? The special occasion speech serves the general purpose of *entertaining, celebrating, commemorating, inspiring, or setting a social agenda*, and includes speeches of introduction, acceptance, and presentation; roasts and toasts; eulogies; and after-dinner speeches, among others.

Note that there is always some overlap in these three types of speeches. An informative speech will have aspects of persuasion in it, and a persuasive speech will also inform. A special occasion speech will include informational and persuasive aspects. Nevertheless, identifying the *primary* function as one of these three purposes will help you narrow your topic and meet your speech goals.

QUICK TIP

To Identify the General Speech Purpose, Consider the Occasion

The speech occasion itself often suggests an appropriate general speech purpose. A town activist, invited to address a civic group about installing solar panels in town buildings, may choose a *persuasive purpose* to encourage the group to get behind the effort. If invited to describe the initiative to the town finance committee, the activist may choose an *informative purpose,* in which the goal is to help the committee understand project costs. If asked to speak at an event celebrating the project's completion, the speaker will choose a *special occasion purpose*. Addressing the same topic, the speaker selects a different general speech purpose to suit each audience and occasion.

◉ Refine the Topic and Purpose

Once you have an idea for a topic and have established a general speech purpose, the next step is to narrow the topic, using your time constraints, audience, occasion, and other relevant factors as guideposts.

Narrow Your Topic

Just as brainstorming and internet tools can be used to discover a topic, they can be instrumental in narrowing one. Using *topic mapping*, you can brainstorm by category (e.g., subtopic). Say your general topic is internships. Some related categories are paid internships, unpaid internships, and cooperative (co-op) education. Ask yourself, "What questions do I have about the topic? Am I more interested in cooperative education or one of the two types of internships? What aspect of internships is my audience most likely to want to hear about?" You can also use trend searching (see p. 48) to narrow your topic.

✓ CHECKLIST
Narrowing Your Topic

- ❏ What is my audience most likely to know about the subject?
- ❏ What do my listeners most likely want to learn?
- ❏ What aspects of the topic are most relevant to the occasion?
- ❏ Can I develop the topic using just two or three main points?
- ❏ How much can I competently research and report on in the time I am given to speak?

Form a Specific Speech Purpose

Once you've narrowed the topic, you need to refine your speech goal beyond the general speech purpose. You know you want to give an informative speech, a persuasive speech, or a special occasion speech, but now you should be able to identify more specifically what you want the speech to accomplish. The **specific speech purpose** describes in action form what you want to achieve with the speech. It does this by spelling out, in a single sentence, what you want the audience to learn, agree with, or perhaps act upon as a result of your speech.

Formulating the specific speech purpose is straightforward. Ask yourself, "What is it about my topic that I want the audience to learn, do, reconsider, or agree with?" Be specific about your aim, and then state it in action form, as in the following, written for a persuasive speech:

Topic (before narrowing):	Binge Drinking
Narrowed Topic:	Describe the nature and prevalence of binge drinking on U.S. campuses and offer solutions to avoid it
General Speech Purpose:	To persuade
Specific Speech Purpose:	To persuade my audience that binge drinking is harmful and convince listeners to consume alcohol safely or not at all

Although the specific purpose statement need not be articulated in the actual speech, it is important to formulate it for yourself in order to keep in mind exactly what you are working to accomplish. Remember the old saying: You've got to know where you are going in order to get there.

Compose a Thesis Statement

While the specific purpose focuses your attention on the outcome you want to achieve with the speech, the **thesis statement** (also called *central idea*) concisely identifies what the speech is *about*. It states the theme of the speech in a single declarative statement, succinctly expressing what the speech will attempt to demonstrate or prove. The main points, the supporting material, and the conclusion all serve to flesh out the thesis. By clearly stating your speech thesis (what it's about), you set in your mind exactly what outcome you want to accomplish (the specific purpose).

The difference between the thesis and specific purpose can be clearly seen in the following examples.

EXAMPLE 1

Speech Topic:	Blogs
General Speech Purpose:	To inform
Specific Speech Purpose:	To inform my audience of three benefits of keeping a blog
Thesis Statement:	Maintaining a blog provides the opportunity to practice writing, a means of networking with others who share similar interests, and the chance to develop basic website management skills.

EXAMPLE 2

Speech Topic:	Service learning courses
General Speech Purpose:	To persuade
Specific Speech Purpose:	To persuade my audience that service learning courses are beneficial for gaining employment after schooling.
Thesis Statement:	Taking service learning courses is a good way to build your résumé and increase your chances of gaining employment after graduation.

In an informative speech, the thesis conveys the scope of the topic, the steps associated with the topic, or the underlying elements of it. It describes what the audience will learn.

In a persuasive speech, the thesis represents what you are going to prove in the address. Notice, too, that in both examples, after you read the thesis you find yourself asking "Why?" or thinking "Prove it!" This will be accomplished by the evidence you give in the speech points (see Chapter 11).

✓CHECKLIST

Identifying the Speech Topic, Purpose, and Thesis

- ❏ Is the topic appropriate to the occasion?
- ❏ Will the topic appeal to the audience's interests and needs?
- ❏ Will I be able to offer a fresh perspective on the topic?
- ❏ Have I identified the general speech purpose—to inform, persuade, or mark a special occasion?
- ❏ Have I identified what I want the audience to gain from the speech—the specific speech purpose?
- ❏ Have I narrowed my topic in line with how much I can competently research and then report on in the time I am given to speak?
- ❏ Does my thesis statement sum up in a single sentence what my speech is about?
- ❏ Does my thesis statement make the claim I intend to make about my topic?

FROM SOURCE TO SPEECH

Narrowing Your Topic to Fit Your Audience

How do you narrow a topic to fit the audience and the speech occasion? Consider the following case study.

A Case Study

Jenny is a member of the campus animal rights club and a student in a public speaking class. She is giving two persuasive speeches this semester: one to her public speaking class and one to the student council, as a representative of her club. For both presentations, Jenny plans to speak on the broad topic of animal rights. But she must narrow this topic considerably to fit each audience and speech occasion.

First, Jenny draws a topic map to generate ideas.

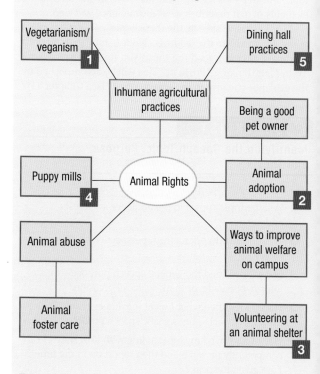

For each presentation, Jenny narrows her topic after considering her audience and the speech occasion.

Public Speaking Class (25–30 people):

- Mixed ages, races, and ethnicities, and an even mix of males and females
- Busy with classes, jobs, sports, and clubs
- Half live in campus housing, where pets are not allowed

Andersen Ross/Getty Images

1 Jenny eliminates vegetarianism because she will be unlikely to change listeners' minds in a six-minute speech.

2 She eliminates animal adoption because it may not be feasible for many students.

3 Volunteering at an animal shelter is an option for all animal lovers, even those who are not allowed to have pets on campus. Jenny argues that students should donate an hour a week to a nearby shelter, so that busy students can still participate.

Student Council (8–10 people):

- Mixed demographic characteristics
- Similar interests: government, maintaining a rich campus life, an investment in ethics and the honor code, and an interest in keeping student affairs within budget

Manfred Rutz/Getty Images

4 Jenny eliminates puppy mills—though the student council may agree that the mills are harmful, they are not in a position to directly address the problem.

5 Jenny zeroes in on dining hall practices, which are directly tied to campus life. Her club's proposed resolution to use free-range eggs in the campus dining hall benefits all students and requires the support of the council—an ideal topic for this audience.

CHAPTER 8

Developing Supporting Material

Good speeches contain relevant, motivating, and audience-centered **supporting material** in the form of examples, stories, testimony, facts, and statistics. (In a persuasive speech, these same supporting materials are referred to as evidence; see Chapter 25.) Supporting material, such as you might discover in a magazine or journal article, engages the audience in your topic, illustrates and elaborates upon your ideas, and provides evidence for your arguments.

◉ Offer Examples

Examples are indispensable tools speakers use to clarify their ideas. An **example** is a typical instance of something. Without examples to illustrate the points a speaker wants to convey, listeners would get lost in a sea of abstract statements. Examples can be *brief* or *extended* and may be either *factual* or *hypothetical*.

Brief examples offer a single illustration of a point. In a speech about restrictions on freedom of expression in China, author Ian McEwan uses the following brief factual example.

> In China, state monitoring of free expression is on an industrial scale. To censor daily the internet alone, the Chinese government employs as many as fifty thousand bureaucrats—a level of thought repression unprecedented in human history.[1]

Sometimes it takes more than a brief example to effectively illustrate a point. **Extended examples** offer extended illustrations of the idea, item, or event being described, thereby allowing the speaker to create a more detailed picture for the audience.

Here, TED speaker Jonathan Drori uses an extended example to illustrate how pollen (the fertilizing element of plants) can link criminals to their crimes:

> [Pollen forensics] is being used now to track where counterfeit drugs have been made, where banknotes have come from. . . . And murder suspects have been tracked using their clothing. . . . Some of the people were brought to trial [in Bosnia] because of the evidence of pollen, which showed that bodies had been buried, exhumed, and then reburied somewhere else.[2]

In some speeches, you may need to make a point about something that could happen in the future if certain events were to occur. Since it hasn't happened yet, you'll need a **hypothetical example** of what you believe the outcome might be. Republican Representative Vernon Ehlers of Michigan offered the following hypothetical example at a congressional hearing on human cloning:

What if in the cloning process you produce someone with two heads and three arms? Are you simply going to euthanize and dispose of that person? The answer is no. We're talking about human life.[3]

◉ Share Stories

One of the most powerful means of conveying a message and connecting with an audience is through a **story**—the telling of a chain of events. Stories (also called **narratives**) help us make sense of our experiences;[4] they tell tales, both real and imaginary, about practically anything under the sun. Stories can be relatively short and simple descriptions of incidents worked into the speech or they can form most of the presentation (see narrative pattern of organization, p. 89). A successful story will strike a chord with and create an emotional connection between speaker and audience members.

All stories possess the essential storytelling elements of *character* (or "protagonist"), *challenge* or *conflict*, and *resolution*, or means of dealing with the challenge. Using these elements, many stories, and especially those that describe overcoming obstacles, work well when they follow a three-part trajectory. First, introduce the protagonist (perhaps yourself) in his or her story setting, or context. Next, recount the challenge or conflict the character faces. A compelling description of the challenge or conflict is crucial in storytelling since everyone can relate to struggle and even failure and how to overcome it. Finally, reveal how the challenge was either dealt with or overcome.

In a speech on helping more young Americans earn college degrees, Melinda French Gates used this format in the following very brief story to illustrate that although some students encounter many barriers to completing degrees, they persevere.

> Last year, we met a young man named Cornell at Central Piedmont Community College in Charlotte, North Carolina. We asked him to describe his typical day. He clocks into work at 11 P.M. When he gets off at 7 the next morning, he sleeps for an hour. In his car. Then he goes to class until 2 o'clock. "After that," Cornell said, "I just crash."[5]

QUICK TIP

Share Stories That Make an Impact

When you include a compelling story in a speech, you will reach the deeper parts of audience members' brains—the hippocampus and amygdala—where emotion and memory work together. Audience members will be more likely to pay attention, remember, and even act on information conveyed in this way.[8]

In just six sentences, Gates includes the elements of character (the student Cornell), challenge (taking classes while working difficult hours), and resolution (getting enough sleep to continue).

Many speakers liberally sprinkle their speeches with **anecdotes**—brief stories of interesting and often humorous incidents based on real life, with a recognizable *moral*—the lesson the speaker wishes to convey. With its offering of wisdom gained through life experiences, the moral is the most important part of an anecdote.[6] For example, in a speech to students at Maharishi University, comedian Jim Carrey talked about how his father's fear of being impractical led him to become an accountant instead of the comedian he wanted to be. This spurred Carrey to take another path:

> So many of us choose our path out of fear disguised as practicality. . . . I learned many great lessons from my father, not the least of which was that you can fail at what you don't want, so you might as well take a chance on doing what you love.[7]

◉ Draw on Testimony

Another potentially powerful source of support for your speech is **testimony**—firsthand findings, eyewitness accounts, and people's opinions. **Expert testimony** includes information from trained professionals in the field. **Lay testimony** is testimony supplied by nonexperts (such as eyewitnesses).

Credibility plays a key role in the effectiveness of testimony, so establish the qualifications of the person whose testimony you use, and inform listeners when and where the testimony was offered (see p. 76 for an example).

QUICK TIP

Use a Variety of Supporting Materials

Listeners respond most favorably to a variety of supporting materials derived from multiple sources to illustrate each main point.[9] Alternating among different types of supporting material—moving from a story to a statistic, for example—will make the presentation more interesting and credible while simultaneously appealing to your audience members' different learning styles.

◉ Provide Facts and Statistics

Most people require some type of evidence before they will accept someone else's claims or position.[10] In Western societies, people especially tend to trust evidence that is based on facts and statistics. **Facts** represent documented occurrences, including actual events, dates, times, people, and places. Listeners are not likely to accept your statements as factual unless you back them up with credible sources.

Statistics are quantified evidence that summarizes, compares, and predicts things. Statistics can clarify complex information and help make abstract concepts concrete for listeners. Audience members will appreciate some statistics in support of your assertions, but they don't want an endless parade of them.

Use Statistics Accurately

Statistics add precision to speech claims—*if* you know what the numbers actually mean and use terms that describe them accurately. Following are some basic statistical terms commonly used in speeches that include statistics.

USE FREQUENCIES TO INDICATE COUNTS   A *frequency* is simply a count of the number of times something occurs:

> On the midterm exam there were 8 A's, 15 B's, 7 C's, 2 D's, and 1 F.

Frequencies can indicate size, describe trends, or help listeners understand comparisons between two or more categories:

- Inside the cabin, the Airbus A380 has room for 525 passengers.[11] (*shows size*)
- Deaths due to opioid overdoses rose from 52,404 in 2015 to roughly 64,000 in 2016.[12] (*describes a trend*)
- In July 2016, the population of the state of Colorado was 49.7 percent female and 50.3 percent male.[13] (*compares two categories*)

USE PERCENTAGES TO EXPRESS PROPORTION   As informative as counts can be, the similarity or difference in magnitude between things may be more meaningfully indicated as a *percentage*—the quantified portion of a whole. Informing an audience that deaths due to opioid overdoses rose in the United States between 2015 and 2016 by nearly 19 percent more quickly shows them the magnitude of the problem than does offering a count.[14] Percentages also help audience members easily grasp comparisons between things, such as the unemployment rate in several states:

> In August 2017, Alaska had the highest rate of unemployment, at 7.2 percent. At 2.3 percent, North Dakota had the lowest rate.[15]

Audience members cannot take the time to pause and reflect on the figures as they would with written text, so consider how you can help listeners interpret the numbers, as in this example:

> As you can see, Alaska's unemployment rate is more than three times greater than that of North Dakota.

USE TYPES OF AVERAGES ACCURATELY   An *average* describes information according to its typical characteristics. Usually we think of the average as the sum of the scores divided by the number of scores. This is the *mean,* the computed average. But there are two other kinds of averages—the *median* and the *mode.*

Consider a teacher whose nine students scored 5, 19, 22, 23, 24, 26, 28, 28, and 30, with 30 points being the highest possible grade. The following illustrates how she would calculate the three types of averages:

- The *mean* score is 22.8, the *arithmetic average,* the sum of the scores divided by 9.
- The *median* score is 24, *the center-most score in a distribution* or the point above and below which 50 percent of the nine scores fall.
- The *mode* score is 28, the *most frequently occurring score* in the distribution.

As a matter of accuracy, in your speeches you should distinguish among these three kinds of averages. Always try to find out whether "average" refers to the mean, median, or mode.

Use Statistics Selectively—and Memorably

Rather than overwhelm the audience with numbers, put a few figures in context to make your message more compelling. For example, instead of only mentioning the actual number of persons using Instagram worldwide (over seven hundred million active monthly users and counting), use a simple ratio to drive home the company's growing reach: "Today, at least 70 percent of businesses in the U.S. use Instagram, nearly double that of one year ago."[16]

Present Statistics Ethically

Offering listeners inaccurate statistics is unethical. Following are steps you can take to reduce the likelihood of using false or misleading statistics:

- *Use only reliable statistics.* Include statistics from the most authoritative source you can locate, and evaluate the methods used to generate the data.
- *Present statistics in context.* Inform listeners of when the data were collected and by whom, the method used to collect the data, and the scope of the research:

    These figures represent data collected by the U.S. Department of Education during 2018 from questionnaires distributed to all public and private schools in the United States with students in at least one of grades 9–12 in the fifty states and the District of Columbia.

- *Avoid cherry-picking.* Politicians are often accused of **cherry-picking**—selecting only those statistics that buttress their own arguments while ignoring competing data.[17] Avoid misrepresenting the truth by offering only one-sided data.
- *Avoid confusing statistics with "absolute truth."* Even the most recent data available will change the next time data are collected. Nor are statistics necessarily any more accurate than the human who collected them. Offer data as they appropriately represent your point, but refrain from declaring that these data are definitive.

CHAPTER 9 ●●●●

Finding Credible Sources in Print and Online

The search for supporting material—for the examples, facts and statistics, opinions, stories, and testimony described in Chapter 8—can be one of the most enjoyable parts of putting together a speech. It is at this stage that you can delve into your subject and select relevant and audience-centered material that supports your speech points.

◉ Assess Your Research Needs

Before beginning your research, review your thesis statement (see p. 52). What do you need to explain, demonstrate, or prove? What mix of evidence—personal knowledge,

---

✔ CHECKLIST
Evaluating Your Research Needs

Do you need . . .

- ❑ Examples to illustrate, describe, or represent your ideas?
- ❑ A story or an anecdote to drive your point home?
- ❑ Firsthand findings, in the form of testimony, to illustrate your points or strengthen your argument?
- ❑ Relevant facts, or documented occurrences, to substantiate your statements?
- ❑ Statistics to quantify evidence, express proportion, and clarify and add context to data?

examples, stories, statistics, and testimony—will help you accomplish this? A little while spent planning a research strategy will save significant time and energy.

◉ Use Library Portals to Access Credible Sources

Rather than relying on sources you find through general search engines such as Google, consider beginning, or certainly continuing, your search at your school library's home page. You might use the web to brainstorm and narrow topics, locate current news on a topic, review reputable blogs, and so forth. Then switch to your school's collection of databases to find peer-reviewed research articles, books, primary source databases, and other vetted material.

Access to these scholarly and other resources is a key benefit of searching for materials within library databases. Libraries purchase access to proprietary databases and other resources that form part of the **deep web**—the large portion of the web that general search engines cannot access because the information is not indexed by them or is fee-based. When you select a database by using a library's portal, you can access its full contents and be assured that the articles and other materials have been vetted for reliability and credibility. The following table lists resources typically found on library portals.

Typical Resources Found on Library Portals
• Full-text databases (newspapers, periodicals, journals)
• General reference works (dictionaries, encyclopedias, atlases, almanacs, fact books, biographical reference works, quotation resources, poetry collections)
• Books, e-books, and monographs
• Archives and special collections (collected papers, objects and images, scholarly works unique to the institution)
• Digital collections (oral histories, letters, old newspapers, image collections, audio and video recordings)
• Video and music collections

◉ Recognize Propaganda, Misinformation, and Disinformation

Discerning the accuracy of information is not always easy. Anyone can post material on the web and, with a little bit of design savvy, make a website look reputable. One way to judge a source's trustworthiness is to ask yourself: Is it reliable *information*, or is it *propaganda, misinformation*, or *disinformation*?[1] (See the table below.)

- **Information** is *data* that is presented in an understandable context. Data are raw and unprocessed facts; information makes sense of data. For example, a patient's vital signs (temperature, blood pressure, pulse, etc.) are data. Interpreting the vital signs in the context of health status is information. Information is neutral unto itself but is subject to manipulation, for purposes both good and bad. It then has the potential to become propaganda, misinformation, or disinformation.

- **Propaganda** is information represented in such a way as to provoke a desired response. Propaganda may be based in fact, but its purpose is to instill a particular attitude or emotion in order to gain support for a cause or issue. Usually presented as advertising or publicity, propaganda encourages you to think or act according to the ideological, political, or commercial perspective of the message source.

Information, Propaganda, Misinformation, and Disinformation	
Information	Data set in a context for relevance.
	Example: A fact
Propaganda	Information represented in such a way as to provoke a desired response.
	Example: A military poster encouraging enlistment
Misinformation	Something that is not true.
	Example: An urban legend
Disinformation	Deliberate falsification of information.
	Example: A falsified profit-and-loss statement

- **Misinformation** always refers to something that is not true. While propaganda may include factual information, misinformation does not. For example, during the U.S. presidential campaign of 2016, rumors circulated that the Pope had endorsed Donald J. Trump, when in fact popes never endorse candidates, and Pope Francis did not veer from this policy. This common form of misinformation, found so often on the internet, is called an *urban legend*— a fabricated story passed along by unsuspecting people.

- **Disinformation** is the deliberate falsification of information. Like misinformation, disinformation thrives on the internet. Doctored photographs and falsified profit-and-loss statements are classic examples of disinformation in action. A contemporary example is ads containing political content posted on social media by Russian agents with the aim of influencing U.S. voters.

Ethical speeches are based on sound information on facts put into context—rather than on misinformation, propaganda, or disinformation.

QUICK TIP

Use Watchdog Sites to Check the Facts

Our most trustworthy elected officials occasionally make false assertions, and even the most reliable news sources publish errors of fact or omission. So whom should you believe—Congresswoman X's dire predictions regarding Social Security or Senator Y's rosier assessment? To check the factual accuracy of information offered by key political players and major journalistic outlets, consult these websites (bearing in mind that they too are not infallible).

- **www.factcheck.org**, sponsored by the Annenberg Public Policy Center
- **www.politifact.com**, sponsored by the *Tampa Bay Times*
- Fact Checker (**www.washingtonpost.com/news/fact-checker/**), sponsored by the *Washington Post*

Investigate a Mix of Primary and Secondary Sources

Nearly all types of speeches can benefit from a mix of the two broad categories of supporting material: primary and secondary sources. **Primary sources** provide firsthand accounts or direct evidence of events, objects, or people. **Secondary sources** provide analysis or commentary about things not directly observed or created. These include the vast world of news, commentary, analysis, and scholarship found in books, articles, and a myriad of sources other than the original.

A speech that contains both primary and secondary sources can be more compelling and believable than one that relies on one source type alone. The firsthand nature of a credible primary source can build trust and engage audience members emotionally. Secondary sources can help listeners put the topic in perspective. A speech on an oil spill, for example, can command more attention if it includes testimony by oil riggers and other eyewitnesses (primary sources) along with analyses of the spill from magazines and newspapers (secondary sources).

Explore Primary Sources

A primary source for a speech may be your own personal experience; government documents and data; a firsthand account found in letters, diaries, old newspapers, photographs, or other sources; a blog; or an interview or survey that you conduct yourself.

CONSIDER PERSONAL KNOWLEDGE AND EXPERIENCE Used effectively, your own knowledge and experience about your topic can serve important functions in a speech, drawing in listeners and creating a sense of connection with them. Sharing experiences and observations about work you've done, people you've known, or places you've visited can add a dimension of authenticity and credibility that a secondhand source might not.

✔ CHECKLIST
Finding Speeches Online

Online, you can find numerous videos and audio files of speeches. These can be useful as models of speeches and primary source material.

❑ American Rhetoric (**www.americanrhetoric.com**) contains 5,000+ speeches.

❑ Gifts of Speech (**gos.sbc.edu**) features speeches by women from around the world since 1848.

❑ Wake Forest University's Political Speeches gateway (**www.wfu.edu/~louden/Political%20Communication/ Class%20Information/SPEECHES.html**) offers links to collections of political speeches.

❑ The United States Senate (**www.senate.gov**) includes speeches by U.S. senators.

❑ *Vital Speeches of the Day* (**www.vsotd.com**) features current speeches delivered in the United States and is published monthly.

ACCESS GOVERNMENT INFORMATION   Many speeches can benefit from citing a statistic from a census or other data set, quoting testimony from a hearing or speech, or otherwise incorporating information discovered in government documents. Nearly all the information contained in these wide-ranging documents, relating to virtually all aspects of social endeavor, comes from highly credible primary sources, so it's well worth the effort to consult them.

- Start at **www.usa.gov**, the official portal to all U.S. government information and services.
- To locate reliable statistics related to your topic, go to FedStats (**fedstats.sites.usa.gov**) and American Fact-Finder (**factfinder.census.gov**).
- To access resources in Spanish, use **www.gobiernousa.gov**. Translations in other languages are also available.

EXPLORE DIGITAL COLLECTIONS   Another source of credible primary research may be found within the online digital collections of libraries, which typically include oral histories, letters, and old newspapers; photographs, prints, and paintings; and audio and video recordings. A presentation on early African American actors, for example, might include a passage from a diary of a nineteenth-century actor and a photograph of him or her on stage. One way to discover a digital collection related to your topic is to enter your topic terms into a general search engine (e.g., "*African American actors*" AND "*digital collections*").

ACCESS BLOGS   A *blog* is a site containing journal-type entries maintained by individuals or groups. Newest entries appear first. Blogs can be useful sources of information about unfolding events and new trends and ideas, if the source is reputable. Many reputable publications, such as *Scientific American* and *The Atlantic*, maintain blog sites for their contributors. If a publication appears likely to contain information about your topic, search for ["*publication name*"] and "blogs."

CONDUCT INTERVIEWS   Oftentimes you can glean considerably more insight into a topic, and get more compelling material to bring to your audience, by speaking personally to someone who has expertise on the subject. Getting the information you need from a subject does require research and advance planning, from deciding on the questions you will ask to how you will record the interview.

- Begin by *learning about the person you will be interviewing* so that you can prepare appropriate and informed questions for him or her.
- *Prepare questions for the interview* in advance of the interview date.

- *Word questions carefully.*
  - Avoid *vague questions,* those that don't give the person being interviewed enough to go on. Vague questions waste the interviewee's time and reflect the interviewer's lack of preparation.
  - Avoid *leading questions,* those that encourage, if not force, a certain response and reflect the interviewer's bias (e.g., "Like most of us, are you going to support candidate X?"). Likewise, avoid *loaded questions,* those that are phrased to reinforce the interviewer's agenda or that have a hostile intent (e.g., "Isn't it true that you've never supported school programs?").
  - Focus on asking *neutral questions,* those that don't lead the interviewee to a desired response. Usually, this will consist of a mix of open, closed, primary, and secondary questions. See p. 45 for more details on open- and closed-ended questions.
- *Establish a spirit of collaboration at the start.*
  - Acknowledge the interviewee and express respect for his or her expertise.
  - Briefly summarize your topic and informational needs.
  - State a (reasonable) goal—what you would like to accomplish in the interview—and reach agreement on it.
  - Establish a time limit for the interview and stick to it.

✓ CHECKLIST

Preparing for the Interview

- ❑ Have I researched my interviewee's background and accomplishments?
- ❑ Do I have a written set of questions?
- ❑ Can the questions be answered within a reasonable time frame?
- ❑ Are my questions relevant to the purpose of my speech?
- ❑ Are my questions posed in a well-thought-out sequence?
- ❑ Are my questions free of bias or hostile intent?
- ❑ Are controversial questions reserved until the end of the interview?
- ❑ Have I obtained advance permission to record the interview?
- ❑ Do I have a working writing implement and ample notepaper, or functioning laptop or tablet?
- ❑ Have I made certain that any recording equipment I plan to use is in working order?

FROM SOURCE TO SPEECH

Evaluating Web Sources

Check the Most Authoritative Websites First

Seek out the most authoritative websites on your topic. For information on legislation, government statistics, health, the environment, and other relevant topics, check government-sponsored sites at the official U.S. government portal, **www .usa.gov**. Government-sponsored sites are free of commercial influence and contain highly credible primary materials.

Evaluate Authorship and Sponsorship

1 *Examine the domain in the web address*—the suffix at the end of the address that tells you the nature of the site: educational (.edu), government (.gov), military (.mil), non-profit organization (.org), business/commercial (.com), and network (.net). A tilde (~) in the address usually indi-cates that it is a personal page rather than part of an insti-tutional website.

2 *Identify the creator of the information.* Is the site operated by an individual, a company, a government agency, or a nonprofit group? If an individual operates the site, does the site provide relevant biographical information, such as links to a résumé or a listing of the author's cre-dentials? Look for contact information. A source that doesn't want to be found is not a good source to cite.

3 *Find out who sponsors the site.* Most credible websites include information about their sponsorship—that is, who pays for the site—often in a section called "About" or "Our Sponsors." Be wary of sites that do not disclose their sponsorship.

4 *Check for signs of bias.* Read critically. Does the author treat all sides of the issue fairly, or does the author favor one viewpoint? If a website uses attention-grabbing head-lines or loaded language that appeals to your emotions, the site is likely biased and may even be propaganda.

Check for Currency

5 *Check for a date that indicates when the page was placed on the web and when it was last updated.* Is the date current?

Check That the Site Credits Trustworthy Sources

6 *Check that the website documents its sources.* Reputable websites document their sources. Investigate these sources, and apply the same criteria to them that you did to the original source document. Verify all information with at least two other independent, reputable sources.

← → C 🔒 Secure | https://www.epa.gov/newsreleases/us-epa-help-bishop-calif-meet-sustainability-g... ☆ 🔲

EPA United States
Environmental Protection
Agency **3**

Search EPA.gov 🔍

Environmental Topics   Laws & Regulations   About EPA

CONTACT US   SHARE (f) (y) (P) (✉)

News Releases

News Releases from Region 09

U.S. EPA to Help Bishop, Calif., Meet Sustainability Goals, Revitalize Downtown

12/15/2016 **5**

Contact Information:
Soledad Calvino (calvino.maria@epa.gov)
415-972-3512 **2**

SAN FRANCISCO – Today, the U.S. Environmental Protection Agency announced that 25 communities across the nation will receive technical assistance to pursue development strategies that advance clean air, clean water, economic development and other local goals. In California, the City of Bishop will receive assistance for identifying strategies and tools to attract redevelopment to the town's center.

"We are thrilled that the City of Bishop will benefit from this program," said Alexis Strauss, EPA's Acting Regional Administrator for the Pacific Southwest. "By providing technical assistance, our Building Blocks program will help local leaders guide their communities towards a prosperous, more sustainable future."

EPA will assist the city in identifying specific opportunities to update its municipal code to allow for increased residential densities and mixed use development to revitalize Bishop's downtown. EPA will also help explore incentives for property owners to invest in improvements, encouraging redevelopment of

United States Evironmental Protection Agency

- *Use active listening strategies (see Chapter 5).*
  - Don't break in when the subject is speaking or inter-ject with leading comments.
  - Paraphrase the interviewee's answers when you are unclear about meaning and repeat back to him or her.
  - Ask for clarification and elaboration when necessary.
- *End the interview by rechecking and confirming.*
  - Confirm that you have covered all the topics (e.g., "Does this cover everything?").
  - Briefly offer a positive summary of important things you learned in the interview.
  - Offer to send the interviewee the results of the interview.

DISTRIBUTE SURVEYS   A *survey* can be useful as both a tool to investigate audience attitudes and a source of primary material for your speech. Surveys are an especially effective source for speech topics focused on the attitudes and behavior of people in your immediate environment, such as fellow students' opinions on issues on or off campus or community members' attitudes toward local initiatives. For guidelines on creating surveys, see Chapter 6.

Explore Secondary Sources

Along with possible primary sources, your speeches will also, if not at times exclusively, rely on secondary sources as found in books, newspapers, periodicals, and reference works (such as encyclopedias, books of quotations, and poetry collections).

WIKIPEDIA—DOS AND DON'TS   When it comes to online research, it is impossible to ignore the presence of Wikipedia, the world's largest experimental free encyclopedia, written collaboratively and often anonymously by anyone who wishes to contribute to it. Though Wikipedia's instant accessibility and vast range make it easy to consult, bear in mind that information may or may not be accurate at any given moment, as people edit material at will. As with any encyclopedia, Wikipedia provides an initial overview of a topic, but to ensure accuracy, use it only as a starting point for further research. The references cited in a Wikipedia article can serve as potential research leads—*if* you follow the links provided and carefully evaluate the information for trustworthiness. Be sure to compare the information in the article to credible sources *not* supplied in the entry itself, and do not offer Wikipedia—or any encyclopedia entry—as a source to audience members.

CHAPTER 10

Citing Sources in Your Speech

Alerting the audience to the sources you use and offering ones that they will find authoritative is a critical aspect of delivering a presentation. When you credit speech sources, you:

- Increase the odds that audience members will believe in your message.
- Demonstrate the quality and range of your research to listeners.
- Demonstrate that reliable sources support your position.
- Avoid plagiarism and gain credibility as an ethical speaker who acknowledges the work of others.
- Enhance your own authority by demonstrating how your own ideas fit into the larger intellectual conversation about the topic.
- Enable listeners to locate your sources and pursue their own research on the topic.

Ethically you are bound to attribute any information drawn from other people's ideas, opinions, and theories—as well as any facts and statistics gathered by others—to their original sources. That is, you are bound to be honest. You need not credit sources for ideas that are **common knowledge**—information that is likely to be known by many people and described in multiple places (though such information must *truly* be widely disseminated; see the "Quick Tip" below).

QUICK TIP

Common Knowledge and Uncommon Facts

One exception to needing to give credit for material in a speech (or a written work) is the use of common knowledge. For example, it is common knowledge that Thomas Jefferson was the third president of the United States. It is not common knowledge that he had a personal library of 6,487 books, which he donated to the Library of Congress after it was attacked and burned down by British troops in 1814. This fact does require acknowledgment of a source—in this case, an article entitled "10 Things You Didn't Know about Thomas Jefferson," published (without a byline) on June 30, 2011, in the *Washington Post*.

◉ Alert Listeners to Key Source Information

An **oral citation** credits the source of speech material that is derived from other people's ideas. For each source, plan on briefly alerting the audience to the following:

1. The *author* or *origin of the source* ("documentary film-maker Ken Burns . . ." or "On the *National Science Foundation* website . . .")

2. The *type of source* (journal article, book, personal interview, website, blog, online video, etc.)

3. The *title* or a *description of the source* ("In the book *Endangered Minds* . . ."; or "In *an article on sharks* . . .")

4. The *date of the source* ("The article, published in the *October 10th, 2018,* issue . . ." or "According to a report on choosing a college major, posted online *September 28, 2018,* on the *Chronicle of Higher Education* website . . .")

Of course, spoken citations need not include complete references (exact titles, full names of all authors, volume and page numbers); doing so will interrupt the flow of your presentation and distract listeners' attention. However, do keep a list of complete references for a bibliography to appear at the end of your speech. (See Appendix A for guidelines on how to document sources in a bibliography.)

Establish the Source's Trustworthiness

Focus on presenting your sources in a way that will encourage audience members to process and believe in the source material. Too often, inexperienced speakers credit their sources in bare-bones fashion, offering a rote recitation of citation elements. For example, a student might cite a source's name, but leave out key details about the source's background that could convince the audience to trust the source.

Discerning listeners will only accept the information you offer if they believe that the sources for it are reliable and accurate, or *credible*. **Source credibility** refers to our level of trust in a source's credentials and track record for providing accurate information. If you support a scientific claim by crediting it to an unknown student's personal blog, for example, listeners won't find it nearly as reliable as if you credited it to a scientist affiliated with a reputable institution.

Be aware that while a source that is credible is usually accurate, this is not always so.[1] Sometimes we have information that contradicts what we are told by a credible source. For instance, a soldier might read an article in the *Washington Post* about a conflict in which he or she participated. The soldier knows the story contains inaccuracies because the soldier was there. In general, however, the soldier finds the *Washington Post* a credible source. Therefore, *since even the most credible source can sometimes be wrong, it is always better to offer a variety of sources, rather than a single source, to support a major point.* This is especially the case when your claims are controversial.

QUICK TIP

Consider Audience Perception of Sources

Not every trustworthy source is necessarily appropriate for every audience. For example, a politically conservative audience may reject information from a liberal publication. Readers of the *Nation*, for example, tend to be liberal, while those who read the *National Review* tend to be more conservative. Thus, audience analysis should factor in your choice of sources. In addition to checking that your sources are reliable, consider whether they will be seen as credible by your particular audience.[2]

Qualify the Source

A simple and straightforward way to demonstrate a source's trustworthiness is to include a brief description of the source's qualifications to address the topic (a **source qualifier**), along with your oral citation—for example, "researcher at Duke Cancer Institute," "columnist for the *Economist*". This will allow the audience to put the source in perspective. To see how you can orally cite sources in ways that listeners will accept and believe, see "Types of Sources and Sample Oral Citations" (p. 74).

◎ Avoid a Mechanical Delivery

Acknowledging sources need not interrupt the flow of your speech. On the contrary, audience members will welcome information that adds backing to your assertions. The key is to avoid a formulaic, or mechanical, delivery. Audience members expect a natural style of delivery of your speech, and this includes delivery of speech sources.

Vary the Wording

Avoid a rote delivery of sources by varying your wording. If you introduce one source with the phrase "According to . . . ," switch to another construction ("As reported by . . .") for the next one. Alternating introductory phrases provides necessary variety.

Vary the Order

Vary the order in which you introduce a citation. Occasionally discuss the findings first, before citing the source. For example, you might state that "Caffeine can cause actual intoxication" and provide evidence to back up this claim before revealing your source—"A chief source for this argument is a report in the July 5, 2018, issue of the *New England Journal of Medicine*. . . ."

◉ Types of Sources and Sample Oral Citations

Following are common types of sources cited in a speech, the specific citation elements to mention, and examples of how you might refer to these elements in a presentation. Each example includes a boldfaced source qualifier describing the source's qualifications to address the topic—for instance, "director of undergraduate studies for four years" or "research scientist at Smith-Kline." Qualifying a source can make the difference between winning or losing acceptance for your arguments.

Book

If a book has *two* or *fewer* authors, state first and last names, title, and date of publication. If *three* or *more authors*, state first and last name of first author and "co-authors."

> *Example:* In his book *Thinking, Fast and Slow,* published in 2011, **psychologist and Nobel Prize winner** Daniel Kahneman claims that . . .

> *Example:* In *The Civic Potential of Video Games*, published in 2009, Joseph Kahne, **noted professor of education and director of the Civic Education Research Group at Mills College**, and his two co-authors, **both educators**, wrote that . . .

Reference Work

For a reference work (e.g., encyclopedia, almanac, directory), note title, date of publication, and author or sponsoring organization.

> *Example:* According to *Literary Market Place 2018*, **the foremost guide to the U.S. book publishing industry**, Karen Hallard and her co-editors report that . . .

Article in a Journal, Newspaper, or Magazine

When citing from an article either online or in print, use the same guidelines as you do for a book.

> *Example:* In an article titled "The False Promise of DNA Testing," published in the June 2016 edition of *Atlantic Monthly* magazine, **journalist and *New York Times* contributing writer** Matthew Shaer argues that forensic testing is becoming ever less reliable.

Website

Name the website, section of website cited (if applicable), and last update.

> *Example:* On its website, last updated November 8, 2017, the Society of Interventional Radiology, **a national organization of physicians and scientists**, explains that radio waves are harmless to healthy cells. . . .

If website content is undated or not regularly updated, review the site for credibility before use, using the criteria listed on pp. 68–69. (If you are citing an online article, use the guidelines under "Article in a Journal, Newspaper, or Magazine" above.)

Blog

Name the blogger, affiliated website (if applicable), and date of posting.

> *Example:* In an April 26, 2017, posting on *Talking Points Memo*, **a news blog that specializes in original reporting on government and politics**, editor Josh Marshall notes that . . .

Television or Radio Program

Name the program, segment, reporter, and date aired.

> *Example:* Judy Woodruff, **PBS NewsHour anchor**, described in a segment on sexual harassment aired on November 14, 2017 . . .

Online Video

Name the online video source, program, segment, and date aired (if applicable).

> *Example:* In a session on mindfulness delivered at the University of Miami on October 9, 2015, and broadcast on YouTube, Jon Kabat-Zinn, **scientist, renowned author, and founding director of the Stress Reduction Clinic** . . .

QUICK TIP

Credit Sources in Presentation Aids

Just as you acknowledge the ideas of others in the verbal portion of your speech, be sure to credit such material used in any accompanying presentation aids. When reproducing copyrighted material, such as a table or photograph, label it with a copyright symbol (©) and the source information. Even if it is not copyrighted, supporting material listed on a visual aid may require citation. You may cite this material orally, print the citation unobtrusively on the aid, or both.

Testimony (Lay or Expert)

Name the person, date, and context in which information was offered.

> *Example:* On June 7, 2016, in congressional testimony before the U.S. Senate Foreign Relations Committee, Victoria Nuland, **Assistant Secretary of State for European and Eurasian Affairs**, revealed that Russian violations of borders . . .

Interview and Other Personal Communication

Name the person and date of the interview or personal communication.

> *Example:* In an interview I conducted last week, Tim Zeutenhorst, **chairman of the Orange City Area Health System Board, at Orange City Hospital in Iowa,** said . . .

> *Example:* In a June 23, 2018, email/Twitter post/letter/memorandum from Ron Jones, **a researcher at the Cleveland Clinic** . . .

✔ CHECKLIST

Offering Key Source Information

- ❑ Have I identified the author or origin of the source?
- ❑ Have I indicated the type of source?
- ❑ Have I offered the title or description of the source?
- ❑ Have I noted the date of the source?
- ❑ Have I qualified the source to establish its reliability and credibility?

part

Organization

LaunchPad
macmillan learning

VIDEO ACTIVITY
Go to LaunchPad to watch a video in
which two students explore how to
outline a speech effectively. Visit
launchpadworks.com

LaunchPad includes:

☑ **LearningCurve** adaptive quizzing

▣ A curated collection of video clips and
full-length speeches

Additional resources, such as presentation
software tutorials and documentation help.

CHAPTER 11 ●●●●

Organizing the Body of the Speech

A speech structure is simple, composed of just three basic parts:
an introduction, a body, and a conclusion. The **introduction**
establishes the purpose of the speech and shows its relevance
to the audience. The **body** of the speech presents main points
that are intended to fulfill the speech purpose. The **conclusion**
brings closure to the speech by restating the purpose, summarizing main points, and reiterating the thesis and its relevance
to the audience. In essence, the introduction of a speech tells
listeners where they are going, the body takes them there, and
the conclusion lets them know the journey has ended.

Chapter 14 describes how to create effective introductions
and conclusions. Here we focus on the elements of the
speech body—*main points, supporting points*, and *transitions*—
and how to arrange them in an outline. In an **outline,** you
separate main and supporting points—the major speech
claims and the evidence to support them—into larger and
smaller divisions and subdivisions. (See also Chapter 13 on
Preparing Outlines for the Speech.)

◉ Use Main Points to Make Your Major Claims

Main points express the key ideas of the speech. Their
function is to represent each of the major ideas or claims
being made in support of the speech thesis. To create main
points, identify the most important ideas of the speech, as
reflected in your thesis. What ideas can you demonstrate
with supporting material? Each of these ideas or claims
should be expressed as a main point.

Restrict the Number of Main Points

Research indicates that audiences can comfortably take in only between two and seven main points.[1] For most speeches, and especially those delivered in the classroom, between two and five main points should be sufficient. As a rule, the fewer main points in a speech, the greater the odds that you will maintain your listeners' attention. If you have too many main points, further narrow your topic (see Chapter 7) or check the points for proper subordination (see pp. 81–82).

QUICK TIP

Save the Best for Last—or First

Listeners have the best recall of speech points made at the beginning of a speech (the "primacy effect") and at the end of a speech (the "recency effect") than of those made in between (unless the ideas made in between are much more striking than the others).[2] If it is especially important that listeners remember certain ideas, introduce those ideas near the beginning of the speech and reiterate them at the conclusion.

Restrict Each Main Point to a Single Idea

A main point should not introduce more than one idea. If it does, split it into two (or more) main points:

Incorrect:	I. We have more free speech on earth than at any previous time in recorded history, but free speech is under serious threat from extremes on all sides, even though freedom of speech sustains all the other freedoms we enjoy.
Correct:	I. We have more free speech than at any previous time in recorded history.
	II. Free speech is under serious threat from extremes on all sides.
	III. Freedom of speech sustains all the other freedoms we enjoy.[3]

Main points should be mutually exclusive of one another. If they are not, consider whether a main point more properly serves as a subpoint.

Express each main point as a *declarative sentence*—one that asserts or claims something. In addition, state your main points (and supporting points; see below) in *parallel form*— that is, in similar grammatical form and style (see p. 83). Phrasing points in parallel form helps listeners understand and retain the points (by providing consistency) and lends power and elegance to your words.

Incorrect:	I. After college, female students who were athletes are more likely to be employed full time than female students who did not engage in athletics.
	II. They are also more likely to thrive physically.
	III. Social well-being is another aspect in which female student athletes score better.
Correct:	I. After college, female student athletes are more likely to be employed full time.
	II. Post graduation, female student athletes are also more likely to thrive in their physical well-being.
	III. After they graduate, female student athletes are more likely to thrive in their social well-being.

Use the Purpose and Thesis Statements as Guides

Main points should flow directly from your specific purpose and thesis statements (see pp. 47–50), as in the following example:

Specific Purpose: What you want the audience to learn or do as a result of your speech	"I want my audience to understand the reasons why meditation is helpful for mental and physical health."
Thesis: The central idea of the speech	"Meditation is an effective means of reducing stress and improving overall mental and physical health."
Main Points:	I. Meditation helps you gain inner peace.
	II. Meditation helps you increase self-awareness.
	III. Regular meditation can improve heart health.

◉ Use Supporting Points to Substantiate Your Claims

Supporting points organize the evidence you have gathered to explain (in an informative speech) or justify (in a persuasive speech) the main points. It is here that you substantiate or prove the main points with examples, narratives, testimony, facts, and statistics discovered in your research (see Chapter 8).

In an outline, supporting points appear in a subordinate position to main points. This is indicated by **indentation**. Just as with main points, order supporting points according to their importance or relevance to the main point.

The most common format for outlining points is the **roman numeral outline**. Main points are enumerated with uppercase roman numerals (I, II, III . . .), supporting points are enumerated with capital letters (A, B, C . . .), sub-supporting points are enumerated with Arabic numerals (1, 2, 3 . . .), and sub-subsupporting points are enumerated with lowercase letters (a, b, c . . .), as seen in the following:

I. Main point
   A. Supporting point
      1. Subsupporting point
         a. Sub-subsupporting point
         b. Sub-subsupporting point
      2. Subsupporting point
         a. Sub-subsupporting point
         b. Sub-subsupporting point
   B. Supporting point
II. Main point

◉ Pay Close Attention to Coordination and Subordination

Outlines reflect the principles of **coordination and subordination**—the logical placement of ideas relative to their importance to one another. Ideas that are *coordinate* are given equal weight; **coordinate points** are indicated by their parallel alignment. An idea that is *subordinate* to another is given relatively less weight; **subordinate points** are indicated by their indentation below the more important points.

Principles of Coordination and Subordination
- Assign equal weight to ideas that are coordinate.
- Assign relatively less weight to ideas that are subordinate.
- Indicate coordinate points by their parallel alignment.
- Indicate subordinate points by their indentation below the more important points.

- Every point must be supported by at least two points or none at all (consider how to address one "dangling" point by including it in the point above it).

◉ Strive for a Unified, Coherent, and Balanced Organization

A well-organized speech is characterized by unity, coherence, and balance. Try to adhere to these principles as you arrange your speech points.

A speech exhibits *unity* when it contains only those points implied by the specific purpose and thesis statements. The thesis is supported by main points, main points are strengthened by supporting points, and supporting points consist of carefully chosen evidence and examples.

A speech exhibits *coherence* when it is organized clearly and logically, with speech points aligned in order of importance (see "Principles of Coordination and Subordination," p. 81). Main points should support the thesis statement, and supporting points should enlarge upon the main points. Transitions serve as mental bridges that help establish coherence.

✓ CHECKLIST

Reviewing Main and Supporting Points

- ❑ Do the main points flow directly from the speech goal and thesis?
- ❑ Do the main points express the key points of the speech?
- ❑ Is each main point truly a main point or a subpoint of another main point?
- ❑ Is each main point substantiated by at least two supporting points—or none?
- ❑ Do you spend roughly the same amount of time on each main point?
- ❑ Are the supporting points truly subordinate to the main points?
- ❑ Does each main point and supporting point focus on a single idea?
- ❑ Are the main and supporting points stated in parallel form?

The principle of *balance* suggests that appropriate emphasis or weight be given to each part of the speech relative to the other parts and to the thesis. Inexperienced speakers may devote overly lengthy coverage to one point and insufficient attention to the others, or may provide scanty evidence in the body of the speech after presenting an impressive introduction. The body of a speech should always be the longest part, and the introduction and conclusion should be of roughly the same length. Stating the main points in parallel form is one aspect of balance. Assigning each main point at least two supporting points is another. If you have only one subpoint, consider how you might incorporate it into the superior point. Think of a main point as a tabletop and supporting points as table legs; without at least two legs, the table cannot stand.

◉ Use Transitions to Give Direction to the Speech

Transitions are words, phrases, or sentences that tie the speech ideas together and enable the listener to follow the speaker as he or she moves from one point to the next. Transitions (also called *connectives*) are a truly critical component of speeches because listeners cannot go back and re-read what they might have missed. Focus on creating transitions to shift listeners from one point to the next. Transitions can take the form of full sentences, phrases, or single words.

Use Transitions between Speech Points

Use transitions to move between speech points—from one main point to the next, and from one subpoint to another.

When moving from one main point to another, full-sentence transitions are especially effective. For example, to move from main point I in a speech about sales contests (*"Top management should sponsor sales contests to halt the decline in sales"*) to main point II (*"Sales contests will lead to better sales presentations"*), the speaker might use the following transition:

> Next, let's look at exactly what sales contests can do for us.

Transitions between supporting points can be handled using single words, phrases, or full sentences as in the following:

> Next, . . .
> First, . . . (second, third, and so forth)
> Similarly, . . .
> We now turn . . .
> If you think that's shocking, consider this . . .

FROM POINT TO POINT

Using Transitions to Guide Your Listeners

Transitions direct your listeners from one point to another in your speech, leading them forward along a logical path while reinforcing key ideas along the way. Plan on using transitions to move between:

- The introduction and the body of the speech
- The main points
- The subpoints, whenever appropriate
- The body of the speech and the conclusion

Introduction

I. Today I'll explore the steps you can take to help achieve carbon neutrality on your campus . . .

(TRANSITION: So how do you go carbon-neutral?)

Body

I. Get informed—examine the steps that other campuses have already taken toward carbon neutrality

(TRANSITION: Looking at what other campuses have done is only part of carbon neutrality, however. Perhaps most important, . . .)

II. Recognize that change starts here, on campus, with you. . . .

While transitions help guide your listeners from point to point, they can also do a lot more, including:

- Introduce main points
- Illustrate cause and effect
- Signal explanations and examples
- Emphasize, repeat, compare, or contrast ideas
- Summarize and preview information
- Suggest conclusions from evidence

Following is an excerpt from a working outline on a speech about achieving carbon neutrality on campus. Note how the student edits himself to ensure that he (1) uses transitions to help listeners follow along and retain his speech points and (2) uses transitions strategically to achieve his goal of persuading the audience.

(TRANSITION: Why is it important for college campuses to become carbon-neutral?)

   I. College campuses generate the carbon equivalent of many large towns . . .

(TRANSITION: As a result . . .)

     A. Colleges have a moral responsibility to their students and their surrounding communities to reduce carbon emissions . . .

     B. Administrators face decisions about mounting energy costs . . .

(TRANSITION: Following are some ideas to create a carbon-neutral campus. First . . .)

   I. Launch a campus-wide campaign to encourage students to reduce their energy use

(TRANSITION: For example . . .)

     A. Provide energy-efficient lightbulbs to students

     B. Encourage students to use bikes and public transit as much as possible, instead of personal cars

     C. Emphasize the importance of shutting off lights and electronic devices when leaving a room . . .

(TRANSITION: Pushing students to take action is a critical part of achieving carbon neutrality. But another key aspect is action by school administrators, who have the power to implement wide-ranging sustainable energy policies . . .)

   II. Lobby administrators to investigate biomass facilities and offshore wind and solar energy sources . . .

     A. Ensure that new campus buildings meet renewable energy standards . . .

     B. Take necessary steps to retrofit older campus buildings . . .

     C. Explore alternative heating . . .

(TRANSITION: So far, we've talked about practical actions we can take to move toward carbon neutrality on campus, but what about beyond the campus?)

   III. Get involved at the town government level

     A. Town-gown communities . . .

     B. Speak up and voice your concerns . . .

(TRANSITION: As you can see, we have work to do . . .)

Conclusion

   I. If we want our children and our children's children to see a healthy earth, we must take action now . . .

Use Internal Previews and Summaries as Transitions

Previews briefly introduce audience members to the ideas that the speaker will address. In a speech introduction, the **preview statement** briefly mentions the main points and thesis of the speech (see p. 11 and p. 10). Within the body itself, speakers use an **internal preview** to draw the audience in with a glimpse of what they will discuss next. An **internal summary** draws together ideas to reinforce them before proceeding to another speech point. Often, a speaker will transition from one major idea or main point to the next using an internal summary and internal preview together.

> We've seen that mountain bikes differ from road bikes in the design of the tires, the seat, the gears, the suspension systems, and the handlebars. (*internal summary*) Now let's take a look at the different types of mountain bikes themselves. As you will see, mountain bikes vary according to the type of riding they're designed to handle—downhill, trails, and cross-country. Let's begin with cross-country. (*internal preview*)

See Chapter 13 for guidance on including transitions in the outline of your speech.

✔ CHECKLIST
Use Transitional Words and Phrases

- ❑ **To show comparisons:** *similarly; in the same way; likewise; just as*
- ❑ **To contrast ideas:** *on the other hand; and yet; at the same time; in spite of; however; in contrast*
- ❑ **To illustrate cause and effect:** *as a result; hence; because; thus; consequently*
- ❑ **To illustrate sequence of time or events:** *first, second, third . . . ; following this; later; earlier; at present; in the past*
- ❑ **To indicate explanation:** *for example; to illustrate; in other words; to simplify; to clarify*
- ❑ **To indicate additional examples:** *not only; in addition to; let's look at*
- ❑ **To emphasize significance:** *most important; above all; remember; keep in mind*
- ❑ **To summarize:** *in conclusion; in summary; finally; let me conclude by saying*

CHAPTER 12

Selecting an Organizational Pattern

Of all of the aspects of speechmaking, the idea of organizational arrangements may seem the most confusing. But selecting and organizing speech points into a pattern is easier and more natural than it might seem. An organizational pattern helps you link points together to maximum effect for your topic and purpose and lets the audience follow your ideas as you wish. Studies confirm that the way you organize your ideas affects your audience's understanding of them, so you'll want to make use of a pattern.[1] A good time to select one is after you've researched the speech and prepared main points.

Speeches make use of at least a dozen different organizational arrangements of main and supporting points. Here we look at six commonly used patterns, five of which are used for all forms of speeches: chronological, spatial, causal (cause-effect), topical, and narrative, and one, the problem-solution pattern, which is typically used for persuasive speeches. In Chapter 23, you will find three additional patterns of organization designed solely for persuasive speeches: *Monroe's motivated sequence, comparative advantage,* and *refutation.*

◉ Arranging Speech Points Chronologically

Some topics lend themselves well to the arrangement of main points according to their occurrence in time relative to one another. The **chronological pattern of arrangement** (also called the *temporal pattern*) follows the natural sequential order of the main points. Topics that describe a series of events in time (such as events leading to development of a vaccine) or develop in line with a set pattern of actions or tasks (such as steps in installing solar panels) call out for this pattern. A speech describing the development of the World Wide Web, for example, immediately calls for a time-ordered sequence of main points:

Thesis Statement:	The internet evolved from a small network designed for military and academic scientists into a vast array of networks used by billions of people around the globe.

Continued on p. 90

One Topic (Patterns of Immigration) Organized Six Ways

Chronological Pattern

Thesis Statement: "Immigration to the U.S. has ebbed and flowed, from the first large wave in 1820 to the most recent wave beginning in 1965."

Sample Main Points:

I.   First large wave occurred between 1790 and 1820: English, Scottish, Irish, Germans, and Spanish.

II. Second wave, largely German, British, and Irish, arrived between 1820 and 1860.

III. Asian immigrants arrived in Western states between 1880 and 1914 in the third wave.

IV. Fourth wave, 1965–present: Asians, Mexicans, South and Central Americans, and Europeans.

Spatial Pattern

Thesis Statement: "Border Patrol sectors—from westernmost San Diego to easternmost Brownsville—have highest apprehension rates for undocumented migrants."[2]

Sample Main Points:

I.   For many years, highest migrant apprehension rates occurred, from west to east, for San Diego, Tucson, and El Paso sectors, but these sectors have seen steep declines in recent years.

II. Along the middle of the border, two Texas sectors—Del Rio and Laredo—have shown modest increases in migrant apprehensions since 2010.

III. Recently, the Rio Grande Valley Sector, at east end of Texas border, has seen increased apprehensions, leading all sectors.

Causal Pattern

Thesis Statement: "U.S. children whose parents are unauthorized immigrants (*cause*) are exposed to risks, including lower preschool enrollment, poverty, and reduced socioeconomic progress." (*effects*)

Sample Main Points:

I.   Children ages 3–4 with unauthorized immigrant parents are less likely to attend preschool.[3]

II. Three-quarters of children with unauthorized parents have incomes under 185 percent of the poverty line.[4]

III. Children with unauthorized parents are more likely to stay in poverty.[5]

Problem-Solution Pattern

Thesis Statement: "Persons who overstay their visas account for about 40 percent of undocumented immigrants in the U.S.[6] (*problem*) To address the issue, we need a biometric (fingerprint) exit system that will identify visa overstayers." (*solution*)

Sample Main Points:

I. Up to five million persons who entered the United States legally remain here with expired visas.[7]

II. The Department of Homeland Security takes fingerprints and photos of entering visitors with visas but has no similar system to track their exits.

III. DHS plans to launch a biometric exit system at high-volume airports in 2018.[8]

Topical Pattern

Thesis Statement: "Debates about immigration often focus on immigrants' role in the labor force, admissions policies, and enforcement policies."

Sample Main Points:

I. Immigrants accounted for nearly 17 percent of the civilian labor force in 2014.[9]

II. Immigration admissions policies are based on reuniting families, admitting skilled workers, and protecting refugees.[10]

III. The Criminal Alien Program (CAP) is the primary immigration enforcement channel.[11]

Narrative Pattern

Thesis Statement: "I came to the U.S. illegally as the child of undocumented immigrants. I am about to graduate high school and want to go to college, but because I am undocumented I cannot apply for aid."

Sample Main Points:

I. I was brought to the United States at age 3 by undocumented parents.

II. I attended U.S. schools through high school.

III. I remain undocumented and cannot apply for college aid.

Main Points:	
	I. The internet was first conceived in 1962 as the ARPANET to promote the sharing of research among scientists in the United States.
	II. In the 1980s, a team created TCP/IP, a language that could link networks, and the internet as we know it was born.
	III. At the end of the Cold War, the ARPANET was decommissioned, and the World Wide Web constituted the bulk of internet traffic.

◉ Arranging Speech Points Using a Spatial Pattern

When describing the physical arrangement of a place, a scene, or an object, logic suggests that the main points can be arranged in order of their physical proximity or direction relative to one another. This calls for a **spatial pattern of arrangement**. For example, you can select a spatial arrangement when your speech provides the audience with a "tour" of a particular place:

Thesis Statement:	El Morro National Monument in New Mexico is captivating for its variety of natural and historical landmarks.
Main Points:	I. Visitors first encounter an abundant variety of plant life native to the high-country desert.
	II. Soon visitors come upon an age-old watering hole that has receded beneath the 200-foot cliffs.
	III. Beyond are the famous cliff carvings made by hundreds of travelers over several centuries of exploration in the Southwest.

In a speech describing a geothermal heating and cooling company's market growth across regions of the country, a speaker might use the spatial arrangement as follows:

Thesis Statement:	Sales of geothermal systems have grown in every region of the country.

Main Points:	I. Sales are strongest in the Eastern Zone.
	II. Sales are growing at a rate of 10 percent quarterly in the Central Zone.
	III. Sales are up slightly in the Mountain Zone.

◉ Arranging Speech Points Using a Causal (Cause-Effect) Pattern

Some speech topics represent cause-effect relationships. Examples include (1) events leading to higher interest rates, (2) reasons students drop out of college, and (3) causes of a disease. The main points in a **causal (cause-effect) pattern** of arrangement usually take the following form:

I. Cause

II. Effect

Sometimes a topic can be discussed in terms of multiple causes for a single effect, or a single cause for multiple effects:

Multiple Causes for a Single Effect (Reasons Students Drop Out of College)	Single Cause for Multiple Effects (Reasons Students Drop Out of College)
I. Cause 1 (lack of funds)	I. Cause (lack of funds)
II. Cause 2 (unsatisfactory social life)	II. Effect 1 (lowered earnings over lifetime)
III. Cause 3 (unsatisfactory academic performance)	III. Effect 2 (decreased job satisfaction over lifetime)
IV. Effect (drop out of college)	IV. Effect 3 (increased stress level)

Some topics are best understood by presenting listeners with the effect(s) before the cause(s). In a speech on health care costs, a student speaker arranges his main points as follows:

Thesis Statement:	In response to rising health care costs, large employers are shifting part of the expense to workers.
Main Points:	I. (*effect*) Workers are now seeing higher co-pays and deductibles.

Main Points: II. (*effect*) Raising the amount employees must contribute has restricted
employer costs to just 5 percent this
year.

                 III. (*cause*) The Affordable Care Act man-
dates that large employers offer more
of their workers health care plans.

                 IV. (*cause*) Rising health care costs have
led to more expensive plans at all
levels of coverage.

QUICK TIP

Blend Organizational Patterns

The pattern of organization for your subpoints can differ
from the pattern you select for your main points. Do
keep your main points in one pattern—this will be the
predominant pattern for the speech—but feel free to use
other patterns for subpoints when it makes sense to do so.
For instance, for a speech about the history of tattooing
in the United States, you may choose a chronological
pattern to organize the main points but use a cause-effect
arrangement for some of your subpoints regarding why
tattooing is so popular today.

◉ Arranging Speech Points Using a Problem-Solution Pattern

The **problem-solution pattern** organizes main points to demonstrate the nature and significance of a problem followed by a
proposed solution. Most often used in persuasive speeches,
the problem-solution pattern can be arranged as simply as
two main points:

     I. Problem (define what it is)

     II. Solution (offer a way to overcome the problem)

But many problem-solution speeches require more than
two points to adequately explain the problem and to substantiate the recommended solution:

     I. The nature of the problem (identify its causes,
incidence, etc.)

     II. Effects of the problem (explain why it's a problem, for
whom, etc.)

III. Unsatisfactory solutions (discuss those that have not worked)

IV. Proposed solution (explain why it's expected to work)

Following is a partial outline of a persuasive speech about cyberbullying arranged in a problem-solution format (for more on using the problem-solution pattern in persuasive speeches, see Chapter 24).

Thesis Statement:	To combat cyberbullying, we need to educate the public about it, report it when it happens, and punish the offenders.
Main Point:	I. Nature of cyberbullying
	A. Types of activities involved
	1. Name-calling, insults
	2. Circulation of embarrassing pictures
	3. Sharing of private information
	4. Threats
	B. Incidence of bullying
	C. Profile of offenders
Main Point:	II. Effects of cyberbullying on victims
	A. Acting out in school
	B. Feeling unsafe in school
	C. Skipping school
	D. Experiencing depression
Main Point:	III. Unsuccessful attempts at solving cyberbullying
	A. Let offenders and victims work it out on their own
	B. Ignore problem, assuming it will go away
Main Point:	IV. Ways to solve cyberbullying
	A. Educate in schools
	B. Report incidents to authorities
	C. Suspend or expel offenders

◉ Arranging Speech Points Topically

When each of the main points is a subtopic or category of the speech topic, try the **topical pattern** of arrangement (also called **categorical pattern**). Consider an informative speech about choosing Chicago as a place to establish a career. You plan to emphasize three reasons for choosing Chicago: the strong economic climate of the city, its cultural variety, and its accessible public transportation. Since these three points are of relatively equal importance, they can be arranged in any order without affecting one another or the speech purpose negatively. For example:

Thesis Statement:	Chicago is an excellent place to establish a career.
Main Points:	I. Accessible transportation
	II. Cultural variety
	III. Multiple industries

This is not to say that when using a topical arrangement, you should arrange the main points without careful consideration. Any number of considerations can factor into your ordering of points, not least of which should be the audience's most immediate needs and interests. Perhaps you have determined that listeners' main concern is the city's attractions for young professionals, followed by an interest in its cultural variety and accessible transportation.

QUICK TIP

Find Freedom with the Topical Pattern

Topical arrangements give you the greatest freedom to structure main points according to the way you wish to present your topic. You can approach a topic by dividing it into two or more categories, for example. You can lead with your strongest evidence or leave your most compelling points until you near the conclusion. If your topic does not call out for one of the other patterns described in this chapter, be sure to experiment with the topical pattern.

◉ Arranging Speech Points Using a Narrative Pattern

Storytelling is often a natural and effective way to get your message across. In the **narrative pattern**, the speech consists of a story or series of short stories, replete with characters, conflict or complications, and resolution (see p. 89).

In practice, a speech built largely upon a story (or series of stories) is likely to incorporate elements of other designs. You might organize the main points of the story in an effect-cause design, in which you first reveal the outcome of what happened (such as a man-made disaster) and then describe the events that led up to the accident (the causes).

Whatever the structure, simply telling a story is no guarantee of giving a good speech. Any speech should include an introduction with a preview and clear thesis, well-organized main points, effective transitions, and a conclusion.

> ## ✔ CHECKLIST
> ### Determining an Organizational Pattern
>
> Does your speech . . .
>
> ❑ Describe a series of developments in time or a set of actions that occur sequentially? Use the *chronological pattern*.
>
> ❑ Describe or explain the physical arrangement of a place, a scene, or an object? Use the *spatial pattern*.
>
> ❑ Explain or demonstrate a topic in terms of its underlying causes or effects? Use the *causal pattern*.
>
> ❑ Demonstrate the nature and significance of a problem and justify a proposed solution? Use the *problem-solution pattern*.
>
> ❑ Stress natural divisions or categories of a topic, in which points can be moved to emphasize audience needs and interests? Use a *topical pattern*.
>
> ❑ Convey ideas through a story, using character, conflict, and resolution? Use a *narrative pattern*, perhaps in combination with another pattern.

CHAPTER 13 ●●●●

Preparing Outlines for the Speech

Outlines are enormously helpful in putting together and delivering a successful speech, providing a framework for your speech materials and a blueprint for your presentation. Plotting points into hierarchical fashion based on their relative importance to one another and using indentation to visually represent this hierarchy will allow you to examine the underlying logic and relationship of ideas to one another.

Speakers can choose among several different types of outline formats. (For a review of the principles and of the mechanics of outlining, see Chapter 11.)

◉ Plan on Creating Two Outlines

As you develop a speech, plan on creating two outlines: a working outline and a speaking, or delivery, outline. Use the **working outline** (also called a *preparation outline*) to organize and firm up main points and, with the research you've gathered, develop supporting points to substantiate them. Completed, the working outline should contain your entire speech, organized and supported to your satisfaction.

Use a **speaking outline** to practice and actually present the speech. Speaking outlines contain the working outline in condensed form and are much briefer. Figure 13.1 provides an overview of the steps involved in outlining a speech.

Use Sentences, Phrases, or Key Words

Speeches can be outlined in sentences, phrases, or key words. (Working outlines typically contain partial or full sentences, reflecting much of the text of the speech; speaking outlines use key words or short phrases.)

In the **sentence outline format**, each main and supporting point is stated in sentence form as a declarative statement

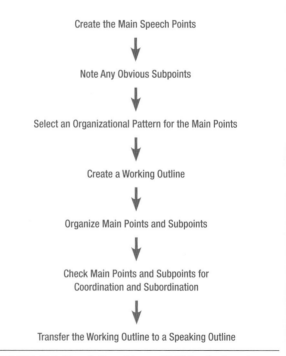

Create the Main Speech Points

↓

Note Any Obvious Subpoints

↓

Select an Organizational Pattern for the Main Points

↓

Create a Working Outline

↓

Organize Main Points and Subpoints

↓

Check Main Points and Subpoints for
Coordination and Subordination

↓

Transfer the Working Outline to a Speaking Outline

FIGURE 13.1 Steps in Organizing and Outlining the Speech

(e.g., one that states a fact or an argument) in much the same way you will express the idea during delivery. Following is an excerpt in sentence format from a speech by Mark B. McClellan on keeping prescription drugs safe:[1]

I. The prescription drug supply is under attack from a variety of increasingly sophisticated threats.

   A. Technologies for counterfeiting—ranging from pill molding to dyes—have improved across the board.

   B. Inadequately regulated internet sites have become major portals for unsafe and illegal drugs.

A **phrase outline** uses partial construction of the sentence form of each point. McClellan's sentence outline would appear as follows in phrase outline form:

I. Drug supply under attack

   A. Counterfeiting technologies more sophisticated

   B. Unregulated internet sites

The **key-word outline** uses the smallest possible units of understanding to outline the main and supporting points. Key-word outlines encourage you to become familiar enough with your speech points that a glance at a few words is enough to remind you of exactly what to say.

I. Threats

   A. Counterfeiting

   B. Internet

Use a Key-Word Outline for Optimal Eye Contact

The type of outline you select will affect how you deliver a speech. The less you rely on reading any outline, the more eye contact you can have with audience members—an essential aspect of a successful speech. For this reason, experts recommend using key-word or phrase outlines over sentence outlines, with key-word outline often being the preferred format. Key-word outlines permit not only the greatest degree of eye contact but also greater freedom of movement and better control of your thoughts and actions than either sentence or phrase outlines. With adequate practice, the key words will jog your memory so that the delivery of your ideas becomes more natural.

◉ Create a Working Outline First

Begin with a working outline before transferring your ideas to a speaking outline containing key words or shortened phrases.

Edit and rearrange items in the working outline as necessary as you work through the mass of information you've collected.

Prepare the body of the speech *before* the introduction, keeping the introduction (and the conclusion) *separate from* the main points (see sample outlines in this chapter). Since introductions serve to preview main points, you will first need to finalize the main points in the body. Introductions must also gain the audience's attention, introduce the topic and thesis, and establish the speaker's credibility (see Chapter 14). To ensure that you address these elements, use such labels as *Attention Getter*, *Topic and Thesis*, *Credibility Statement*, and *Preview Statement* (see the Sample Working Outline below).

SAMPLE WORKING OUTLINE

The following working outline is from a speech delivered by public speaking student Zachary Dominque. It includes all elements of the speech, including transitions and reminders to show presentation aids (SHOW SLIDE) in red. (In practice, working outlines may or may not include delivery cues; speaking outlines do include them. See p. 96). Next to each mention of a source requiring credit is a note in parentheses (e.g., "For bibliography: ABC of Mountain Biking"). This allows you to maintain a bibliography. The speech is organized topically, according to natural subdivisions of a topic (see p. 93).

The History and Sport of Mountain Biking

Zachary Dominque
St. Edwards University

Topic:	Mountain Biking
General Speech Purpose:	To inform my listeners about the sport of mountain biking
Specific Purpose:	To help my audience gain an overview of and appreciation for mountain biking
Thesis Statement:	Mountain biking is a relatively new, exciting, and diverse sport.

Introduction

(Attention getter)

    I. Imagine that you're on a bike, plunging down a steep, rock-strewn mountain, yet fully in control.

II. Adrenaline courses through your body as you hurtle through the air, touch down on glistening pebbled streams and tangled grasses, and rocket upward again.

III. You should be scared, but you're not; in fact, you're having the time of your life.

IV. Like we say, Nirvana.

V. How many of you like to bike—ride to campus, bike for fitness, or cycle just for fun?

VI. You might own a bike with a lightweight frame and thin wheels, and use it to log some serious mileage— or possibly a comfort bike, with a nice soft seat and solid tires.

(Credibility statement.)

VII. Good morning, folks. My name is Zachary Dominque, and I'm a mountain biker.

VIII. I've been racing since I was eight years old and won state champion three years ago, so this topic is close to my heart.

(Preview)

IX. Today, I'm going to take you on a tour of the exciting sport of mountain biking: I'll be your engine—your driver—in mountain bike–speak.

X. Our ride begins with a brief overview of mountain biking; then we'll do a hopturn—a turn in reverse—to learn about the sport's colorful history.

XI. Pedalling ahead in this beautiful autumn air, we'll chat about the various differences in design and function between mountain bikes and road bikes.

XII. We'll conclude our tour at a local bike shop, where you can compare downhill, trail, and cross-country mountain bikes.

XIII. These are the three main types of mountain bikes, designed for the three major types of mountain biking.

XIV. I hope by then that you'll catch a little bit of mountain biking fever and see why I find it such an exciting, intense, and physically challenging sport.

(TRANSITION) Mountain biking is a sport that can be extreme, recreational, or somewhere in between. But no matter what kind of rider you are, it's always a great way to get out in the natural world and get the adrenaline going. To start, let me briefly define mountain biking.

Body

I. The website ABC of Mountain Biking offers a good basic definition: "Mountain biking is a form of cycling on off-road or unpaved surfaces such as mountain trails and dirt roads; the biker uses a bicycle with a sturdy frame and fat tires." (**For bibliography**: ABC of Mountain Biking)

   A. The idea behind mountain biking is to go where other bikes won't take you.

      1. Mountain bikers ride on backcountry roads and on single-track trails winding through fields or forests.

      2. They climb up steep, rock-strewn hills and race down over them.

      3. The focus is on self-reliance, because these bikers often venture miles from help.

   B. According to the National Bicycle Dealers Association website, in 2012 mountain bikes accounted for 25 percent of all bikes sold in the United States.

      1. If you factor in sales of the comfort bike, which is actually a mountain bike modified for purely recreational riders, sales jump to nearly 38 percent of all bikes sold. (**For bibliography**: National Bicycle Dealers Assn)

      2. Some 50 million Americans love riding their mountain bikes, according to data collected by the New England Mountain Bike Association. (**For bibliography:** New England Mountain Bike Assn)

(TRANSITION)   So you see that mountain biking is popular with a lot of people. But the sport itself is fairly new.

II. The history of mountain biking is less than 50 years old, and its founders are still around.

   A. The man in this picture is Gary Fisher, one of the founders of mountain biking. (SHOW GF SLIDE 1)

   B. According to *The Original Mountain Bike Book*, written in 1998 by pioneering mountain bikers Rob van der Plas and Charles Kelly, they, along with Fisher, Joe Breeze, and other members of the founding posse from the Marin County, California, area, were instrumental in founding the modern sport of mountain biking in the early 1970s. (**For bibliography**: *Original MB Book*)

   C. Mountain bikes—called MTBs or ATBs (for all-terrain bikes)—didn't exist then as we now know them, so as you can see in this picture of Gary Fisher, he's riding a modified one-speed Schwinn cruiser. (SHOW SCHWINN SLIDE 2)

1. Cruisers, or "ballooners," aren't made to go off road at all.

2. Nothing equips them to navigate trails, and their brakes aren't remotely equipped to handle stops on steep descents.

3. But this is the type of bike Fisher and others started out with.

D. By the mid-1970s, growing numbers of bikers in California got into using modified cruisers to race downhill on rocky trails.

1. They'd meet at the bottom of Mount Tamalpais, in Corte Madera, California. (SHOW MT TAM SLIDE 3)

2. They'd walk their bikes a mile or two up its steep slopes, and hurl on down.

E. As even more people got involved, Charles Kelly and others organized the famed Repack Downhill Race on Mt. Tam.

1. Held from 1976 to 1979, the Repack race became a magnet for enthusiasts and put the sport on the map, according to *The Original Mountain Bike Book*.

(TRANSITION) The reason why the race was called "Repack" is a story in itself.

2. The trail in the Repack race plummeted 1,300 feet in less than 2 miles.

   a. Such a steep drop meant constant braking, which in turn required riders to replace, or "repack," their bikes' grease after nearly each run, according to the Marin Museum of Biking website. (**For bibliography**: Marin Museum)

   b. As Breeze recounts in his own words: "The bikes' antiquated hub coaster brake would get so hot that the grease would vaporize, and after a run or two, the hub had to be repacked with new grease." (SHOW BIKE SLIDE 4)

(TRANSITION) As you might imagine, these early enthusiasts eventually tired of the routine.

F. The bikers had tinkered with their bikes from the start, adding gearing, drum brakes, and suspension systems.

G. In 1979, Joe Breeze designed a new frame—called the "Breezer"—which became the first actual mountain bike.

H. By 1982, as van der Plas and Kelly write in *The Original Mountain Bike Book*, standardized production of mountain bikes finally took off.

(TRANSITION)   Now that you've learned a bit of the history of mountain biking, let's look at what today's mountain bike can do. To make things clearer, I'll compare them to road bikes. Road bikes are the class of bikes that cyclists who compete in the Tour de France use.

III. Mountain bikes and road bikes are built for different purposes. (SHOW MB & RB SLIDE 5)

A. Mountain bikes are built to tackle rough ground, while road bikes are designed to ride fast on paved, smooth surfaces.

1. To accomplish their task, mountain bikes feature wide tires with tough tread.

2. In contrast, road bike tires are ultrathin and their frames extremely lightweight.

   a. If you take a road bike off-road, chances are you'll destroy it.

   b. Without the knobby tread and thickness found on mountain bike tires, road bike tires can't grip onto the rocks and other obstacles that cover off-road courses.

B. The handlebars on the bikes also differ, as you can see here.

1. Mountain bikes feature flat handlebars; these keep us in an upright stance, so that we don't flip over when we hit something.

2. The drop handlebars on road bikes require the cyclist to lean far forward; this position suits road cycling, which prizes speed.

C. The gears and suspension systems also differentiate mountain bikes from road bikes.

1. Mountain bikes use lower gears than road bikes and are more widely spaced, giving them more control to ride difficult terrain.

2. As for suspension, road bikes generally don't have any kind of suspension system that can absorb power.

   a. That is, they don't have shock absorbers because they're not supposed to hit anything.

   b. Imagine riding over rocks and roots without shocks; it wouldn't be pretty.

3. Many mountain bikes have at least a great front shock absorbing suspension system.

   a. Some have rear-suspension systems.

   b. Some bikes have dual systems.

(TRANSITION)   I hope by now you have a sense of the mountain bike design. But there are finer distinctions to draw.

IV. There are actually three different types of mountain bikes, designed to accommodate the three major kinds of mountain biking—downhill, trails, and cross-country.

(TRANSITION)   Let's start with downhill. (SHOW DH SLIDE 6)

A. Downhill bikes have the fewest gears of the three types of mountain bikes and weigh the most.

   1. That's because downhill biking is a daredevil sport—these bikers are crazy!

   2. They slide down hills at insane speeds, and they go off jumps.

B. As described on the website Trails.com, downhill racers catch a shuttle going up the mountain, then speed downhill while chewing up obstacles. (**For Bibliography:** Trails.com)

C. Think of downhill racing as skiing with a bike.

(TRANSITION)   Now let's swing by trail biking. (SHOW TB SLIDE 7)

D. Trail bikes look quite different than either downhill or cross-country bikes.

   1. They have very small wheels, measuring either 20, 24, or 26 inches, and smaller frames.

   2. These differences in design help trail bikers do what they do best: jump over obstacles—cars, rocks, and large logs.

E. The trail biker's goal is to not put a foot down on the ground.

F. Trail bike racing is one of the few types of biking that's done by time, not all at a mass start.

(TRANSITION)   The third major type of mountain biking, cross-country, or XC cycling, is my sport. (SHOW XC SLIDE 8)

G. Cross-country biking is also the most common type of mountain biking—and the one sponsored by the Olympics.

 1. That's right. According to Olympic.org, in 1996, mountain biking became an Olympic sport. (**For Bibliography:** Olympic.org)

 2. This was just two decades after its inception.

H. With cross-country, you get the best of all worlds, at least in my humble opinion.

 1. The courses are creative, incorporating hills and valleys and rough to not-so-rough terrain.

 2. If done competitively, cross-country biking is like competing in a marathon.

 3. Done recreationally, it offers you the chance to see the great outdoors while getting, or staying, in great shape.

 I. Cross-country bikes come in two forms.

 1. XC bikes are very lightweight, with either full or partial suspension.

 2. The Trails/Marathon XC hybrid bikes are a bit heavier, with full suspension; XC bikes are designed for seriously long rides.

(TRANSITION)   Well, it has been quite a tour, folks. (***Signals close of speech***)

Conclusion

 I. Our course began with an overview of mountain biking and a hopturn into a brief history of the sport.

 II. We also learned about the differences between mountain bikes and road bikes, and the three major categories of mountain bikes. (***Summarizes main points***)

III. To me, mountain biking, and especially cross-country, is the perfect sport—fulfilling physical, spiritual, and social needs.

IV. It's a great sport to take up recreationally. (***Leaves audience with something to think about***)

 V. And if you decide to mountain bike competitively, just remember: Ride fast, drive hard, and leave your blood on every trail. (***Memorable close***)

Works Cited

International Olympic Committee. 2015. "Cycling, Mountain Biking." March 2015. **www.stillmed.olympic .org/AssetsDocs/OSC%20Section/pdf/QR_sports_summer /Sports_Olympiques_VTT_eng.pdf.**

Marin Museum of Biking. n.d. "History of Mountain Biking." Accessed October 11, 2017. **www.mmbhof.org /mtn-bike-hall-of-fame/history.**

National Bicycle Dealers Association. 2015. "Industry Overview, 2015." Accessed November 28, 2017. **www.nbda .com/articles/industry-overview-2012-pg34.htm.**

New England Mountain Bike Association. 2013. "CT NEMBA's Trail School." April 7, 2013. **www.nemba.org /news/ct-nembas-trail-school.**

Trails.com. n.d. "Mountain Bikes and Biking." Accessed October 11, 2017. **www.trails.com/mountain-bikes-and-biking.html.**

Van der Plas, Rob, and Charles Kelly. 1998. *The Original Mountain Bike Book.* Minneapolis: Motorbooks.

◉ Prepare a Speaking Outline for Delivery

Using the same numbering system as the working outline, condense long phrases or sentences into key words or short phrases, including just enough words to jog your memory. Include any **delivery cues** that will be part of the speech (see below). Place the speaking outline on large (at least 4 × 6-inch) notecards, 8.5 × 11-inch sheets of paper, or in a speaker's notes software program or app (see Chapter 21). Print large enough, or use large enough fonts, so that you can see the words at a glance. (For accuracy's sake, even in phrase or key-word outlines, direct quotations may be written out verbatim, as seen in this outline.)

Delivery Cue	Example
Transitions	(TRANSITION)
Timing	(PAUSE) (SLOW DOWN)
Speaking Rate/ Volume	(SLOWLY) (LOUDER)
Presentation Aids	(SHOW MODEL) (SLIDE 3)
Source	(ATLANTA CONSTITUTION, August 2, 2018)
Statistic	(2018, boys to girls = 94,232; U.S. Health & Human Services)
Quotation	Eubie Blake, 100: "If I'd known I was gonna live this long, I'd have taken better care of myself."

SAMPLE SPEAKING OUTLINE
The History and Sport of Mountain Biking

Zachary Dominque
St. Edwards University

Introduction

    I. Imagine on bike, plunging rock-strewn, yet control.

    II. Adrenaline, hurtle, touch downstream, rocket.

    III. Scared, but not—time of life.

    IV. Nirvana.

    V. How many bike, fitness, fun?

    VI. Might own lightweight, thin wheels, serious mileage—or comfort, soft seat, solid tires.

    VII. Morning, Zachary, MTBer.

    VIII. Eight; champion, heart.

    IX. Today, tour, exciting sport of . . . engine, driver, MTB-speak.

    X. Ride begins brief overview; do hopturn—colorful history.

    XI. Pedaling ahead autumn, chat differences between mountain, road.

    XII. Conclude shop, compare MTBs.

    XIII. Three types bikes, designed for three . . .

    XIV. Hope catch fever, exciting, intense, and physically.

(TRANSITION)   MTB sport extreme . . . in-between. But no matter, always great way natural world, adrenaline. Start, define.

Body

    I. *ABC/MB def*: "MTB is a form of cycling on off-road or unpaved surfaces such as mountain trails and dirt roads; the biker uses a bicycle with a sturdy frame and fat tires."

      A. The idea—go where others.

        1. MTBs ride backcountry, single-track winding fields, forests.

        2. Climb steep, rock-strewn, race down.

        3. Self-reliance, miles from help.

      B. National Bicycle Dealers Assoc., 2013 MTBs 25 percent sold.

        1. Factor comfort, actually MTB modified recreational, sales 38 percent.

        2. 50 million love riding, data gathered NE MTB Assn.

(TRANSITION)   So MTB popular people. But fairly new.

II. History MTB less 50, founders.

A. Gary Fisher, founders MTB. (SHOW GF SLIDE 1)

B. *Original Mountain Bike Book*, written 1998 by van
der Plas, Kelly; they, along with Fisher, Breeze, other
members posse Marin, instrumental founding modern
sport early 1970s.

C. MTBs or ATBs (terrain)—didn't exist, so picture Fisher,
modified Schwinn cruiser. (SHOW SCHWINN SLIDE 2)

1. Cruisers, "ballooners," off-road.

2. Nothing equips navigate, brakes equipped stops
descents.

3. But bike Fisher, others started.

D. Mid-1970s, growing numbers using modified race
downhill.

1. Meet bottom Tamalpais, CA. (SHOW MT TAM
SLIDE 3)

2. Walk bikes mile up steep, hurl.

E. Even involved, Kelly, others organized Repack.

1. 1976–1979, magnet enthusiasts, on map,
Original MTB.

(TRANSITION)   Reason called "Repack" story itself.

2. Trail plummeted 1,300 feet 2 miles, Breeze article
MTB Fame website.

a. Such drop constant braking, required riders replace,
"repack," grease each run.

b. Breeze recounts: "The bikes' antiquated hub coaster
brake would get so hot that the grease would
vaporize, and after a run or two, the hub had to
be repacked with new grease." (SHOW BIKE
SLIDE 4)

(TRANSITION)   Might imagine, early enthusiasts tired.

F. Bikers tinkered, gearing, drum, suspension.

G. 1979, Breeze new frame—"Breezer"—first actual MTB.

H. 1982, as van der Plas, Kelly write in *Original MTB*,
standardized took off.

(TRANSITION)   Now learned history, let's look today's can
do. Clearer, compare road. Class cyclists Tour
de France use.

III. MTB, road built different purposes. (SHOW MB &
RB SLIDE 5)

  A. MTB tackle rough, road designed fast, paved, smooth.

    1. Accomplish task, wide tire, tough tread.

    2. In contrast, road ultrathin, frames lightweight.

      a. Take off-road, destroy.

      b. Without knobby tread, thickness MTB tires, road
can't grip rocks, obstacles.

  B. Handlebars differ.

    1. MTB flat; upright stance, don't flip.

    2. Drop handlebars require forward; suits road cycling,
prizes speed.

  C. Gears, suspension also differ.

    1. MTB lower gears, widely spaced—more control
difficult terrain.

    2. As for suspension, road don't, absorb power.

      a. That is, don't have shock, not supposed to.

      b. Imagine without shocks; wouldn't be pretty.

    3. Many MTBs at least a great front.

      a. Some rear.

      b. Some dual.

(TRANSITION)   Hope sense MTB design, but finer
distinction . . .

IV. Actually three types MTB, accommodate three kinds.

(TRANSITION)   Let's start with downhill. (SHOW DH
SLIDE 6)

  A. Downhill fewest gears, weigh most.

    1. Because downhill daredevil—crazy!

    2. Slide insane, off jumps.

  B. Trails.com, downhill racers catch shuttle going up,
speed downhill chewing up.

  C. Think racing skiing bike.

(TRANSITION)   Now let's swing by trail biking. (SHOW TB
SLIDE 7)

  D. Trail bikes look different than either.

    1. Small wheels, 20, 24, or 26, smaller frames.

    2. Differences design help trail do best—jump
obstacles—cars, rocks, large logs.

E. Trail goal not foot on ground.

F. Trail racing few types done by time, not mass.

(TRANSITION)   Third major type MTB, cross-country, or XC.
(SHOW XC SLIDE 8)

G. Cross-country most common—Olympics.

1. That's right. In 1996 . . .

2. Just two decades inception.

H. With XC, best all worlds, humble.

1. Courses creative, incorporating hills, valleys, rough, not-so.

2. Competitively, XC like marathon.

3. Recreationally, chance see outdoors, shape.

I. XC two forms.

1. Lightweight, full or partial.

2. Trails/Marathon XC hybrids heavier, full suspension; designed seriously long.

(TRANSITION)   Quite tour.

Conclusion

I. Course began overview, hopturn history sport.

II. Also learned differences: mountain, road, three major categories of MTB, three types MTB accommodate fans.

III. To me, MTB, especially XC, perfect—fulfilling physical, spiritual, social needs.

IV. Great take up recreationally.

V. Decide bike competitively, remember: ride fast, drive hard, leave blood.

✓ CHECKLIST

Steps in Creating a Speaking Outline

❑ Create the outline on sheets of paper, large notecards, or software app.

❑ Write large and legibly using at least a 14-point font or easy-to-read ink and large letters.

❑ For each main and subpoint, choose a key word or phrase that will jog your memory accurately.

❑ Include delivery cues.

❑ Write out full quotations or other critical information.

❑ Using the speaking outline, practice the speech at least five times, or as needed.

part

Starting, Finishing, and Styling

VIDEO ACTIVITY
Go to LaunchPad to watch a video about
a student who used an ineffective example
in her speech. Visit **launchpadworks.com**

LaunchPad includes:

☑ **LearningCurve** adaptive quizzing

▶ A curated collection of video clips and
full-length speeches

Additional resources, such as presentation
software tutorials and documentation help.

CHAPTER 14 ●●●●

Developing the Introduction and Conclusion

A compelling introduction and conclusion, although not a
substitute for a well-developed speech body, are nevertheless
essential to the success of any speech. A good opening
previews what's to come in a way that engages listeners in
the topic and speaker. An effective conclusion ensures that the
audience remembers key points and reacts in a way that
the speaker intends.

◎ Preparing the Introduction

The choices you make about the introduction can affect the
outcome of the entire speech. In the first several minutes
(one speaker pegs it at twenty seconds),[1] audience members
will decide whether they are interested in the topic of your
speech and whether they will believe what you say. A speech
introduction serves to:

- Arouse the audience's attention and willingness to listen.
- Introduce the topic, purpose, and main points.
- Establish your credibility to speak on the topic.
- Motivate the audience to accept your speech goals.

✓ CHECKLIST

Guidelines for Preparing the Introduction

❑ Prepare the introduction after you've completed the
speech body so you will know exactly what you need
to preview.

❑ Keep the introduction brief—as a rule, no more than
10–15 percent of the entire speech.

❑ Practice delivering your introduction until you feel
confident you've got it right.

Gain Audience Attention

An introduction must first of all win the audience's attention. They must believe the speech will interest them and offer them something of benefit. Techniques for doing this include sharing a compelling quotation or story, establishing common ground, providing unusual information, posing a question, and using humor.

USE A QUOTATION   In a recent commencement address, Twitter executive Wayne Chang advised graduates: "Make your own rules, hack the system, and change the world."[2] Quotations such as this, which touch upon a theme of the speech, will likely arouse interest. Quotations can be drawn from literature, poetry, and film, or directly from people you know.

TELL A STORY   Noted speechwriter William Safire once remarked that stories are "surefire attention getters."[3] Stories, or *narratives*, personalize issues by encouraging audience identification and involvement. Speeches that begin with brief stories of meaningful and entertaining incidents can boost speaker credibility and promote greater understanding and retention of the speaker's message[4] (see also p. 57). You can relate an entire story (if brief) in the introduction or, alternatively, offer part of a longer one, indicating you will return to it further on in the speech.

QUICK TIP

Show Them the Transformation

Stories often feature transformation—how people overcome obstacles or otherwise experience change.[5] One powerful means of gaining audience involvement is to tell a story in which others were changed by adopting beliefs and behaviors similar to those you are proposing in your speech. If you can think of a story that does this, your message is likely to be doubly persuasive.

ESTABLISH COMMON GROUND   Audiences are won over when speakers express interest in them and show that they share in the audience's concerns and goals. Refer to the occasion that has brought you together, and use your knowledge of the audience to touch briefly on areas of shared experience. This creates goodwill and a feeling of common ground (or *identification;* see also Chapter 6).

OFFER UNUSUAL INFORMATION   "Nearly one in 100 people are now displaced from their homes."[6] Surprising audience members with startling facts and statistics is one of the surest ways to get their attention. Offering statistics, for example, is a powerful means of illustrating consequences and relationships that can quickly bring points into focus, as in this opener by Chef James Oliver: "Sadly, in the next eighteen minutes when I do our chat, four Americans that are alive will be dead from the food they eat."[7]

POSE QUESTIONS "How long do you think our water supply will last?" Posing questions such as this can be an effective way to draw the audience's attention to what you are about to say. Questions can be real or rhetorical. **Rhetorical questions** do not invite actual responses. Instead, they make the audience think.

USE HUMOR—PERHAPS Handled well, humor can build rapport and set a positive tone for the speech. But humor can also easily backfire. Simply telling a series of unrelated jokes without making a relevant point will detract from your purpose, and few things turn an audience off more quickly than tasteless humor. Strictly avoid humor or sarcasm that belittles others—whether on the basis of race, sex, ability, or otherwise. A good rule of thumb is that speech humor should always match the rhetorical situation.

Preview the Topic, Purpose, and Main Points

Once you've gained the audience's attention, use the introduction to provide a **preview**, or brief overview, of the speech *topic*, *purpose*, and *main points*. First, declare what your speech is about (topic) and what you hope to accomplish (purpose).

Topic and purpose are clearly revealed in this introduction by Marvin Runyon, former postmaster general of the United States:

> This afternoon, I want to examine the truth of that statement—"Nothing moves people like the mail, and no one moves the mail like the U.S. Postal Service." I want to look at where we are today as a communications industry, and where we intend to be in the days and years ahead.[8]

Once you've revealed the topic and purpose, briefly preview the main points of the speech. This helps audience members mentally organize the speech as they follow along. Simply tell the audience what the main points will be and in what order you will address them. Save your in-depth discussion of each one for the body of your speech.

Robert L. Darbelnet, former CEO of the American Automobile Association, effectively introduces his topic, purpose, and main points with this preview:

> My remarks today are intended to give you a sense of AAA's ongoing efforts to improve America's roads. Our hope is

that you will join your voices to ours as we call on the federal government to do three things:

Number one: Perhaps the most important, provide adequate funding for highway maintenance and improvements.

Number two: Play a strong, responsible, yet flexible role in transportation programs.

And number three: Invest in highway safety.

Let's see what our strengths are, what the issues are, and what we can do about them.[9]

Establish Credibility as a Speaker

During the introduction, audience members make a decision about whether they are interested not just in your topic but also in you. They want to feel that they can trust what you have to say—that they can believe in your *ethos*, or good character. To build credibility, offer a simple statement of your qualifications for speaking on the topic. Briefly emphasize some experience, knowledge, or perspective you have that is different from or more extensive than that of your audience: "I've felt passionate about preserving open space ever since I started volunteering with the Land Trust four summers ago."

Motivate the Audience to Accept Your Goals

A final, and critical, function of the introduction is to motivate the audience to care about your topic and make it relevant to them. You may choose to convey what the audience stands to gain by the information you will share or convince audience members that your speech purpose is consistent with their motives and values. A student speech about the value of interview training shows how this can be accomplished:

Why do you need interview training? It boils down to competition. As in sports, when you're not training, someone else is out there training to beat you. All things being equal, the person who has the best interviewing skills has got the edge.

✓ CHECKLIST

How Effective Is Your Introduction?

Does your introduction . . .

❏ Capture the audience's attention?

❏ Stimulate their interest in what's to come?

❏ Establish a positive bond with listeners?

❏ Alert listeners to the speech topic, purpose, and main points?

❏ Establish your credibility?

❏ Motivate listeners to accept your speech goals?

◎ Preparing the Conclusion

Just as a well-crafted introduction gets your speech effectively out of the starting gate, a well-constructed conclusion lets you drive home your purpose and leave the audience inspired to think about and even to act upon your ideas. The conclusion serves to:

- Signal the end of the speech and provide closure.
- Summarize the key points.
- Reiterate the thesis or central idea of the speech.
- Challenge the audience to remember and possibly act upon your ideas.
- End the speech memorably.

Signal the End of the Speech and Provide Closure

People who listen to speeches are taking a journey of sorts, and they want and need the speaker to acknowledge the journey's end. They look for logical and emotional closure.

One signal that a speech is about to end is a transitional word or phrase: *finally, looking back, in conclusion, let me close by saying* (see Chapter 11). You can also signal closure by adjusting your manner of delivery; for example, you can vary your tone, pitch, rhythm, and rate of speech to indicate that the speech is winding down (see Chapters 17 and 18).

✓ CHECKLIST
Guidelines for Preparing the Conclusion

❑ As with the introduction, prepare the conclusion after you've completed the speech body.

❑ Do not leave the conclusion to chance. Include it with your speaking outline.

❑ Keep the conclusion brief—as a rule, no more than 10–15 percent, or about one-sixth, of the overall speech. Conclude soon after you say you are about to end.

❑ Carefully consider your use of language. More than in other parts of the speech, the conclusion can contain words that inspire and motivate (see Chapter 15 on use of language).

❑ Practice delivering your conclusion until you feel confident you've got it right.

❑ Once you've signaled the end of your speech, conclude in short order (though not abruptly).

Summarize the Key Points

One bit of age-old advice for giving a speech is "Tell them what you are going to tell them (in the introduction), tell them (in the body), and tell them what you told them (in the conclusion)." The idea is that emphasizing the main points three times will help the audience remember them. A restatement of points in the conclusion brings the speech full circle and gives the audience a sense of completion. Consider how executive Holger Kluge, in a speech titled "Reflections on Diversity," summarizes his main points:

> I have covered a lot of ground here today. But as I draw to a close, I'd like to stress three things.
>
> First, diversity is more than equity. . . .
>
> Second, weaving diversity into the very fabric of your organization takes time. . . .
>
> Third, diversity will deliver bottom line results to your businesses and those results will be substantial. . . .[10]

Reiterate the Topic and Speech Purpose

The conclusion should reiterate the topic and speech purpose—to imprint it on the audience's memory. In the conclusion to a speech about the U.S. immigration debate, civil defense lawyer Elpidio Villarreal reminds his listeners of his central idea:

> Two paths are open to us. One path would keep us true to our fundamental values as a nation and a people. The other would lead us down a dark trail; one marked by 700-mile-long fences, emergency detention centers and vigilante border patrols. Because I really am an American, heart and soul, and because that means never being without hope, I still believe we will ultimately choose the right path. We have to.[11]

Challenge the Audience to Respond

A strong conclusion challenges audience members to put to use what the speaker has shared with them. In an *informative speech*, the speaker challenges audience members to use what they've learned in a way that benefits them. In a *persuasive speech*, the challenge usually comes in the form of a call to action. Here the speaker challenges listeners to act in response to the speech, see the problem in a new way, or change both their actions and their beliefs about the problem.

Emma Watson, United Nations Women Goodwill Ambassador, makes a strong call to action at the conclusion of her speech at a special event for the HeForShe campaign.

We are struggling for a uniting word, but the good news is we have a uniting movement. It is called HeForShe. I am inviting you to step forward, to be seen to speak up, to be the "he" for "she." And to ask yourself if not me, who? If not now, when?[12]

QUICK TIP

Bring Your Speech Full Circle

Picking up on a story or an idea you mentioned in the introduction can be a memorable way to conclude a speech and bring the entire presentation full circle. You can provide the resolution of the story or reiterate the link between the moral (lesson) of the story and the speech theme.

Make the Conclusion Memorable

A speech that makes a lasting impression is one that listeners are most likely to remember and act on. To accomplish this, make use of the same devices for capturing attention described for use in introductions—quotations, stories, startling statements, questions, references to the audience and the occasion, and humor.

✓ CHECKLIST

How Effective Is Your Conclusion?

Does your conclusion . . .

❑ Alert the audience, with a transition, that the speech is ending?

❑ Actually come to an end soon after you say you will finish?

❑ Last no more than about one-sixth of the time spent on the body of the speech?

❑ Remind listeners of the speech topic, purpose, and main points?

❑ Include a challenge or call to action to motivate the audience to respond to your ideas or appeals?

❑ Provide a sense of closure and make a lasting impression?

CHAPTER 15 ●●●●

Using Language

Words are the public speaker's tools of the trade, and the ones you choose to style your speech will play a crucial role in creating a dynamic connection with your audience. The right words and **rhetorical devices** (techniques of language) will help your listeners understand, believe in, and retain your message.

◉ Use an Oral Style

Speeches require an **oral style**—the use of language that is simpler, more repetitious, more rhythmic, and more interactive than written language.[1] As Jayne Benjulian, former chief speechwriter at Apple, has noted, "Every speech has language meant to be spoken. They are monologues. . . . Speeches are an oral medium."[2] Speeches therefore must be prepared for the ear—to be *heard* rather than read. This is particularly important because unlike readers, listeners have only one chance to get the message.

Strive for Simplicity

To ensure understanding, express yourself simply, without pretentious language or unnecessary **jargon** (the specialized, "insider" language of a given profession). Speak in commonly understood terms and choose the simpler of two synonyms: *guess* rather than *extrapolate*; *use* rather than *utilize*. Use fewer rather than more words, and shorter sentences rather than longer ones. As speechwriter Peggy Noonan notes in her book *Simply Speaking*:

> Good hard simple words with good hard clear meanings are good things to use when you speak. They are like pickets in a fence, slim and unimpressive on their own but sturdy and effective when strung together.[3]

Former First Lady Michelle Obama, in a speech at the Democratic Convention, used the simplest, jargon-free language to describe her party's response to its opponents: "When they go low, we go high."[4] Each word contains just one syllable, yet the audience roared with understanding and approval.

Make Frequent Use of Repetition

Repetition is key to oral style, serving to compensate for natural lapses in listening and to reinforce information. Even very brief speeches repeat key words and phrases. Repetition adds emphasis to important ideas, helps listeners follow your logic, and infuses language with rhythm and drama.

> ## QUICK TIP
>
> ### Experiment with Phrases and Sentence Fragments
>
> In line with an oral style, experiment with using phrases and sentence fragments in place of full sentences. This speaker, a physician, demonstrates how short phrases can add punch to a speech: "I'm just a simple bone-and-joint guy. I can set your broken bones. Take away your bunions. Even give you a new hip. But I don't mess around with the stuff between the ears. . . . That's another specialty."[5]

Use Personal Pronouns

Audience members want to know what the speaker thinks and feels, and to be assured that he or she recognizes them and relates them to the message. The direct form of address, using the personal pronouns such as *we, us, I,* and *you,* helps to create this feeling of recognition and inclusion. Note how Sheryl Sandberg, Chief Operating Officer of Facebook, uses personal pronouns to begin a speech on why there are too few women leaders (italics added):

> So for any of *us* in this room today, let's start out by admitting *we're* lucky. *We* don't live in the world *our* mothers lived in, *our* grandmothers lived in, where career choices for women were so limited. . . . But all that aside, *we* still have a problem. . . . Women are not making it to the top of any profession anywhere in the world.[6]

◉ Choose Concrete Language and Vivid Imagery

Concrete words and vivid imagery engage audience members' senses, making a speech come alive for listeners. **Concrete language** is specific, tangible, and definite. Concrete nouns such as *iceberg, stone, lawn,* and *butter* describe things we can physically sense (see, hear, taste, smell, and touch). In contrast, **abstract language** is general or nonspecific, leaving meaning open to interpretation. Abstract nouns, such as *peace, freedom,* and *love,* are purely conceptual; they have no physical reference. Politicians use abstract language to appeal to mass audiences, or to be noncommittal: "We strive for peace." In most speaking situations, however, listeners will appreciate concrete nouns and verbs.

Note how concrete nouns and adjectives that modify them add precision and color:

Abstract: The old road needed repair.

Concrete: The rutted road was pitted with muddy craters.

Offer Vivid Imagery

Imagery is concrete language that brings into play the senses of smell, taste, sight, hearing, and touch to paint mental pictures. Vivid imagery is more easily recalled than colorless language,[7] and speeches containing ample imagery also elicit more positive responses than those that do not.[8]

Adding imagery into your speech need not be difficult if you focus on using strong, active verbs and colorful adjectives. Rather than *walk*, you can say *saunter*; in place of *look*, use *gaze*. Replace passive forms of the verb "to be" (e.g., *is, are, was, were, will be* . . .) with more active verb forms. Rather than "the houses were empty," use "the houses *stood* empty." You can use descriptive adjectives to modify nouns (as in "*dilapidated* house") and use adverbs to modify verbs. President Franklin D. Roosevelt famously did this when he characterized the nation's struggles during World War II as "this dark hour,"[9] conveying with one simple adjective the gravity of the times.

Choose Strong Verbs

Mundane Verb	Colorful Alternative
look	*behold, gaze, glimpse, peek, stare*
walk	*stride, amble, stroll, skulk*
throw	*hurl, fling, pitch*
sit	*sink, plop, settle*
eat	*devour, inhale, gorge*

Use Figures of Speech

Figures of speech make striking comparisons that help listeners visualize, identify with, and understand the speaker's ideas. Such figures as similes, metaphors, and analogies are key to making a speech both memorable and persuasive.

A **simile** explicitly compares one thing to another, using *like* or *as*: "He works *like a dog*," and "rusted-out factories scattered *like tombstones across the landscape*."[10]

A **metaphor** also compares two things, but does so by describing one thing as actually *being* the other: "Time is a thief" and "Drain the swamp" (with government bureaucracy being the swamp).

An **analogy** is simply an extended metaphor or simile that compares an unfamiliar concept or process to a more familiar one. For example, African American minister Phil Wilson used metaphoric language when he preached about the dangers of AIDS:

> Our house is on fire! The fire truck arrives, but we won't come out, because we're afraid the folks from next door will see that we're in that burning house. AIDS is a fire raging in our community and it's out of control![11]

Avoid Clichés, Mixed Metaphors, and Faulty Analogies

Used properly, similes and metaphors express ideas compactly and cleverly. However, avoid those that are predictable and stale, known as **clichés**, such as "sold like hotcakes" (a clichéd simile) and "pearly white teeth" (a clichéd metaphor). Beware, too, of using **mixed metaphors**, or combining two or more unrelated (and incompatible) images: For example, "Burning the midnight oil at both ends" incorrectly joins the metaphor "burning the midnight oil" and "burning the candle at both ends."

Analogies, too, can mislead audience members if used carelessly. A **faulty analogy** is an inaccurate or misleading comparison suggesting that because two things are similar in some ways, they are necessarily similar in others. (See p. 163 on using analogies.)

◉ Choose Words That Build Credibility

Audiences expect speakers to be competent and credible. To project these qualities, use language that is appropriate, accurate, assertive, and unbiased.

Use Words Appropriately

The language you use in a speech should be appropriate to the audience, the occasion, and the subject matter. Formal occasions call for more formal language, but no matter what the occasion, listeners will expect you to avoid obvious grammatical errors and substandard usage (as well as any form of suggestive language, bathroom humor, and obscene references). Done carefully, it may be appropriate to mix regionalisms or **vernacular language** (language specific to particular regions of a country) or even slang into your speech. Even alternating between two languages, called *code-switching*, may be appropriate. The key is to ensure that your meaning is clear and your use is suitable for your audience. Consider the following excerpt:

> On the gulf where I was raised, *el valle del Rio Grande* in South Texas—that triangular piece of land wedged between the river *y el golfo* which serves as the Texas–U.S./Mexican border—is a Mexican *pueblito* called Hargill.[12]

Use Words Accurately

Audiences lose confidence in speakers who misuse words. Check that your words mean what you intend, and beware especially of **malapropisms**—the inadvertent, incorrect uses of a word or phrase in place of one that sounds like it[13]. ("It's a strange receptacle" for "It's a strange spectacle").

Use the Active Voice

Voice is the feature of verbs that indicates the subject's relationship to the action. Speaking in the active rather than passive voice will make your statements—and the audience's perception of you as the speaker—clear and assertive instead of indirect and weak. A verb is in the *active voice* when the subject performs the action, and in the *passive voice* when the subject is acted upon or is the receiver of the action:

Passive:	A test was announced by Ms. Carlos for Tuesday.
	A president is elected every four years.
Active:	Ms. Carlos announced a test for Tuesday.
	The voters elect a president every four years.

Use Inclusive, Unbiased Language

Focus on using language that reflects respect for audience members' cultural beliefs, norms, and traditions. Review and eliminate any language that reflects unfounded assumptions, negative descriptions, or stereotypes of a given group's age, class, gender identity, sexual orientation, ability, and ethnic, racial, or religious characteristics. Consider whether certain seemingly well-known names and terms may be foreign to some listeners, and include brief explanations for them. Sayings specific to a certain region or group of people—termed **colloquial expressions** or *idioms*—such as "back the wrong horse" and "ballpark figure" can add color and richness to a speech, but only if listeners understand them.

Word your speech with gender-neutral language: Avoid the third-person generic masculine pronouns (*his, he*) in favor of inclusive pronouns such as *his or her, he or she, they, their, we, our, you, your,* or other gender-neutral terms that your audience will understand.

QUICK TIP

Denotative versus Connotative Meaning

When drafting your speech, choose words that are both denotatively and connotatively appropriate to the audience. The **denotative meaning** of a word is its literal, or dictionary, definition. The **connotative meaning** of a word is the special (often emotional) association that different people bring to bear on it. For example, you may agree that you are *angry* but not *irate,* and *thrifty* but not *cheap.* Consider how the connotative meanings of your word choices might affect the audience's response to your message, including those of non-native speakers of English.

◉ Choose Words That Create a Lasting Impression

Oral speech that is artfully arranged and infused with rhythm draws listeners in and leaves a lasting impression on audience members. It is surprisingly easy to achieve this effect with rhetorical devices such as repetition, alliteration, and parallelism.

Use Repetition to Create Rhythm

Repeating key words, phrases, or even sentences at various intervals throughout a speech creates a distinctive rhythm and thereby implants important ideas in listeners' minds. Repetition works particularly well when delivered with the appropriate voice inflections and pauses.

In a form of repetition called **anaphora**, the speaker repeats a word or phrase at the beginning of successive phrases, clauses, or sentences. In his speech delivered in 1963 in Washington, DC, Dr. Martin Luther King Jr. repeated the phrase "I have a dream" eleven times in eight successive sentences, each with an upward inflection followed by a pause. Speakers have made use of anaphora since earliest times. For example, Jesus preached (italics added):

Blessed are the poor in spirit . . .
Blessed are the meek . . .
Blessed are the peacemakers . . .[14]

Repetition can focus attention on the theme of the speech. Speakers may do this by using both anaphora and *epiphora* in the same speech. In **epiphora** (also called *epistrophe*), the repetition of a word or phrase appears at the end of successive statements. In a speech to his New Hampshire supporters, former President Barack Obama used both anaphora and epiphora to establish a theme of empowerment (italics added):

> *It was* a creed written into the founding documents that declared the destiny of a nation: *Yes, we can.*

> *It was* whispered by slaves and abolitionists as they blazed a trail toward freedom through the darkest of nights: *Yes, we can.*

> *It was* sung by immigrants as they struck out from distant shores and pioneers who pushed westward against an unforgiving wilderness: *Yes, we can.*[15]

Use Alliteration for a Poetic Quality

Alliteration is the repetition of the same sounds, usually initial consonants, in two or more neighboring words or syllables. Alliteration lends speeches a poetic, musical rhythm. A classic example is Jesse Jackson's "Down with dope, up with hope." More recently, President Donald J. Trump threatened to respond to North Korean aggression with "fire and fury."

Experiment with Parallelism

Parallelism is the arrangement of words, phrases, or sentences in a similar form. Parallel structure helps emphasize important ideas, and can be as simple as orally numbering points ("first, second, and third"). Like repetition, parallelism also creates a sense of steady or building rhythm. Speakers often make use of three parallel elements, called a *triad*, as in Abraham Lincoln's famous ". . . of the people, by the people, and for the people . . . ."

Parallelism in speeches often makes use of **antithesis**—setting off two ideas in balanced (parallel) opposition to each other to create a powerful effect:

> One small step for a man, one giant leap for mankind.
> —*Neil Armstrong on the moon, 1969*

> For many are called, but few are chosen.
> —*Matthew 22:14*

✓ CHECKLIST

Using Effective Oral Style

❑ Use familiar words and easy-to-follow sentences.

❑ Root out biased language.

❑ Avoid unnecessary jargon.

❑ Use fewer rather than more words to express your thoughts.

❑ Clarify meaning and make memorable comparisons with *similes*, *metaphors*, and *analogies*.

❑ Use the active voice.

❑ Repeat key words, phrases, or sentences at the beginning of successive sentences (*anaphora*) and at their close (*epiphora*).

❑ Experiment with *alliteration*—words that repeat the same sounds, usually initial consonants, in two or more neighboring words or syllables.

❑ Experiment with *parallelism*—arranging words, phrases, or sentences in similar form.

part

Delivery

CHAPTER 16 ●●●●

Methods of Delivery

For most of us, anticipating the actual delivery of a speech feels unnerving. In fact, effective delivery rests on the same natural foundation as everyday conversation, except, obviously, that it is more rehearsed and purposeful. By focusing on four key qualities of effective delivery, you can reduce your fears and make your presentations more authentic.

◉ Keys to Effective Delivery

Effective delivery is the controlled use of voice and body to express the qualities of naturalness, enthusiasm, confidence, and directness.[1] Audiences respond most favorably to speakers who project these characteristics during delivery. As you practice delivering your speech, focus on these key qualities:

- *Strive for naturalness.* Rather than behaving theatrically, act naturally. Think of your speech as a particularly important conversation.

- *Show enthusiasm.* Inspire your listeners by showing enthusiasm for your topic and for the occasion. An enthusiastic delivery helps you feel good about your speech, and it focuses your audience's attention on the message.

- *Project a sense of confidence.* Focus on the ideas you want to convey rather than on yourself. Inspire the audience's confidence in you by appearing confident to them.

- *Be direct.* Engage directly with audience members. Demonstrate your interest and concern for listeners by establishing eye contact, using a friendly tone of voice, and animating your facial expressions, especially positive ones such as smiling and nodding whenever appropriate. (See Chapters 17 and 18 on techniques for using voice and body in a speech.)

◉ Select a Method of Delivery

For virtually any type of speech or presentation, you can choose from four basic methods of delivery: speaking from manuscript, speaking from memory, speaking impromptu, and speaking extemporaneously.

Speaking from Manuscript

When **speaking from manuscript**, you read a speech *verbatim*—that is, from prepared written text that contains the entire speech, word for word. As a rule, speaking from manuscript restricts eye contact and body movement, and may also limit expressiveness in vocal variety and quality. Watching a speaker read a speech can be monotonous and boring for the audience.

If you must read from prepared text—for example, when you need to convey a precise message, when you will be quoted and must avoid misinterpretation, or when addressing an emergency and conveying exact descriptions and direction—do what you can to deliver the speech naturally:

- Vary the rhythm of your words (see Chapter 17).
- Become familiar enough with the speech so that you can establish some eye contact.
- Use a large font and double- or triple-space the manuscript so that you can read without straining.
- Consider using some compelling presentation aids (see Chapter 20).

Speaking from Memory

The formal name for **speaking from memory** is *oratory*. In oratorical style, you put the entire speech, word for word, into writing and then commit it to memory. Memorization is not a natural way to present a message. True eye contact with the audience is unlikely, and the potential for disaster exists because there is always the possibility of forgetting. Some kinds of brief speeches, however, such as toasts and introductions, can be well served by memorization. Sometimes it's helpful to memorize a part of the speech, especially when you use direct quotations as a form of support. If you do use memorization, practice that portion of your speech so completely that you can convey enthusiasm and directness.

Speaking Impromptu

Speaking impromptu is a type of delivery that is unpracticed, spontaneous, or improvised, and involves speaking on relatively short notice with little time to prepare. Many occasions require that you make remarks on the spur of the moment. An instructor may ask you to summarize key points from an assignment, for example, or a boss may invite you to take the place of an absent co-worker who was scheduled to speak on a new project.

Try to anticipate situations that may require you to speak impromptu, and prepare some remarks beforehand. Otherwise, maximize the time you do have to prepare on the spot:

- *Think first about your listeners.* Consider their interests and needs, and try to shape your remarks accordingly. For example, who are the people present, and what are their views on the topic?
- *Listen to what others around you are saying.* Take notes in a key-word or phrase format (see p. 105) and arrange them into main points from which you can speak.
- *Acknowledge the previous speaker.* If your speech follows someone else's, acknowledge that person's statements. Then make your points.
- *Stay on the topic.* Don't wander off track.
- *Use transitions.* Use signal words such as *first, second,* and *third* to organize points and help listeners follow them.

As much as possible, try to organize your points into a discernible pattern. If addressing a problem, for example, such as a project failure or glitch, consider the *problem-solution pattern*—state problem(s), then offer solution(s); or the *cause-effect pattern* of organizational arrangement—state cause(s) first, then address effect(s); see Chapter 12 for various ways of using these patterns. If called upon to defend one proposal as superior to another, consider using the *comparative advantage pattern* to illustrate various advantages of your favored proposal over the other options (see p. 189).

Speaking Extemporaneously

When **speaking extemporaneously**, you prepare and practice in advance, giving full attention to all facets of the speech—content, arrangement, and delivery alike. However, instead of memorizing or writing the speech word for word, you speak from an outline of key words and phrases that isolates the main ideas that you want to communicate (see Chapter 13).

Because extemporaneous delivery is most conducive to achieving a natural, conversational quality, most speakers prefer it among the four types of delivery. Knowing your ideas well enough to present them without memorization or manuscript gives you greater flexibility in adapting to the specific speaking situation. You can modify wording, rearrange your points, change examples, or omit information in keeping with the audience and the setting. You can have more eye contact, more direct body orientation, greater freedom of movement, and generally better control of your thoughts and actions than any of the other delivery methods allow.

Speaking extemporaneously does present a possible drawback. Occasionally, even a glance at your speaking notes may fail to jog your memory on a point you wanted to cover, and you find yourself searching for what to say next. The remedy for this potential pitfall is frequent practice—rehearsing the speech about six times—using a key word or phrase outline (see p. 105).

Choosing a Method of Delivery

When . . .	Method of Delivery
You want to avoid being misquoted or misconstrued, or you need to communicate exact descriptions and directions . . .	Consider *speaking from manuscript* (read the part of your speech requiring precise wording from fully prepared text).
You must deliver a short special occasion speech, such as a toast or an introduction, or you plan on using direct quotations . . .	Consider *speaking from memory* (memorize part or all of your speech).
You are called upon to speak without prior planning or preparation . . .	By definition, you will be *speaking impromptu*— (organizing your thoughts with little or no lead time). Follow the guidelines on p. 129.
You have time to prepare and practice developing a speech or presentation that achieves a natural conversational style . . .	Consider *speaking extemporaneously* (develop your speech in working outline and then practice and deliver it with a phrase or key-word speaking outline).

> ✓ **CHECKLIST**
>
> **Tips for Successful Delivery**
>
> ❏ Strive for naturalness.
> ❏ Show enthusiasm.
> ❏ Project a sense of confidence and composure.
> ❏ Engage your audience by being direct.
> ❏ If you must read from a prepared text, do so naturally.
> ❏ In general, don't try to memorize entire speeches.
> ❏ When speaking impromptu, maximize any preparation time.

CHAPTER 17 ●●●●

Your Voice in Delivery

Used properly in the delivery of a speech, your voice is a powerful instrument of expression that conveys who you are and delivers your message with confidence. As you practice, you can learn to control each of the elements of vocal delivery: volume, pitch, speaking rate, pauses, vocal variety, and pronunciation and articulation.

◉ Adjust Your Speaking Volume

Volume, the relative loudness of a speaker's voice while delivering a speech, is usually the most obvious vocal element we notice about a speaker, and with good reason. We need to hear the speaker at a comfortable level. The proper volume for delivering a speech is somewhat louder than that of normal conversation. Just how much louder depends on three factors: (1) the size of the room and of the audience, (2) whether or not you use a microphone, and (3) the level of background noise. Speaking at the appropriate volume is critical to how credible your listeners will perceive you to be, so check that audience members can hear you. Be alert to signals that your volume is slipping or is too loud and make the necessary adjustments.

◉ Vary Your Intonation

Pitch is the range of sounds from high to low (or vice versa). Anatomy determines a person's natural pitch—a bigger or smaller voice box produces a lower- or higher-pitched voice.

QUICK TIP

Breathe from Your Diaphragm

To project your voice so that it is loud enough to be heard by everyone in the audience, breathe deeply from your diaphragm rather than more shallowly from your vocal cords. The reason? The strength of your voice depends on the amount of air the diaphragm—a large, dome-shaped muscle encasing the inner rib cage—pushes from the lungs to the vocal cords. With full but relaxed breaths, the depth of your voice will improve and help your voice sound more confident.

But within these natural constraints, you can and should control pitch through **intonation**—the rising and falling of sound across phrases and sentences. Intonation is important in speechmaking because it powerfully affects the meaning associated with spoken words. For example, say "Stop." Now, say "Stop!" Varying intonation conveys two very distinct meanings.

As you speak, intonation conveys your mood, level of enthusiasm, and commitment to the audience and occasion. Without intonation, speaking becomes monotonous—a death knell to any speech.

To avoid a monotone voice, practice and listen to your speeches with a recording device, such as a smart phone or computer. You will readily identify instances that require better intonation.

◉ Adjust Your Speaking Rate

Speaking rate is the pace at which you convey speech. The normal rate of speech in face-to-face conversation for native English-speaking adults is roughly between 120–130 and 160–170 words per minute, but there is no standard or ideal rate. If the overall rate is too slow, the audience will get fidgety, bored, and even sleepy. If too fast, listeners will appear irritated and confused, because they can't catch what you're saying. The audience may see you as unsure about your control of the speech.[1] If you tend to speak either too quickly or too slowly, choose 160 words from your speech and time yourself for one minute as you speak them aloud. If you fall very short of finishing, increase your pace. If you finish well before the minute is up, slow down. Practice until you achieve a comfortable speaking rate.

Use a Natural Conversational Pace

Experts recommend using your natural conversational pace when delivering a speech, but varying the pace and vocal emphasis at different points.[2] Focus on slowing your pace during serious points and picking it up during lighter ones. Think about "punching" key phrases with emphatic intonation. Experiment with and practice these variations in pacing and vocal emphasis until they feel natural.

◉ Use Strategic Pauses

Many novice speakers are uncomfortable with pauses. Like intonation, however, pauses can be important strategic elements of a speech. **Pauses** enhance meaning by providing a type of punctuation, emphasizing a point, drawing attention to a thought, or just allowing listeners a moment to contemplate what is being said.

As you practice delivering your speech, focus on avoiding unnecessary and undesirable **vocal fillers** such as *uh*, *hmm*, *you know*, *I mean*, and *it's like*. These so-called disfluencies will make you appear unprepared and cause audience members to be distracted from the message. Rather than vocal fillers, use silent pauses for strategic effect.

◉ Strive for Vocal Variety

Rather than operating separately, all the vocal elements described so far—volume, pitch, speaking rate, and pauses—work together to create **vocal variety**. Indeed, the real key to effective vocal delivery is to vary all these elements with a tone of enthusiasm. For example, as the great civil rights leader Martin Luther King Jr. spoke the now famous words "I have a dream," his pauses were immediately preceded by a combination of reduced speech rate and increased volume and pitch. Vocal variety comes quite naturally when you are excited about what you are saying to an audience, when you feel it is important and want to share it with them.

◉ Carefully Pronounce and Articulate Words

Few things distract an audience more than improper pronunciation or unclear articulation of words. **Pronunciation** is the correct formation of word sounds—examples of mispronunciation include, *aks* for *asked* (askt), and *jen-yu-wine* for

✓ CHECKLIST

Practice Check for Vocal Effectiveness

- ❑ As you practice, is your vocal delivery effective?
- ❑ Is your voice too loud? Too soft?
- ❑ Do you avoid speaking in a monotone? Do you vary the stress or emphasis you place on words to clearly express your meaning?
- ❑ Is your rate of speech comfortable for listeners?
- ❑ Do you avoid unnecessary vocal fillers, such as *uh, hmm, you know, I mean,* and *it's like*?
- ❑ Do you use silent pauses for strategic effect?
- ❑ Does your voice reflect a variety of emotional expressions? Do you convey enthusiasm?

genuine (jen yu **in**). **Articulation** is the clarity or forcefulness with which the sounds are made, regardless of whether they are pronounced correctly. Incorrect pronunciation and poor articulation are largely a matter of habit.

A common pattern of poor articulation is **mumbling**—slurring words together at a low level of volume and pitch so that they are barely audible. Sometimes the problem is **lazy speech**. Common examples are saying *fer* instead of *for* and *wanna* instead of *want to.*

Like any habit, poor articulation can be overcome by unlearning the problem behavior:

- If you mumble, practice speaking more loudly and with emphatic pronunciation.
- If you tend toward lazy speech, put more effort into your articulation.
- Consciously try to say each word clearly and correctly.
- Practice clear and precise enunciation of proper word sounds. Say *articulation* several times until it rolls off your tongue naturally.
- Do the same for these words: *want to, going to, Atlanta, chocolate, sophomore, California.*

◉ Use Dialect (Language Variation) with Care

Every culture has subcultural variations on the preferred pronunciation and articulation of its languages, called **dialects**. In the United States, there is so-called Standard English, Black English, regional varieties of Spanglish (a mix of Spanish and English, such as Tex-Mex), and other regional variations in the South, New England, and along the Canadian border. Although dialects are neither superior nor inferior to standard language patterns, the audience must be able to understand and relate to the speaker's language. As you practice your delivery, ensure that your pronunciation and word usage can be understood by all audience members, or take the time to share with them any special meanings you may wish to convey.

✓ CHECKLIST
Tips on Using a Microphone

❏ Learn how to use and perform a sound check with the microphone well before delivering your speech.

❏ When you first speak into the microphone, ask listeners if they can hear you clearly.

❏ Speak directly into the microphone; with many mics, if you turn your head or body, you won't be heard.

❏ When wearing a hands-free *lavaliere microphone* (also called a *lapel microphone* or *personal microphone*) clipped to clothing, speak as if you were addressing a small group. The amplifier will do the rest.

❏ When using a *handheld* or *fixed microphone*, beware of *popping*, a sound that occurs when you use sharp consonants, such as *p*, *t*, and *d*, and the air hits the mike. To prevent popping, move the microphone slightly below your mouth and several inches away.

CHAPTER 18 ●●●●

Your Body in Delivery

As we listen to a speaker, we simultaneously use our eyes and ears to evaluate messages sent by his or her **nonverbal communication**—body movements, physical appearance, and qualities of voice. As we listen to a speaker's words, we respond at the same time to his or her visual and vocal cues. Thus it is vital to plan not only the words you will say but also the physical manner in which you will deliver them.

◉ Pay Attention to Body Language

Research confirms the importance of **body language**—facial expressions, eye behavior, gestures, and general body movements during the delivery of a speech. For example, audiences are more readily persuaded by speakers who emphasize eye contact, nod at listeners, and stand with an open body position than by those who minimize these nonverbal cues.[1]

Animate Your Facial Expressions

From our facial expressions, audiences can gauge whether we are excited about, disenchanted by, or indifferent to our speech—and the audience to whom we are presenting it.

Few behaviors are more effective for building rapport with an audience than *smiling*.[2] A smile is a sign of mutual welcome at the start of a speech, of mutual comfort and interest during the speech, and of mutual goodwill at the close of a speech. In addition, smiling when you feel nervous or otherwise uncomfortable can help you relax and gain heightened composure. Of course, facial expressions need to correspond to the tenor of the speech. Doing what is natural and normal for the occasion should be the rule.

✔ CHECKLIST

Tips for Using Effective Facial Expressions

- ❑ Use animated expressions that feel natural and express your meaning.
- ❑ Never use expressions that are out of character for you or inappropriate to the speech occasion.
- ❑ In practice sessions, loosen your facial features with exercises such as widening your eyes and moving your mouth.
- ❑ Establish rapport with the audience by smiling naturally when appropriate.

Maintain Eye Contact

If smiling is an effective way to build rapport, maintaining eye contact is mandatory in establishing a positive relationship with your listeners. Having eye contact with the audience is one of the most, if not *the* most, important physical actions in public speaking, at least in Western cultures. Eye contact does the following:

- Maintains the quality of directness in speech delivery.
- Lets people know they are recognized.
- Indicates acknowledgment and respect.
- Signals to audience members that you see them as unique human beings.

While it may be impossible to look at every listener, you can make the audience feel recognized by using a technique called **scanning**—moving your gaze from one listener to another and from one section to another, pausing to gaze at one person long enough to complete one thought. Be certain to give each section of the room equal attention. Some experienced speakers recommend that your eyes should focus on the back row, giving the audience the impression you are taking them all in.

Use Gestures That Feel Natural

Words alone seldom suffice to convey what we want to express. Physical gestures fill in the gaps, as in illustrating the size or shape of an object (e.g., by showing the size of it by extending two hands, palms facing each other), or expressing the depth of an emotion (e.g., by pounding a fist on a podium). Gestures should arise from genuine emotions and should conform to your personality.[3]

Create a Feeling of Immediacy

In most Western cultures, listeners learn more from and respond most positively to speakers who create a perception of physical and psychological closeness, called **nonverbal immediacy**,

---

✓ CHECKLIST
Using Gestures Effectively

- ❑ Use natural, spontaneous gestures.
- ❑ Avoid exaggerated gestures, but use gestures that are broad enough to be seen by each audience member.
- ❑ Eliminate distracting gestures, such as fidgeting with pens, jingling coins in pockets, drumming your fingers on a podium or table, or brushing back hair from your eyes.
- ❑ Analyze your gestures for effectiveness in practice sessions.
- ❑ Practice movements that feel natural to you.

between themselves and audience members.[4] The following behaviors encourage immediacy:

- Make frequent eye contact.
- Animate your facial expressions.
- Smile when appropriate.
- Use natural body movements.
- Use vocal variety.
- Maintain upright but not stiff posture.
- Use natural hand and arm gestures.

QUICK TIP

Use Movement to Connect

Audience members soon tire of listening to a **talking head** who remains steadily positioned in one place behind a microphone or a podium, so even in formal situations, use natural body movements. Use your physical position vis-à-vis audience members to adjust your relationship with them, establishing a level of familiarity and closeness that is appropriate to the rhetorical situation. Movement toward listeners stimulates a sense of informality and closeness; remaining behind the podium fosters a more formal relationship of speaker to audience.

Maintain Good Posture

A speaker's posture sends a definite message to the audience. Listeners perceive speakers who slouch as being sloppy, unfocused, or even weak. Strive to stand erect, but not ram-rod straight. The goal should be to appear authoritative but not rigid.

◉ Practice the Delivery

Practice is essential to effective delivery. The more you practice, the greater your comfort level will be when you actually deliver the speech. More than anything, it is uncertainty that breeds anxiety. By practicing your speech using a fully developed speaking outline (see Chapter 13), you will know what to expect when you actually stand in front of an audience.

Focus on the Message

The primary purpose of any speech is to get a message across, not to display extraordinary delivery skills. Keep this goal foremost in your mind. Psychologically, too, focusing on your message is likely to make your delivery more natural and confident.

FROM WEAK TO CONFIDENT DELIVERY

Enhancing Your Delivery with Body Language

Positive and natural nonverbal behaviors—including frequent eye contact, animated facial expressions (including smiling), natural hand and arm gestures, relaxed but erect posture, and vocal variety that avoids a monotone—encourage audience members' trust and willingness to seriously consider your message.

In her first speech (top), student speaker Teresa stood behind a podium. The audience couldn't see her gestures, and her delivery was stiff and uninspired. After practicing the speech about six times (bottom), Teresa improved her delivery by assuming a more confident posture, using open hand and arm gestures, and moving from the podium.

The first time she delivered her speech (top), student speaker Charlotte read continuously from notecards and failed to make eye contact and engage nonverbally with the audience. After practice (bottom), Charlotte effectively connects with her audience with eye contact, a smile, and a gesture toward her presentation aid. She keeps her hands and arms around the middle of her body, above the waistline, which helps speakers project a sense of confidence and authority.

Plan Ahead and Practice Often

If possible, begin practicing your speech at least several days before you are scheduled to deliver it.

- Practice with your speaking notes, revising those parts of the speech that aren't satisfactory, and altering the notes as you go.
- Record the speech (see the Quick Tip below).
- Time each part of your speech—introduction, body, and conclusion (see Chapter 14 for guidelines).
- Include any presentation aids you plan to use.
- Practice the speech about five times in its final form.
- Try to simulate the actual speech setting, paying particular attention to seating arrangement and projecting your voice to fill the space.
- Practice in front of at least one volunteer, and seek constructive criticism.
- Schedule your practice sessions early in the process so that you have time to prepare.
- Dress appropriately for the rhetorical situation.

QUICK TIP

Record Two Practice Sessions

Videorecording two practice sessions can provide valuable feedback. As you watch your initial recording, make notes of the things you'd like to change. Before rerecording, practice several more times until you are comfortable with the changes you've incorporated. No one is ever entirely thrilled with his or her image on video, so try to avoid unnecessary self-criticism. Videorecord your speech a second time, paying close attention to the areas of speech delivery that you want to improve.

part

Presentation Aids

LaunchPad
macmillan learning

VIDEO ACTIVITY
Go to LaunchPad to watch a video about a student speaker who needs to improve his presentation slides. Visit **launchpadworks.com**

LaunchPad includes:

☑ **LearningCurve** adaptive quizzing

▶ A curated collection of video clips and full-length speeches

Additional resources, such as presentation software tutorials and documentation help.

CHAPTER 19 ●●●●

Speaking with Presentation Aids

Used judiciously, presentation aids can help listeners to understand and retain information that is otherwise difficult or time-consuming to convey in words. Indeed, research confirms that most people process information best when it is presented both with words and graphics—a principle dubbed the **multimedia effect**.[1] However, no matter how powerful a photograph, chart, or other aid may be, if it is unrelated to a speech point, is poorly designed, or simply duplicates what the speaker says, the audience will become distracted and actually retain *less* information than without it.[2]

◯ Select an Appropriate Aid

A **presentation aid** can be an object, model, picture, graph, chart, table, audio, video, or multimedia. Choose the aid, or combination of aids, that will help your audience grasp information most effectively.

Props and Models

A **prop** can be any object, inanimate or even live, that helps demonstrate the speaker's points. A **model** is a three-dimensional, scale-size representation of an object. Presentations in engineering, architecture, and many other disciplines often make use these aids. When using a prop or model:

- In most cases, keep the prop or model hidden until you are ready to use it.
- Make sure it is big enough for everyone to see (and read, if applicable).
- Practice your speech using the prop or model.

Pictures

Pictures (two-dimensional representations) include photographs, line drawings, diagrams, maps, and posters. A *diagram* or *schematic drawing* explains how something works or is constructed or operated. *Maps* help listeners visualize geographic areas and understand relationships among them; they also illustrate the proportion of one thing to something else in different areas. Pictures, including photographs, can strengthen many types of presentations, including those using persuasive appeals, but avoid using shocking images that will upset viewers.

Graphs, Charts, and Tables

A **graph** represents relationships among two or more things. A *line graph* uses points connected by lines to demonstrate how something changes or fluctuates in value. A *bar and column graph* uses bars of varying lengths to compare quantities or magnitudes. *Pie graphs* depict the division of a whole into slices. Each slice constitutes a percentage of the whole.

Pictograms use picture symbols (icons) to illustrate relationships and trends; for example, a generic-looking human figure repeated in a row can demonstrate increasing enrollment in college over time.

✓ CHECKLIST
Create Effective Line, Bar, and Pie Graphs

❑ Label the axes of line graphs, bar graphs, and pictograms.

❑ Start the numerical axis of the line or bar graph at zero.

❑ Compare only like variables.

❑ Assign a clear title to the graph.

❑ Clearly label all relevant points of information in the graph.

❑ When creating multidimensional bar graphs, do not compare more than three kinds of information.

❑ In pie graphs, restrict the number of pie slices to a maximum of seven.

❑ Identify and accurately represent the values or percentages of each pie slice.

❑ In pictograms, clearly indicate what each icon symbolizes.

❑ Make all pictograms the same size.

A **chart** visually organizes complex information into compact form. A **flowchart** diagrams the progression of a process or relationship, helping viewers visualize a sequence or directional flow. A **table** (tabular chart) systematically groups data in column form, allowing viewers to examine and make comparisons about information quickly.

Audio, Video, and Multimedia

Audio and video clips—including short recordings of sound, music, or speech; video clips; and multimedia, which combines audio, video, stills, animation, and text into a single production—can powerfully engage audience members and and help them understand and relate to your message.[3] (See Chapter 21 for guidelines on embedding audio and video into a slide deck.)

When incorporating audio and video into your presentation:

- Cue the audio or video clip to the appropriate segment before the presentation.
- Keep clips short—total 30–60 seconds per clip.
- As with any type of presentation aid, use clips to support one or more key points, but don't rely on them to replace your role as speaker.
- Embed video clips directly into your slides.
- Alert audience members beforehand to what will be played, and discuss its relevance to speech points when it concludes.
- Use the audio or video clip in a manner consistent with copyright.

QUICK TIP

Reasons to Use Video as an Aid

Video adds more drama, engages more senses, and communicates more information in less time than other media—*if* it is relevant to the speech. When deciding to include video as a presentation aid, consider whether it will serve one or more of these functions:

- Encourage audience identification with the topic
- Elicit a desired emotional response
- Make an idea tangible (by, for example, demonstrating it)
- Provide testimony that adds credibility to your claims

◎ Options for Showing Presentation Aids

Today, nearly all presenters generate tables, charts, and other aids using presentation software programs such as Microsoft PowerPoint and Apple Keynote (and their online counterparts such as Prezi). They then project slides using LCD panels and projectors or a DLP (digital light processing) device. On the more traditional side, display options include flip charts, chalkboards and whiteboards, and handouts.

Flip Charts

A **flip chart** is simply a large pad of paper on which you can write or draw. This aid is often prepared in advance; then, as you progress through the speech, you flip through the pad to the next exhibit. You can also write and draw on the pad as you speak. Sometimes a simple drawing or word written for emphasis can be as or more powerful than a highly polished slide.

Chalkboards and Whiteboards

On the lowest-tech end of the spectrum lies the writing board on which you can write with chalk (on a chalkboard) or with nonpermanent markers (on a whiteboard). Reserve the writing board for impromptu explanations, such as presenting simple processes that are done in steps, or for engaging the audience in short brainstorming sessions. If you have the time to prepare a speech properly, however, don't rely on a writing board. They force the speaker to turn his or her back to the audience, make listeners wait while you write, and require legible handwriting that will be clear to all viewers.

QUICK TIP

Hold the Handouts

A **handout** conveys information that either is impractical to give to the audience in another manner or is intended to be kept by audience members after the presentation. To avoid distracting listeners, unless you specifically want them to read the information as you speak, wait until you are finished before you distribute the handout. If you do want the audience to view a handout during the speech, pass it out only when you are ready to talk about it.

> ✅ **CHECKLIST**
> **Incorporating Presentation Aids into Your Speech**
>
> ❏ Practice with the aids and the equipment used to display them until you are confident that you can handle them without causing undue distractions.
>
> ❏ Talk to your audience rather than to the screen or object—avoid turning your back to the audience.
>
> ❏ Maintain eye contact with the audience.
>
> ❏ Place the aid to one side rather than behind you, so that the entire audience can see it.
>
> ❏ Display the aid only when you are ready to discuss it.
>
> ❏ If you use a pointer, once you've indicated your point, put it down.
>
> ❏ In case problems arise, be prepared to give your presentation without the aids.

CHAPTER 20 ●●●●

Designing Presentation Aids

The quality of a speaker's presentation aids is a critical factor in the audience's perception of his or her credibility, or *ethos*. Well-designed aids signal that the speaker is prepared and professional; poorly designed aids create a negative impression that is difficult to overcome.

As you prepare aids (such as slides made with Microsoft PowerPoint or similar programs), focus on keeping elements easy to view and designed in a consistent manner. Audience members can follow only one piece of information at a time, and visuals that are crowded or difficult to decipher will divert attention from your message.[1]

◉ Keep the Design Simple

Audience members should be able to process the message in your slides quickly—master presenter Nancy Duarte suggests in three seconds—so that they can return their attention to the speaker.[2] Thus it is important to restrict text to a minimum and present only one major idea per slide:

- *Follow the six-by-six rule*. Use no more than six words in a line and six lines on one slide. This will keep the audience's attention on you (see the table on p. 149).

- *Word text in active verb form.* Use the active voice and parallel grammatical structure, for example "Gather Necessary Documents; Apply Early" (see Chapter 15 on language).
- *Avoid clutter.* Allow plenty of white space, or "visual breathing room" for viewers.[3]
- *Create concise titles.* Use titles that summarize content and reinforce your message.

Cluttered Aid	Easy-to-Read Aid
Buying a Used Car	Buying a Used Car
1. Prepare in advance— know the market value of several cars you are interested in before going to shop.	1. Know the car's market value.
2. Do not get into a hurry about buying the first car you see—be patient, there will be others.	2. Don't hurry to buy.
3. It is recommended that you shop around for credit before buying the car.	3. Shop for credit before buying.
4. Inspect the car carefully, looking for funny sounds, stains, worn equipment, dents, etc.	4. Inspect the car carefully.
5. Ask for proof about the history of the car, including previous owners.	5. Get proof of the car's history.

QUICK TIP

Beware of "Chartjunk"

Certain kinds of information—especially statistical data and sequences of action—are best understood when visually presented. However, avoid what design expert Edward Tufte coined as *"chartjunk"*[4]—slides jammed with too many graphs, charts, and meaningless design elements that obscure rather than illuminate information. Use fewer rather than more slides and only those design elements that truly enhance meaning.

◉ Use Design Elements Consistently

Apply the same design decisions you make for one presentation aid to all of the aids you display; this will ensure that viewers aren't distracted by a jumble of unrelated visual elements. Carry your choice of design elements—color, fonts, upper- and lowercase letters, styling (boldface, underlining, italics), general page layout, and repeating elements such as titles and logos—through each aid.

◉ Select Appropriate Typeface Styles and Fonts

A *typeface* is a specific style of lettering, such as Arial or Times New Roman. Typefaces come in a variety of *fonts*, or sets of sizes (called the *point size*), and upper and lower cases. Designers divide the thousands of available typefaces into two major categories: serif and sans serif. *Serif typefaces* include small flourishes, or strokes, at the tops and bottoms of each letter. *Sans serif typefaces* are more blocklike and linear; they are designed without these tiny strokes.

Consider these design guidelines when selecting type:

- Check the lettering for legibility, taking into consideration the audience's distance from the visual. On slides, experiment with 36-point type for major headings, 24-point type for subheadings, and *at least* 18-point type for text.
- Lettering should stand apart from the background. Use either dark text on light background or light text on dark background.
- Use a common typeface that is simple and easy to read and is not distracting.
- Use standard upper- and lowercase type rather than all capitals.
- Use no more than two different typefaces in a single aid.
- Use **boldface**, <u>underlining</u>, or *italics* sparingly.

QUICK TIP

Using Serif and Sans Serif Type

For reading a block of text, serif typefaces are easier on the eye. Small amounts of text, however, such as headings, are best viewed in sans serif type. Thus, consider a sans serif typeface for the heading and a serif typeface for the body of the text. If you include only a few lines of text, use sans serif type throughout.

◉ Use Color Carefully

Skillful use of color can draw attention to key points, influence the mood of a presentation, and make things easier to see. Conversely, poor color combinations will set the wrong mood, render an image unattractive, or make it unreadable. Note the effect of these color combinations:

Effects of Color Combinations	
Color	Effect in Combination
Yellow	Warm on white, harsh on black, fiery on red, soothing on light blue
Blue	Warm on white, hard to see on black
Red	Bright on white, warm or difficult to see on black

Color affects both the legibility of text and the mood conveyed. Following are some tips for using color effectively in your presentation aids:

- Keep the *background color* constant across all slides or other aids.
- Use *bold, bright colors* to emphasize important points.
- For typeface and graphics, use colors that contrast rather than clash with or blend into the background color; check for visibility when projecting. Audiences will remember information just as easily if white text appears on dark background or dark text on light background, so long as the design is appealing.[5]
- Limit colors to no more than three, with maximum of four in complex and detailed aids.

◉ Consider Subjective Interpretations of Color

Colors can evoke distinct associations for people, so take care not to summon an unintended meaning or mood. For example, control engineers see red and think danger, while a financial manager will think unprofitability.

Consider, too, that the meanings associated with certain colors may differ across cultures. Western societies don black for funerals, while the Chinese use white. If you are presenting in a cross-cultural context, check the meanings of colors for the relevant nationalities.

> ✓ **CHECKLIST**
>
> **Apply the Principles of Simplicity and Continuity**
>
> ❑ Concentrate on presenting one major idea per visual aid.
> ❑ Apply design decisions consistently to each aid.
> ❑ Use type that is large enough for audience members to read comfortably.
> ❑ Use color judiciously to highlight key ideas and enhance readability.
> ❑ Check that colors contrast rather than clash.

CHAPTER 21 ●●●●

Using Presentation Software

Public speakers can use a variety of powerful software tools to create and display high-quality visual aids. These programs include the familiar Microsoft PowerPoint and its Apple counterpart, Keynote, and online programs such as Prezi.

◉ Give a Speech, Not a Slide Show

Frequently we hear someone say, "I'm giving a PowerPoint (or a Prezi or Keynote) presentation today," instead of "I'm giving a speech." Some speakers hide behind presentation media, focusing attention on their aids rather than on the audience. They might mistakenly believe that the display itself is the presentation, or that it will somehow save an otherwise poorly planned speech. It can be easy to become so involved in generating fancy aids that you forget your primary mission: to communicate through the spoken word and your physical presence. Speaker and message must take center stage.

◉ Develop a Plan

Often the best place to begin planning your slides is your speaking outline (see p. 106). Think through which points might be better explained with some kind of visual: Decide what the content of your slides should be, how many slides you'll need, and how to arrange them. Review and edit slides as necessary using *Slide Sorter* view (in PowerPoint), *Light table* or *Outline* view (in Keynote), or *path tool* (in Prezi).

⚡ **LaunchPad** For detailed guidance on creating presentations in PowerPoint, Keynote, and Prezi, go to launchpadworks.com

◉ Avoid Technical Glitches

Technical errors are always a hazard with presentation software and any hardware required to run it. Common risks include a projector malfunctioning, a presentation file being incompatible with an operating system, an internet connection failing, or a computer drive freezing. Follow these steps to avoid such problems.

1. Save all presentation files to a reliable source—flash drive, CD, DVD, website, or email—that you can access on the presentation computer.

2. Save all presentation files (images, sound, videos) into the same folder in the source location.

3. Familiarize yourself with the presentation computer before you give the speech to facilitate smooth operation during the presentation.

4. Check that the operating system of the presentation computer (e.g., Windows 10, Mac OS High Sierra) is compatible with the the aids.

5. Confirm that the version of the software used to create the aids corresponds to the software on the presentation computer; this will prevent distortions in your graphics, sound, and video.

6. Prepare both a digital backup and a set of printed handouts of the aids.

◉ Find Media for Presentations

You can import photos, illustrations, clip art, video, or sound directly into your aids by downloading your own files or those from the internet. For downloadable digital images, try the following websites:

- Google images (images.google.com)
- Getty Images (www.gettyimages.com)
- Flickr Creative Commons (www.flickr.com/creative commons): access to photographs shared by amateur and hobbyist photographers
- American Memory (memory.loc.gov/ammem/index.html): free access to still and moving images depicting the history of the American experience

The following sites offer downloadable music files and audio clips:

- SoundCloud (www.soundcloud.com)
- Jamendo (www.jamendo.com)

FROM SLIDE SHOW TO PRESENTATION

Getting Ready to Deliver a PowerPoint, Keynote, or Prezi Presentation

To avoid technical glitches, practice delivering your speech with your presentation software and ensure compatibility with the venue's equipment.

Check the Venue

Before your speech, take stock of the equipment and room layout. See the annotated photo for tips on achieving a smooth delivery with digital aids.

1 **Power sources.** Ensure that cords can reach the presentation equipment, and consider taping them to the floor to keep them out of the way.

2 **Computer needs and compatibility.** Check that you can display all aids, from the slide show to audio and video clips, on the presentation computer. If possible, practice at least once on this computer.

(clockwise from bottom) (top) Purestock/Getty Images
(bottom left) Jeff Presnail/Getty Images/Getty Images;
(bottom center) cinoby/Getty Images; (bottom right) Caspar
Benson/Getty Images

3 **Internet access.** Have wireless log-in information available and/or a cable that reaches the internet jack.

4 **Backup plan.** Create a contingency plan in case of computer failure; for example, print overhead transparencies from slide show, prepare to put information on a whiteboard, or create handouts.

5 **Audio.** Determine how you will broadcast any audio aids, and check speaker volume before the speech.

Position Yourself Carefully

Choose a place to stand that gives the audience clear sightlines to you and your slide show. Stand so that you can face forward even when changing slides or gesturing toward your aids. This helps you connect with your audience and project your voice clearly, and it prevents you from reading off your slides.

Mark Wilson/Getty Images

Needs improvement: This speaker's sideways stance discourages eye contact and indicates that he may be reading off his slides.

Macmillan Learning

Good placement: This speaker can access the computer or gesture toward the slides without blocking the audience's sightlines.

- MP3.com (www.mp3.com)
- SoundClick (www.soundclick.com)
- Audio Archive (www.archive.org/details/audio)
- The Daily.WAV (www.dailywav.com)

The following sites contain useful video clips:

- YouTube (www.youtube.com)
- CNN Video (www.cnn.com/video) and ABC News Video (abcnews.go.com/video): especially useful for speech topics on current events or timely social issues
- New York Times (www.nytimes.com/video)
- Google Videos (video.google.com)

◉ Avoid Copyright Infringement

Abide by copyright restrictions when using visual and audio materials from the internet or other sources. Some material is available under fair-use provisions (see p. 27). Even if fair use applies, cite the source of the material in your presentation. Consult your school's information technology (IT) office for statements of policy pertaining to copyrighted and fair-use materials, especially from undocumented sources such as peer-to-peer (P2P) sharing.

- Cite the source of all copyrighted material in your presentation. For example, include a bibliographic footnote on the slide containing the material.
- Be wary of sites purporting to offer "royalty free" media objects; there might actually be other costs associated with the materials.
- When time, resources, and ability allow, create and use your own pictures, video, or audio for your presentation slides.

✓ CHECKLIST

Tips for Successfully Using Presentation Software in Your Speech

- ❑ Don't let the technology get in the way of relating to your audience.
- ❑ Talk to your audience rather than to the screen.
- ❑ Maintain eye contact as much as possible.
- ❑ Have a backup plan in case of technical errors.
- ❑ If you use a pointer (laser or otherwise), turn it off and put it down as soon as you have made your point.
- ❑ Incorporate the aids into your practice sessions until you are confident that they strengthen, rather than detract from, your core message.

part ⑦

Types of Speeches

VIDEO ACTIVITY
Go to LaunchPad to watch a video
of a student speaker who lacks
credibility with his audience. Visit
launchpadworks.com

LaunchPad includes:

✓ **LearningCurve** adaptive quizzing

▶ A curated collection of video clips and
full-length speeches

Additional resources, such as presentation
software tutorials and documentation help.

CHAPTER 22 ●●●●

Informative Speaking

To *inform* is to communicate knowledge. People are naturally curious about the world, and with its goal of increasing the audience's knowledge and deepening their understanding of a topic, **informative speaking** is an ideal vehicle for satisfying this instinct. Informative speeches bring new issues to light, offer fresh insights on familiar subjects, or provide novel ways of thinking about a topic. Your speech might be an analysis of an issue, a report of an event, or a physical demonstration of how something works. As long as the audience learns something, the options are nearly limitless.

QUICK TIP

Enlighten Rather Than Advocate

Whereas a persuasive speech explicitly seeks to modify attitudes or convince an audience to adopt a specific position, an informative speech stops short of this, focusing instead on sharing knowledge and deepening understanding.[1] Although there are always elements of persuasion in an informative speech, and vice versa, if you keep this general speech purpose in mind, you will be able to deliver a speech whose primary function is to enlighten rather than to advocate.

◉ Use Audience Analysis

Audience members must be able to identify with your informative topic and see how they can benefit from the information you give them. You therefore need to gauge the audience's knowledge of your topic and their likely interests and needs with respect to it. Then adapt your speech accordingly. (See Chapter 6.) If speaking about collecting vintage guitars, for example, you might tell a specialized audience of collectors the "inside story" of a sale. For a general audience, you might instead provide an overview of the guitar brands collectors seek, and the most prized models and prices they fetch.

◉ Present New and Interesting Information

Audiences want to learn something new from the speaker. To satisfy this drive, offer information that is fresh and compelling. Seek out unusual (but credible) sources, novel (but sound) interpretations, moving stories, compelling examples, and striking facts. If a speech does not offer audience members anything new, they will feel that their time has been wasted and will rightly be offended.[2]

QUICK TIP

Don't Overwhelm the Audience

As important as offering new information is not overwhelming audience members with too much of it. Most people will recall less than half of the information you tell them, so focus on what you most want to convey and trim material that is not vital to your central idea.[3]

◉ Look for Ways to Increase Understanding

Audience members cannot put the speaker on "pause" in order to digest information, so help them to stay on track with these basic speechmaking techniques described in previous chapters:

- Prepare a well-organized *introduction* that clearly previews the thesis and main points and a *conclusion* that summarizes them; this will help listeners anticipate and remember information (see Chapter 14).
- Make liberal use of *transition words and phrases* (first, next, "I'll now turn . . .") to signal points and verbally map the flow of ideas. Use *internal previews* to forecast key points and *internal summaries* to reinforce them (see p. 86).

- Use rhetorical devices such as *repetition* and *parallelism* to reinforce information and drive home key ideas (see Chapter 15).
- Choose an *organizational pattern* to help listeners mentally organize ideas and see relationships among them (see Chapters 12 and 24).
- Use *presentation aids* selectively to help listeners hear and see related (but not duplicated) information, as, for instance, in charts and diagrams (see Chapters 19–21).

QUICK TIP

Make the Introduction Motivating

Early on in your informative speech, give audience members a reason to care about your message. Use the introduction to point out the topic's relevance to them and to describe any concrete benefits they will gain by listening to you. Expand upon these points in the speech body, and reiterate them once more in the conclusion.

◉ Subject Matter of Informative Speeches

When searching for topics for an informative speech, it can be useful to brainstorm using the following broad subject categories: *people, events, concepts, issues, processes,* or *objects or phenomena.* These are not hard-and-fast divisions—a speech can be about both the *process* of dance and the *people* who perform it, for example—but they do indicate the range of potential subject matter suited to an informative purpose, as seen in the table on p. 161.

◉ Decide How to Communicate Your Information

Typically, we communicate information by defining, describing, demonstrating, and/or explaining it. Some speeches rely on a single approach (e.g., they focus on *demonstrating* how something works or *explaining* what something means). Many speeches combine strategies. As you prepare your speech, ask yourself, "How much emphasis should I give to defining my topic, describing it, demonstrating it, or explaining its meaning?"

Subject Categories of Informative Speeches

Subject Category	Sample Topics
Speeches about People	
Address impact of individuals or groups of people who have made a difference	• Athletes • Activists • Authors • You, the speaker
Speeches about Current or Historical Events	
Address noteworthy occurrences, past and present	• Refugee asylum seekers • The rise and fall of the Islamic State • The Battle of Britain
Speeches about Concepts	
Address abstract or complex ideas, theories, or beliefs	• Cybersecurity • String theory • Nanotechnology
Speeches about Issues	
Address social problems or matters in dispute, about which you want to raise awareness rather than advocate a position	• Speech codes on campus • Regulating drones • Gun violence
Speeches about Processes	
Demonstrate and/or explain how something is done, how it is made, or how it works	• Production of algae-based biofuels • Visualization in sports • Core-power yoga
Speeches about Objects or Phenomena	
Address aspects of non-human subjects (their history and function, for example)	• Self-driving cars • UNESCO World Heritage Sites in the United States • The El Niño phenomenon

DEFINITION When your topic is new to the audience and/ or addresses a complex concept (What is a fractal?), or when addressing a controversial issue such as free speech or the Electoral College, pay particular attention to providing adequate definitions. Few things are more frustrating to audience members than spending the entire speech listening to something they don't quite grasp because it was inadequately defined. To *define* something is to identify its essential qualities and meanings. You can approach definition in a number of ways, including the following:

- Defining something by what it does (*operational definition*): The Electoral College is a system of voting for the U.S. presidency that includes 538 electors representing the states.
- Defining something by describing what it is not (*definition by negation*): The Electoral College is not a place but a process.
- Defining something by providing several concrete examples (*definition by example*): Electors include elected officials, state party leaders, or people in the state who have a personal or political affiliation with their party's presidential candidate.[4]
- Defining something by comparing it to something with which it has something in common (*definition by analogy*): The Electoral College is like the World Series in baseball.
- Defining something by illustrating its root meaning (*definition by word origin*): The word *elector* derives from the Latin *eligere*, "to choose or pick out."

DESCRIPTION   Whether offering your audience a "virtual tour" of the top of Mount Everest or describing the physical ravages caused by drug abuse, the point of description is to provide a mental picture for the audience. Use *concrete words* and *vivid imagery* to help listeners visualize your depictions (see Chapter 15).

DEMONSTRATION   Sometimes the purpose of an informative speech is to explain how something works or to provide an actual demonstration, similar to "how-to" videos and podcasts. A speech may not include an actual physical demonstration (e.g., how to use Apple's Clips App), but the speaker will nevertheless rely on a verbal demonstration of the steps involved.

EXPLANATION   Many informative speech topics are built on *explanation*—providing reasons or causes, demonstrating relationships, and offering interpretation and analysis. The classroom lecture is a classic example of explanation in an informative context (see Chapter 30). But numerous kinds of speeches rely on explanation, from those that address difficult or confusing theories and processes (What is the relationship between the glycemic index and glycemic load?) to those that present ideas that challenge conventional thinking (Why do researchers say that sometimes emotion makes us more rather than less logical?). See the checklist on p. 164 for strategies for explaining complex ideas.

◉ Take Steps to Reduce Confusion

New information can be hard to grasp, especially when it addresses a difficult concept (such as *equilibrium* in engineering), a difficult-to-envision process (such as *cash-flow management* in business), or a counterintuitive idea—one that challenges commonsense thinking (such as *drinking a glass of red wine a day can be healthy*).

Useful for almost any speech, the following strategies for communicating information are especially helpful when attempting to clarify complex information, as in scientific and technical concepts.

Use Analogies to Build on Prior Knowledge

Audience members will understand a new concept more easily if the speaker uses an **analogy** to relate it to something that they already know. For example, to explain the unpredictable paths that satellites often take when they fall to earth, you can liken the effect to dropping a penny into water: "Sometimes it goes straight down, and sometimes it turns end over end and changes direction. The same thing happens when an object hits the atmosphere."[5]

In the following excerpt from a speech about nanotechnology, Wolfgang Porod explains the size of a nanometer by comparing it to the diameter of the moon. Note how he attempts to reduce confusion by first *defining* the root *nano* and then comparing it to the size of the moon:

> What is a nano and what is special about a nano? *Nano* is a prefix derived from the Greek word for dwarf and it means one billionth of something. So a nanosecond is a billionth of a second. A nanometer is a billionth of a meter. Now, just saying that doesn't really tell you that much. So what does it mean to have the length scale of a billionth of a meter? Well, imagine the diameter of the moon. It just happens to be, roughly . . . a billion meters. So take that and shrink it down to the length scale of a meter, which is what it means to go a billion size scales. So a nanometer is a billionth of a meter.[6]

QUICK TIP

Use Analogies Accurately

Linking the unfamiliar with the familiar through analogy aids understanding. But no analogy can exactly represent another concept; at a certain point, the similarities will end.[7] To ensure accuracy, state the limits of the comparison. The statement "The heart is like a pump, *except the heart is much more complex*" demonstrates that, though similar, a heart and a pump are not the same.[8]

✓ CHECKLIST

Strategies for Explaining Complex Information

To explain a *concept or term*:

❑ Use analogies that link concepts to something familiar.
❑ Define terms in several ways.
❑ Simplify terminology wherever possible.

To explain a *process or structure*, do all of the above *and*:

❑ Make ample use of presentation aids, including models and drawings.

To explain a counterintuitive idea, do all of the above *and*:

❑ Address the commonly-held assumption first.
❑ Acknowledge its plausibility.
❑ Demonstrate its limitations using familiar examples.

Appeal to Different Learning Styles

Audience members are more likely to follow your points if you reinforce them with other media. The reason for this is that people have different **learning styles**, or preferred ways of processing information. One learning theory model suggests four preferences: visual, aural, read/write, and kinesthetic.[9] Few of us are not helped by visual reinforcement, so consider that most of the audience will appreciate visual aids. Many of us are *multimodal learners*, in that we combine two or more preferences.

Audience analysis can sometimes give you a sense of the types of learners in an audience. For example, mechanics of all types have strong spatial visualization abilities and thus would be classified as visual learners; they may also be kinesthetic learners who want to "test" things for themselves, perhaps by handling actual models. Often, however, you may not have enough information to determine your listeners' learning style, so plan on conveying and reinforcing information in a variety of modes as suggested in the following table.

Communicating Information to Different Types of Learners	
Type	Advice for Communicating Information
Visual (Learns through visual aids)	Include pictures, charts, tables, or videos.
Aural (Learns through the spoken word)	Use colorful and concrete language and strong examples and stories.
Read/Write (Learns through written text)	Use text-based slides (but observe the six-by-six rule; see p. 148) and perhaps handouts.
Kinesthetic (Learns through hands-on contact)	Use real-life demonstrations, models, simulations, and other hands-on applications.

◉ Arrange Points in a Pattern

Informative speeches can be organized using any of the patterns described in Chapter 12, including the topical, chronological, spatial, cause-effect, and narrative patterns. (Note that although the *problem-solution* pattern may be used in informative speeches, it is usually a more logical candidate for persuasive speeches.) A speech about the Impressionist movement in painting, for example, could be organized *chronologically*, in which main points are arranged in sequence from the movement's early period to its later falling out of favor. It could be organized *causally* (cause-effect), by demonstrating that Impressionism came about as a reaction to the art movement that preceded it. It could also be organized *topically* (by categories), by focusing on the major figures associated with the movement, famous paintings linked to it, or notable contemporary artists who paint in the style.

SAMPLE INFORMATIVE SPEECH

This informative speech by Saundra Dixon describes the quest to achieve carbon neutrality on college campuses. In terms of categories of informative subject matter described in this chapter (see p. 161), carbon neutrality is both a concept and a process. To ensure understanding of this fairly complex idea, which might be unfamiliar to her audience, Saundra is careful to define potentially confusing or unknown terms, including, of course, the topic term. Saundra chose a topic that could easily veer into persuasive territory. On the whole, however, she avoids advocacy, focusing instead on increasing the audience's awareness of this movement. She introduces her speech with a powerful quotation and a short but effective preview of her thesis and main points. Organizationally, the speech follows the topical pattern, moving from one aspect of the topic to another (see p. 93). With strong supporting material in the form of real-life examples, as well as testimony from credible publications and reports, Saundra is able to convey a good deal of information in an engaging way.

Going Carbon Neutral on Campus

Saundra Dixon

 LaunchPad See Saundra deliver her speech in LaunchPad:
launchpadworks.com

"Climate change is real. It is happening right now. It is the most urgent threat facing our entire species, and we need to work collectively together and stop procrastinating."

> Beginning the speech with a quote from a well-known actor and activist effectively captures the audience's attention and gets them interested in the topic.

These words, from Leonardo DiCaprio in his 2016 Academy Awards acceptance speech, reflect the consensus of the worldwide scientific community, the Catholic Church, and the U.S. military. Human-caused climate change is indeed one of the greatest global challenges of our lifetimes. To address this challenge, colleges and universities are engaging in a range of actions to become carbon neutral.

During this presentation, I will explain the scope of the campus movement toward carbon neutrality. First I'll give a brief overview of carbon neutrality. Second,

I'll describe what institutions of higher learning are doing to move towards carbon neutrality. Third, I'll share with you some specific means by which colleges and universities are attempting to achieve carbon neutrality. Led by student involvement, carbon neutrality at colleges of all sizes is one step in meeting the challenge of human-caused climate change.

In her preview statement, Saundra states the thesis and main points.

To begin: What is carbon neutrality, and why is it important? According to a 2014 assessment by the Intergovernmental Panel on Climate Change, it is 100 percent certain that the Earth's climate is warming, and 95–100 percent certain that human-caused activities are responsible for the warming. The United Nations Human Rights Council identifies climate change as an immediate and far-reaching human rights issue due to its likely impact on poor and marginalized countries. A 2016 study by the think tank Demos estimates that unchecked climate change will cost the Millennial generation $8.8 trillion dollars in total lost lifetime income.

With this transition, Saundra moves into the speech body.

By citing data from authoritative government and other sources, Saundra boosts her credibility.

These forecasts may sound bleak, but the good news is that steps can and are being taken to prevent these things from happening. This is where carbon neutrality comes in.

Carbon neutrality means taking as much carbon-based pollution out of the atmosphere as we put in. We emit carbon in the form of carbon dioxide and methane gas, through activities like burning coal or natural gas for energy and dedicating large swaths of land to raising livestock. Reducing carbon output requires the use of renewable energy sources—like wind and solar—and altering habits of consumption, including eating a diet that is more plant-based. Carbon neutrality also requires that we offset or cancel out carbon-based pollution with such carbon-absorbing activities as, for example, preserving forests and wetlands. In other words, being carbon neutral means balancing the carbon equation and not causing additional carbon pollution.

Saundra carefully defines carbon neutrality.

As I've mentioned, individuals can take steps to reduce carbon-based pollution, such as switching to

Here Saundra approaches persuasive territory, yet still she mostly informs, rather than advocates.

renewable energy at home and eating a more plant-based diet. However, the biggest impacts will come from actions by groups and institutions, including colleges. If just one large school shifts to carbon neutrality, it can do more to reduce the impact of climate change than thousands of carbon-neutral individuals.

In fact, many colleges in the United States and around the world are already taking big steps towards carbon neutrality. Over 500 U.S. colleges have signed the American College and University Presidents' Climate Commitment and have actively pledged to become carbon neutral by a specific date, which varies by school. According to Second Nature, the nonprofit organization overseeing this Climate Commitment,

Saundra supports her topic with excellent examples of colleges that are achieving carbon neutrality.

some colleges have already become 100 percent carbon neutral, such as College of the Atlantic, Green Mountain College, Colby College, and Middlebury College.

Those four schools have something in common: They are all relatively small liberal arts colleges, mostly located in rural areas. Some of the methods that these schools have successfully implemented to reduce carbon are difficult to scale up at larger schools. For example, Middlebury College uses a biomass gasification plant that superheats wood chips to create steam for heating, air conditioning, and hot water. The Middlebury campus in Vermont has a total enrollment of just over 2,500 students. The amount of wood chips that would be needed to power such a plant at a larger school would be prohibitive, forcing larger schools to seek other solutions to reduce their carbon footprint.

That's not to say that larger schools are getting left behind in the race for carbon neutrality. Colorado State University, a campus of over 30,000 students, is also home to a 30-acre field of solar panels—which the university claims generate enough electricity to power 949 homes—as well as a steam turbine that cuts the school's carbon emissions by 2,600 tons every year. Meanwhile, Stanford University successfully met its goal of reducing carbon emissions by 68 percent by the end of 2016 and pledged to meet even more ambitious emission goals in subsequent years. Finally, the entire ten-campus University of California system has pledged to become carbon neutral by 2025. Whether small or large, and whether early or recent adopters, colleges nationwide have begun doing their part to reduce their carbon outputs.

So far, we've seen that carbon neutrality is important and that there is a widespread commitment to moving towards carbon neutrality on college campuses. Let's look now at more specific ways in which students and administrators are achieving carbon neutrality.

> In this transition, Saundra internally summarizes previous points and previews her next point.

First and foremost, energy efficiency is the key to reducing emissions. Energy efficiency requirements for new buildings and retrofits for aging ones can go a long way towards this end. Colleges are switching to locally appropriate renewable energy, and some are even generating their own energy using solar arrays or wind farms. Additionally, administrators can choose to bring locally sourced food to campus dining halls, which cuts down on carbon emitted during food transportation. Speaking of transportation, another easy step that students can take is to use public transit and campus shuttles instead of personal cars whenever possible.

The other side of carbon neutrality is absorbing existing carbon emissions. To do this, some colleges are turning to off-site options. Preserving undeveloped land, for example, provides a natural system to absorb emissions. Meanwhile, purchasing carbon offsets pays for carbon-reducing projects elsewhere, such as reforestation, carbon dioxide or methane capture,

> Saundra fails to offer a needed definition for *carbon offsets*. Clearly defining potentially unfamiliar terms is crucial in any speech.

and clean energy development. For example, Green Mountain College partners with local energy company Native Energy and with the Seneca Meadows Landfill in upstate New York to obtain carbon offsets.

Perhaps the biggest barrier to carbon neutrality is the up-front cost. Building energy-efficient cafeterias, lecture halls, and dormitories isn't cheap, but it can be a smart business investment. In a 2015 *New York Times* commentary, journalist David Bornstein observed that the University of New Hampshire invested $600,000 in energy efficiency projects that resulted in $1.3 million in savings in just five years. Colleges are finding ways to implement these projects not only because it saves the environment, but also because it saves them money in the long run.

> Saundra supports her point with evidence from a source she establishes as credible.

Finally, students and administrators committed to carbon neutrality are taking other steps right now without spending a cent. Energy-saving competitions between dormitories on campus—like those sponsored by the nonprofit group Alliance to Save Energy—reduce energy costs, cut carbon emissions, and increase clean energy awareness and engagement among students. So do student groups tasked with turning off lights in unoccupied rooms, and coalitions between students, staff, and administration to reduce food waste. Schools are using all of these strategies as they to move toward carbon neutrality.

Today we've explored what carbon neutrality is and how it can be achieved. We learned about the steps college communities are taking to work towards carbon neutrality. Human-caused climate change isn't just about our future. It is happening right now. As I've described today, so too are efforts by students

Saundra uses this transition to signal the conclusion.

and educators to curb it. Carbon neutrality—the balancing of carbon-based pollution with carbon absorption—can help to address human-caused climate change. In the words of Bob Best, Head of Energy and Sustainability at the investment management company JLL: "From students and faculty to parents and alumni, environmental sustainability is now one of the pillars of a university's public image." Colleges and

By concluding with a quotation, Saundra reinforces her thesis and makes the speech memorable.

universities recognize this reality and overwhelmingly support carbon neutrality initiatives. Through a mixture of emissions reduction and emissions capture, on- and off-site, small and large colleges have already been successful in moving towards a greener tomorrow.

Works Cited

Bornstein, David. 2015. "Investing in Energy Efficiency Pays Off." *New York Times,* February 6, 2015. http://opinionator.blogs.nytimes.com/2015/02/06/investing-in-energy-efficiency-pays-off/.

Colorado State University. "Sustainability in Facilities Management." Accessed January 24, 2018. http://www.fm.colostate.edu/sustain/energy.html.

Core Writing Team. 2014. *Climate Change 2014 Synthesis Report.* Geneva: Intergovernmental Panel on Climate Change.

Demos. 2016. "The Price Tag of Being Young: Climate Change and Millennials' Economic Future." August 22, 2016. http://www.demos.org/publication/price-tag-being-young-climate-change-and-millennials-economic-future.

Jones Lang LaSalle. 2017. "Carbon-Neutral Campus: Navigating the Road to Zero." April 13, 2017. http://www.us.jll.com/united-states/en-us/news/4487/lessons-for-higher-education-carbon-neutral-goals.

Second Nature. 2018. "Reporting Platform." Accessed January 24, 2018. http://reporting.secondnature.org/institution/data/.

Stanford University. "Sustainable Stanford 2016–17 Year in Review." Accessed January 24, 2018. https://sustainability-year-in-review.stanford.edu/2017/.

United Nations Human Rights Office of the High Commissioner. "Human Rights and Climate Change." Accessed January 24, 2018. http:// www.ohchr.org/EN/Issues/HRAndClimateChange/Pages/HRClimateChangeIndex.aspx.

Woodside, Ruby. 2016. "New England Colleges Demonstrate Excellence." *Second Nature*, December 9, 2016. http://secondnature.org/2016/12/09/new-england-colleges-demonstrate-excellence/.

CHAPTER 23 ●●●●

Principles of Persuasive Speaking

To persuade is to advocate, to ask others to accept your views. A **persuasive speech** is meant to influence audience members' attitudes, beliefs, values, and/or behavior by appealing to some combination of their needs, desires, interests, and even fears.

When you speak persuasively, you aim to produce some shift in the audience's emotions and reasoning about an issue—to arouse involvement and perhaps motivate action for an issue or a cause, or to strengthen (or weaken) beliefs about a certain controversy. Whatever the topic, the goal is to reinforce, stimulate, or change the audience's attitudes and beliefs about the issue in question to more closely match your own.

◉ Persuasive Speeches Appeal to Human Psychology

Success in persuasive speaking requires attention to human psychology—to what motivates people. Audience analysis is therefore extremely important in persuasive appeals, both to identify what your target audience cares about and to build common ground (see Chapter 6). But persuasion is a complex process, and getting people to change their minds, even a little, is challenging.

Research confirms that you can increase the odds of influencing the audience in your direction if you:

- Set modest goals. Expect minor rather than major changes in your listeners' attitudes and behavior.[1]
- Establish your credibility and build common bonds to encourage the audience's trust in and identification with you (see p. 38).
- Make your message personally relevant to the audience.
- Expect to be more successful when addressing an audience whose position differs only moderately from your own.[2] The more strongly audience members feel about a given issue, the less likely they are to be persuaded of an alternative viewpoint.[3]
- If asking for the audience to support a position or cause, demonstrate positive consequences of your position.
- Consider using stories. Audiences react positively to them, both cognitively and behaviorally.[4]

Persuasion is both ancient art and modern science, with roots in Greek and Roman *rhetoric,* as persuasion was first named, and branches in contemporary social science. Both classical and contemporary perspectives recognize that successful persuasion requires a balance of reason and emotion, and that audience members must be well disposed toward the speaker.

◉ Classical Persuasive Appeals: Ethos, Pathos, and Logos

Aristotle explained that persuasion could be brought about by the speaker's use of three types of *persuasive appeals* or "proofs"—termed logos, pathos, and ethos. The first appeal uses *reason and logic,* the second targets listeners' *emotions,* and the third enlists the *ethical character* of the speaker. According to Aristotle, and generations who followed him to the present day, effective persuasive speeches make use of all of these appeals.

Appeal to Reason

Many persuasive speeches focus on issues that require considerable thought. Aristotle used the term *logos* to refer to persuasive appeals directed at the audience's systematic reasoning on a topic. Does lowering the federal corporate income tax rate create jobs? Should community colleges be tuition-free? When you ask audience members to reach a conclusion regarding a complicated issue, they will look to you to provide factual evidence and logical reasons—to offer appeals to logos. You can evoke logos in a speech with evidence and reasoning within the framework of an argument. Persuasive speeches contain one or more arguments (see Chapter 24 on constructing arguments).

Appeal to Emotion

A second powerful means of persuasion is *pathos*—appealing to listeners' emotions. Feelings such as love, compassion, anger, and fear underlie many of our actions and motivate us to think and feel as we do. Appealing to these emotions helps establish a personal connection with the audience and makes your claims more relatable.

One means of evoking emotion or pathos in a speech is to appeal to the audience's physical senses through the use of *vivid imagery*. Another way to stir feeling is to call upon *shared values,* such as patriotism, selflessness, faith, and hope. Infusing parts of the speech with *repetition* and *parallelism,* which creates rhythm and drama, also arouses emotion (see Chapter 15 on Using Language).

You can see how these techniques operate in the following excerpt from the famous "Fight on the Beaches" speech by Winston Churchill, delivered on June 4, 1940, to the British House of Commons. Here Churchill sought to motivate the nation for the battles ahead through his use of vivid descriptions of the enemy ("odious apparatus of Nazi rule") and of where he would take the battles ("on the seas and the oceans"; "in the fields and in the streets"); through his appeals to the values of patriotism and hope ("we shall not flag or fail"; "we shall never surrender") and through his unforgettable use of repetition and parallelism ("We shall…"):

> Even though large tracts of Europe and many old and famous States have fallen or may fall into the *grip of the Gestapo* and all the *odious apparatus* of Nazi rule, *we shall not flag or fail. We shall go on* to the end, *we shall fight* in France, *we shall fight* on the seas and oceans, *we shall fight* with growing confidence and growing strength in the air, *we shall defend* our Island, whatever the cost may be, *we shall fight* on the beaches, *we shall fight* on the landing grounds, *we shall fight* in the fields and in the streets, *we shall fight* in the hills; *we shall never surrender. . . .*[5]

QUICK TIP

Base Emotional Appeals on Sound Reasoning

Although emotion is a powerful means of moving an audience, relying solely on naked emotion to persuade will fail most of the time. What actually persuades is the interplay between emotion and logic.[6] Emotion gets the audience's attention and arouses their feelings—either positive or negative—about the issue in question. Reason provides the justification for these feelings, and emotion and reason together may dispose audience members to believe in or act upon your suggestions.

Appeal to Credibility

No matter how well-reasoned a message is or which strong emotions its words target, if audience members have little regard for you as the speaker, they won't respond positively to your appeals. Aristotle termed this effect of the speaker *ethos*, or ethical *character*. Ethos is about establishing your authority as a speaker and person.

A persuasive appeal based on ethos contains three elements. The first is *competence*, or demonstrating mastery of the subject matter. Second is *moral character*, as reflected in an honest presentation of the message. Third is *goodwill*, as demonstrated by the speaker's interest in and concern for the needs of the audience relative to the speech.

Applying Aristotle's Three Persuasive Appeals

Appeal to Logos	Targets audience members' rationality using factual evidence and logical reasoning
Appeal to Pathos	Targets audience members' emotions using dramatic storytelling and techniques of language such as vivid imagery, repetition, and parallelism, and figures of speech such as metaphor
Appeal to Ethos	Targets audience members' feelings about the speaker's character through demonstrations of trustworthiness, competence, and concern for their welfare

◎ Contemporary Persuasive Appeals: Needs and Motivations

Current research confirms the persuasive power of ethos, pathos, and logos in persuasive appeals.[7] Advertisers consciously create ads aimed at evoking an emotional response (pathos) in consumers, that convince us that their company or product is reliable or credible (ethos), and that offer factual reasons (logos) for why we should buy something.[8] At the same time, modern-day scholars have developed additional strategies for reinforcing or changing attitudes, including (1) targeting audience members' *motivations* for feeling and acting as they do, (2) appealing to audience members' *needs*, and (3) appealing to how they are likely to *mentally process* the persuasive message.

Appeal to What Motivates Audience Members

Winning over audience members to your point of view requires appealing to their **motives**, or predispositions to behave in certain ways.[9] Motives arise from needs and desires that we seek to satisfy (see below). If as a speaker you can convince listeners that taking an action you propose will reward them in some way, you are likely to encourage receptivity to change.

Appeal to Audience Members' Needs

Our multibillion-dollar advertising industry focuses on one goal: appealing to consumers' needs. Likewise, one very effective way to persuade audience members is to point to some need they want fulfilled and show them a way to fulfill it. According to psychologist Abraham Maslow's classic **hierarchy of needs**, each of us has a set of basic needs ranging from essential, life-sustaining ones to less critical, self-improvement ones.[10] Our needs at the lower, essential levels (physiological and safety needs) must be fulfilled before the higher levels (social, self-esteem, and self-actualization needs) become important and motivating. Using Maslow's hierarchy to persuade your listeners to to refrain from texting while driving, for example, you would appeal to their need for safety.

Following are Maslow's five basic needs, along with suggested actions a speaker can take to appeal to them.

Maslow's Hierarchy of Needs	
Need	Speech Action
Physiological needs (to have access to basic sustenance, including food, water, and air)	• Plan for and accommodate the audience's physiological needs—are listeners likely to be hot, cold, hungry, or thirsty?
Safety needs (to feel protected and secure)	• Appeal to safety benefits— voting for a clean air bill will remove a threat or protect audience members from harm.
Social needs (to find acceptance; to have lasting, meaningful relationships)	• Appeal to social benefits— adopting a healthier diet will lead to being more physically fit and attractive to peers.
Self-esteem needs (to feel good about ourselves; self-worth)	• Appeal to emotional benefits— volunteering as a high school mentor will make listeners feel better about themselves.
Self-actualization needs (to achieve goals; to reach our highest potential)	• Appeal to your listeners' need to fulfill their potential—daily meditation reduces stress and increases self-awareness.

Encourage Mental Engagement

Audience members will mentally process your persuasive message by one of two routes, depending on the degree of their involvement in the message.[11] According to the **elaboration likelihood model of persuasion (ELM)**, when listeners are motivated and able to think critically about a message, they engage in **central processing**. That is, listeners who seriously consider what your message means to them are the ones most likely to act on it. When audience members lack the motivation or ability to judge your argument based on its merits, they engage in **peripheral processing** of information—they pay little attention and respond to the message as being irrelevant, too complex to follow, or just plain unimportant. Listeners may buy into your message, but they do so not on the strength of the arguments but on the basis of such superficial factors as reputation, entertainment value, or the speaker's personal style. These listeners

Do You Encourage Central Processing?	
Do you:	**Example**
Link your argument to listeners' concerns and emphasize direct consequences?	"Hybrid cars may not be the best-looking or fastest cars on the market, but when gas prices rise, they save you money."
Present your message at an appropriate level of understanding?	For a *general audience*: "The technology behind hybrid cars is simple." For an *expert audience*: "To save even more gas, you can turn an EV into a PHEV with a generator and additional batteries."
Do you demonstrate common bonds and stress your credibility?	"It took me a while to convince myself to buy a hybrid, but once I did, I found I saved nearly $3,000 this year."

are unlikely to experience any meaningful changes in attitudes or behavior. Central processing produces more long-lasting changes in audience perspective.

Demonstrate Speaker Credibility

You've seen the qualities of speaker competence, moral character, and goodwill that the ancients described in terms of ethos (see p. 38). A contemporary term for ethos is **speaker credibility**. Research verifies the vital importance of ethos, or speaker credibility, in gaining an audience's trust. For example, studies confirm a direct relationship between attitude change and listeners' perceptions of the speaker's level of competence and preparation.[12] Speakers perceived as high in credibility will also be regarded as more truthful than those perceived to have low credibility.[13]

STAGES IN SPEAKER CREDIBILITY   For audience members, credibility builds in phases as the speaker moves through the speech. It begins with the impressions audience members form even before the speaker begins to speak.

   Initial credibility is based on factors such as information provided about the speaker ahead of the event and, as the speech begins, on his or her physical appearance and non-verbal behavior. Listeners assign more credibility to speakers who dress appropriately and establish eye contact than to those who do not take these steps.

Once into the speech, audience members will assign speakers more or less credibility based on their actual message, including the quality of evidence and the skill with which the speech is delivered. This is called **derived credibility**, since it derives from actual performance. Here is where competence plays a major role.

Listeners continue to make judgments about credibility up until and even after the conclusion of the speech. **Terminal credibility** encompasses the totality of the audience's impressions, including that of the strength of the speaker's conclusion as well as the overall speech performance. Ending abruptly, without a good summation, and hurrying away from the venue will negatively impact terminal credibility.[14]

✓ CHECKLIST

Tips for Increasing Speaker Credibility

- ❏ Strive to make a positive first impression.
- ❏ Enlighten your audience with new and relevant information.
- ❏ For topics that involve a lot of facts and analysis, emphasize your expertise.
- ❏ For topics of a more personal nature, emphasize your commonality with the audience.

Consider Cultural Orientation

The audience's cultural orientation—its core values, cultural norms, cultural premises, and emotions—will significantly affect their responses to persuasion.

🔀 **LaunchPad** To learn more about the role of culture in persuasion, see the section on Cultural Orientation in LaunchPad: launchpadworks.com

CHAPTER 24

Constructing the Persuasive Speech

In persuasive speeches, one or more arguments serve as the framework for the speaker's appeals. An **argument** is a stated position, with support for or against an idea or issue. In an argument, you ask listeners to accept a conclusion about some state of affairs, support it with evidence, and provide reasons demonstrating that the evidence supports the claim. The core elements of an argument consist of a claim, evidence, and warrants:[1]

1. The **claim** (also called a **proposition**) states the speaker's conclusion about some state of affairs. The claim answers the question: "What are you trying to prove?"

2. The **evidence** substantiates the claim, answering the question: "What is your proof for the claim?"

3. The **warrant** provides reasons or justifications for why the evidence supports the claim. It is a line of reasoning that provides a rationale for accepting that the evidence for the claim is valid, or *warranted*.

◎ Identify the Nature of Your Claims

You can construct arguments for a persuasive speech based on three different kinds of claims: of fact, of value, and of policy. Your speech may contain only one type of claim or,

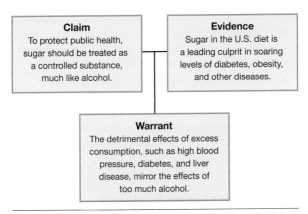

Claim
To protect public health, sugar should be treated as a controlled substance, much like alcohol.

Evidence
Sugar in the U.S. diet is a leading culprit in soaring levels of diabetes, obesity, and other diseases.

Warrant
The detrimental effects of excess consumption, such as high blood pressure, diabetes, and liver disease, mirror the effects of too much alcohol.

FIGURE 24.1 Core Components of Argument

often, consist of several arguments addressing different kinds of claims.

- **Claims of fact** focus on whether something is or is not true or whether something will or will not happen. They usually address issues for which two or more competing answers exist, or those for which an answer does not yet exist (called a *speculative claim*). An example of the first is "Global warming is causing more extreme weather patterns." An example of the second is "Drones will deliver groceries to most homes in the United States by 2025."
- **Claims of value** address issues of judgment. Speakers arguing claims of value try to show that something is right or wrong, good or bad, worthy or unworthy. Examples include "Is assisted suicide ethical?" and "Is any painting worth $100 million?" Evidence in support of a value claim tends to be more subjective than for a fact claim.
- **Claims of policy** recommend that a specific course of action be taken or approved. Legislators regularly construct arguments based on claims of policy: "Should we pass a law restricting the use of assault weapons/genetically modified foods/firecrackers?" Anyone can argue for a claim of policy as long as he or she advocates for or against a given plan. In claims of policy the word *should* appears; it speaks to an "ought" condition, proposing that certain better outcomes would be realized if the proposed condition were met.

✔ CHECKLIST

Identify the Nature of Your Claim

- ❑ When addressing whether something is or is not true, or whether something will or will not happen, frame your conclusion as a *claim of fact*.
- ❑ When addressing issues that rely upon individual judgment of right and wrong for their resolution, frame your conclusion as a *claim of value*.
- ❑ When proposing a specific outcome or solution to an issue, frame your conclusion as a *claim of policy*.

◉ Use Convincing Evidence

As in claims, you can choose among different types of evidence to support these claims.

Offer Secondary Sources ("External Evidence")

The most common form of evidence is secondary sources—
the examples, narratives, testimony, facts, and statistics
described in Chapter 8. Sometimes called "external evidence"
because the knowledge comes from outside the speaker's
own experience, secondary or external sources are most
powerful when they impart new information that the audience has not previously used in forming an opinion.[2]

Offer Speaker Expertise as Evidence

When the audience will find your opinions credible, consider
using your own experience and knowledge as evidence.
Offered along with other forms of evidence, speaker expertise can encourage audience identification and add credibility
to a claim. Following is an example:

Claim:	Young adults need the protection of a health insurance plan.
Speaker Expertise as Evidence:	Being young and healthy, I didn't believe I needed insurance . . . until I required surgery costing thousands of dollars.
Warrant:	The young and healthy are also vulnerable and need to protect themselves against unforeseen events.

Note that in this example, the warrant could just as easily be
implied as stated. Some claims require carefully stated warrants; others can be implied.

Offer Evidence That Appeals to Audience Needs and Motivations

Even seemingly overwhelming evidence may not be enough
to convince audience members of certain claims unless they
see how it relates to their own needs and motivations. This is
especially important when asking the audience to act on your
suggestions, but it can be important for many different kind
of claims. When urging changes in a health behavior such as
diet, for example, offer evidence that listeners are likely to
find personally useful and motivating. If making a claim of
policy that your college administration should change its free
speech policies, you might cite evidence that relates directly
to the students: "In our college, the administration's Student
Code of Conduct infringes on your First Amendment rights
of freedom of expression by . . ."

◉ Select Warrants

As with claims and evidence, you can use different types of warrants or lines of reasoning to justify the links you make between claim and evidence.

- **Motivational warrants** offer reasons targeted at the audience's needs and emotions. In Aristotle's terms, the motivational warrant makes use of *pathos,* or *emotional appeals.* Motivational warrants often are implied rather than stated outright:

Claim:	You can easily afford to join Organization X dedicated to ending the hunger of thousands of children.
Evidence:	The price of one soft drink can feed a child for a week.
Motivational Warrant:	You don't want any child to starve or go without proper medical care.

- **Authoritative warrants** rely on the audience's beliefs about the credibility of the *source of the evidence;* this appeal is based on *ethos.* The success or failure of authoritative warrants rests on how highly the audience regards the authority figure.

Claim:	We should contribute financially to an agency that feeds hungry children.
Evidence:	Any amount we give, however small, will go far in meeting the agency's objectives.
Authoritative Warrant:	The agency is sponsored by Senator X.

- **Substantive warrants** target the audience's faith in the speaker's factual evidence as justification for the argument; this warrant is based on *logos* and appeals to the audience's rational thinking on a matter:

Claim:	Climate change is linked to stronger hurricanes.
Evidence:	We have seen a consistent pattern of stronger hurricanes and warmer oceans.
Substantive Warrant:	Hurricanes and tropical storms get their energy from warm water.

Substantive warrants frequently make use of two types of reasoning: causation and analogy. In **causal reasoning**, the speaker argues that one event, circumstance, or idea (the cause) is the reason (effect) for the other. The example on p. 182 about climate change offers an instance of causal reasoning, or **warrant by cause**. The warrant proves the relationship of cause (climate change) to effect (stronger hurricanes) on the factual basis of the process of hurricane formation.

A second type of reasoning used in substantive warrants, **reasoning by analogy**, compares two similar cases and implies that what is true in one case is true in the other. The assumption is that the characteristics of Case A and Case B are similar, if not the same, and that what is true for B must also be true for A. Arguments based on **warrant by analogy** occur frequently in persuasive speeches, especially those addressing claims of policy.

Claim:	Lifting economic sanctions on Iran in exchange for a suspension in its pursuit of nuclear weapons risks creating another North Korea.
Evidence:	North Korea used the loosening of sanctions to redouble its nuclear program, just as the Iranians are doing now.
Warrant by analogy:	Iran, like North Korea, is an anti-American regime and sponsor of terror that cannot be trusted to do as they say.

QUICK TIP

Include a Call to Action

In any speech asking audience members to do something, be sure to include a **call to action** in the conclusion of your speech (see p. 117). Make an explicit appeal to take the specific action—buy only those products that meet fair-trade conditions, register to vote, join a charity, and so forth. Lower barriers to action by telling the audience precisely what they need to do to accomplish the act, and remind them of the benefits to themselves of taking the action.

◉ Counterarguments: Addressing the Other Side

All attempts at persuasion are subject to counterargument. A persuasive speaker can choose to offer only one side of the argument(s) or acknowledge opposing views. A **one-sided message** does not mention opposing claims; a **two-sided message** mentions opposing points of view and sometimes refutes them. Research suggests that two-sided messages generally are more persuasive than one-sided messages, as long as the speaker adequately refutes opposing claims.[3]

If listeners are aware of opposing claims and you ignore them, you risk a loss of credibility. This is especially the case when speaking with people who disagree with your position. Yet you need not painstakingly acknowledge and refute all opposing claims. Instead, raise and refute the most important counterclaims and evidence that the audience would know about. Ethically, you can ignore counterclaims that don't significantly weaken your argument.[4]

Persuasion scholar Herbert Simons describes four types of potential audiences, from hostile to critical to sympathetic to uninformed. Following are various counterargument strategies for appealing to each type.[5]

Counterargument Strategies for Appealing to Different Audience Types	
Audience Type	**Counterargument Strategy**
Hostile audience or those who strongly disagree	• Raise counterarguments, focusing on those the audience is most likely to disagree with and try to win support.
Critical and/or conflicted audience	• Address major counterarguments and refute them; introduce new evidence.
Sympathetic audience	• If time permits, briefly address only most important counterarguments.
Uninformed, less educated, or apathetic audience	• Briefly raise and refute only key counterarguments the audience may hear in future.

*Audience types based on Herbert Simons, *Persuasion in Society*, 2nd ed. (New York: Routledge, 2011).

> ✔ **CHECKLIST**
>
> ## Strategies for Addressing Counterarguments
>
> ❑ Gently challenge preconceptions associated with the counterarguments, but do not insult the audience.
>
> ❑ Acknowledge counterclaims the audience is most likely to disagree with and demonstrate why those claims are weaker than your argument.
>
> ❑ If you can introduce new evidence to demonstrate that the counterclaim is outdated or inaccurate, do so.
>
> ❑ Consider where in the speech to introduce the counterclaims. When addressing a hostile audience about a controversial topic, addressing the counterclaim early in the speech and revisiting it just before the conclusion works well; otherwise, you can address counterclaims just before the conclusion.

◉ Avoid Fallacies in Reasoning

A **logical fallacy** is either a false or erroneous statement or an invalid or deceptive line of reasoning.[6] In either case, you need to be aware of fallacies in order to avoid making them in your own speeches and to be able to identify them in the speeches of others. Many fallacies of reasoning exist; the table on pp. 186–187 lists several that occur frequently in communication.

◉ Strengthen Your Case with Organization

Once you've developed your arguments, with claims as main points, focus on structuring your speech using one of the organizational patterns described in Chapter 12 and those designed specifically for persuasive speeches (see this chapter). There is no one "right" way to organize a persuasive speech—or any kind of speech—only choices that will be more or less effective for your topic and purpose (see also the table on p. 88).

Following are some criteria to consider when choosing an organizational pattern.

What Do Your Claims and Evidence Suggest?

The nature of your claims and evidence may make a suitable pattern easy to spot. A claim of policy arguing that "junk" foods in school cafeterias should be limited implies that unrestricted

Continued on p. 188

Common Logical Fallacies

Logical Fallacy	Examples
Begging the question An argument that is stated in such a way that it cannot help but be true, even though no evidence has been presented.	"Intelligent Design is the correct explanation for biological change over time because we can see godly evidence in our complex natural world."
Ad hominem argument An argument that targets a person instead of the issue at hand in an attempt to incite an audience's dislike for that person.	"How can you accept my opponent's position on education when he has been divorced?"
Bandwagoning An argument that uses (unsubstantiated) general opinion as its (false) basis for asserting the truth of something.	"Nikes are superior to other brands of shoes because everyone wears Nikes."
Either-or fallacy (*"false dichotomy"*) An argument stated in terms of only two alternatives, even though there may be many additional alternatives.	"Either you're with us or against us."
Red herring An argument that introduces an irrelevant or unrelated topic into the discussion to divert attention from the issue at hand.	"The previous speaker suggests that Medicare is in shambles. I disagree and recommend that we study why the young don't respect their elders."
Hasty generalization An argument that uses an isolated instance to make an unwarranted general conclusion.	"My neighbor who works at Walmart is untrustworthy; therefore, Walmart is not a trustworthy company."

Logical Fallacy	Examples
Post hoc ergo propter hoc (also called *post hoc* and *fallacy of false cause*) An argument suggesting a causal relationship between two states or events due to the order in which the event occurred, rather than taking other factors into consideration.	"The child was vaccinated in June and became ill the following week, clearly as a result of the vaccine."
Faulty analogy An argument claiming that two phenomena are alike when in fact the things compared are not similar enough to warrant the comparison.	"Banning guns for law-abiding citizens because criminals use them to kill people is like banning cars because some people use them to drive drunk and kill people."[7]
Non sequitur (*"does not follow"*) An argument in which the conclusion does not follow from the evidence.	"Because they live in the richest country in the world, they must be extremely wealthy."
Slippery slope A faulty assumption that one case will lead to a series of events or actions.	"Helping refugees from Syria today will force us to help refugees across the Middle East and worldwide."
Appeal to tradition An argument which bases its acceptance on historical tradition—on the fact that if something has traditionally been done, it must be done "right."	"A marriage should be between a man and a woman because that is how it has always been."

sales of these foods represent a *problem* and that limiting them represents a *solution*; many such claims of policy fit naturally into the problem-solution pattern. However, perhaps your research convincingly points to several advantages associated with limiting junk food and several disadvantages associated with not doing so. In this event, the *comparative advantage pattern*, in which you offer a series of compelling advantages associated with limiting junk food over not doing so (see p. 189 in this chapter) might serve your topic and purpose well. It is up to you to determine which pattern will best suit the speech.

What Response Do You Seek?

You can also hone in on a pattern by considering the response you seek from the audience. Do you want them to actually do something—buy a product, donate to a cause? If so, you may select the action-oriented *Monroe's motivated sequence* (see p. 190). If your goal is to strengthen attitudes regarding solving a certain issue, you might select the *problem-solution* or *cause-effect* pattern.

What is the Audience's Disposition?

Considering audience attitudes can also help you select a pattern. How receptive to or critical of your claims is the audience likely to be? Where does your target audience stand relative to your topic? The refutation pattern, for example (see p. 191), is particularly effective when persuading audience members hostile to your position.

Each of these criteria can help in selecting a pattern, as can simple experimentation. Often an effective choice will become apparent fairly quickly.

Problem-Solution Pattern of Arrangement

One commonly used design for persuasive speeches, especially (but not restricted to) those based on *claims of policy*, is the *problem-solution pattern*. Here you organize speech points to demonstrate the nature and significance of a problem and then to provide justification for a proposed solution:

    I. Problem (define what it is)

    II. Solution (offer a way to overcome the problem)

But many problem-solution speeches require more than two points to adequately explain the problem and to support the recommended solution. Thus a **problem-cause-solution pattern** may be in order:

    I. The nature of the problem (define what it is)

    II. Reasons for the problem (explain why it's a problem, for whom, etc.)

    III. Proposed solution (explain why it's expected to work)

When arguing a claim of policy, it may be important to demonstrate the proposal's feasibility using a four-point *problem-cause-solution-feasibility pattern*. This organization can be seen in the following claim of policy about the Social Security program:

Thesis Stated as Need or Problem:	Serious financial challenges to our nation's Social Security program require that we take steps to ensure it will be able meet its obligations to citizens.
Main Points:	**I.** To keep Social Security funded, we need to raise both the full benefits age and early eligibility age. (*Need/problem*)
	II. People are living longer in retirement, thus collecting Social Security over a longer period. (*Causes of the problem; can offer single or multiple causes*)
	III. Congress should raise early eligibility age from 62 to 67 and normal retirement age from 67 to 70. (*Solution to the problem*)
	IV. Social Security programs in countries X and Y have done this successfully. (*Evidence of solution's feasibility*)

Comparative Advantage Pattern of Arrangement

Another way to organize speech points is to show how your viewpoint or proposal is superior to one or more alternative viewpoints or proposals. The **comparative advantage pattern** is most effective when your audience is already aware of the issue or problem and agrees that a need for a solution (or an alternative view) exists.

Using the comparative advantage pattern, the main points in a speech addressing the best way to control the deer population might look like these:

Thesis:	Rather than hunting, fencing, or contraception alone, the best way to reduce the deer population is by a dual strategy of hunting *and* contraception.
	I. A combination strategy is superior to hunting alone because many areas are too densely populated by humans to permit hunting; in such cases, contraceptive darts and vaccines can address the problem. (*Advantage over alternative #1*)

    II. A combination strategy is superior to relying solely on fencing because fencing is too expensive for widespread use. (*Advantage over alternative #2*)

    III. A dual strategy is superior to relying solely on contraception because only a limited number of deer are candidates for contraceptive darts and vaccines. (*Advantage over alternative #3*)

Monroe's Motivated Sequence

The **motivated sequence pattern**, developed in the mid-1930s by Alan Monroe,[8] is a five-step sequence that begins with arousing listeners' attention and ends with calling for action. This pattern is particularly effective when you want the audience to do something—buy a product, donate to a cause, and so forth.

STEP 1: ATTENTION The *attention step* addresses listeners' core concerns, making the speech highly relevant to them.

STEP 2: NEED The *need step* isolates the issue to be addressed. If you can show the members of an audience that they have an important need that must be satisfied or a problem that must be solved, they will have a reason to listen to your propositions.

STEP 3: SATISFACTION The *satisfaction step* identifies the solution. This step begins the crux of the speech, offering the audience a proposal to reinforce or change their attitudes, beliefs, and values regarding the need at hand.

STEP 4: VISUALIZATION The *visualization step* provides the audience with a vision of anticipated outcomes associated with the solution. The purpose of this step is to carry audience members beyond accepting the feasibility of your proposal to seeing how it will actually benefit them.

STEP 5: ACTION Finally, in the *action step* the speaker asks audience members to act according to their acceptance of the message. This may involve reconsidering their present way of thinking about something, continuing to believe as they do but with greater commitment, or implementing a new set of behaviors.

For an example of using Monroe's motivated sequence in a speech, see "Becoming a Socially Conscious Consumer" on p. 192.

Refutation Pattern of Arrangement

Similar to debate, the **refutation pattern** addresses each main point and then refutes (disproves) an opposing claim to your position. This pattern can effectively address counterarguments (see p. 184).

Refutation may influence audience members who either disagree with you or are conflicted about where they stand. Note that it is important to refute *strong* rather than *weak* objections to the claim, since weak objections won't sway the audience.[9] Consider this pattern when you are confident that the opposing argument is weak and vulnerable to attack.

Main points in a refutation pattern are arranged in a format similar to this:

Main Point I:	State the opposing position.
Main Point II:	Describe the implications or ramifications of the opposing claim.
Main Point III:	Offer arguments and evidence for your position.
Main Point IV:	Contrast your position with the opposing claim to drive home the superiority of your position.

📖 **LaunchPad** For more details on the refutation pattern of arrangement, see the section "Refutation Pattern of Arrangement" in LaunchPad: launchpadworks.com

SAMPLE PERSUASIVE SPEECH

In this carefully planned persuasive speech, Jacob Hahn offers strong evidence and reasons for his claims in support of socially responsible consumerism. Jacob organizes the speech using Monroe's five-step motivated sequence. He begins with the attention step, making the speech relevant to listeners, and ends with the action step, demonstrating clearly what audience members can do. Note Jacob's persuasive use of language throughout, especially in the strong imagery that helps listeners visualize the tragedy that occurred in a factory in Bangladesh ("bodies, bricks, and garments left in the rubble") and use of personal pronouns to involve audience members personally.

Becoming a Socially Conscious Consumer

Jacob Hahn

📶 **LaunchPad** See Jacob deliver his speech in LaunchPad:

launchpadworks.com

It started with a few cracks in the wall. But then, on April 24, 2013, it became the worst disaster in the history of the garment industry. According to BBC News, on that day the Rana Plaza garment factory in Dhaka, Bangladesh, completely collapsed, leading to the deaths of over 1,100 people.

> Jacob starts the persuasive speech with a dramatic story line ("a few cracks . . .") that serves as an effective attention-getter.

Along with the bodies, bricks, and garments left in the rubble, questions remained about who was to blame for the tragedy. Sure, there were the obvious culprits—the plaza owner, the construction company. But there were other suspects too. What about the companies whose goods were manufactured there? As Emran Hossain and Dave Jamieson pointed out in their May 2, 2013, *Huffington Post* article, garment industry insiders partially blame Western retailers for the tragedy. They claim that it is retailer demand for low-priced labor that creates these poorly constructed and unsafe work factories, which then leads to disasters like the factory collapse.

> Continuing with the "story" keeps the audience involved and wanting to know more.

The thousands of miles that separate us from tragedies like this can make them seem unrelated to our everyday lives. But what if they are not? What if, by purchasing the products these companies make, individuals such as you and I are also somewhat responsible for what happened?

> **Step 1**, the **attention** step of Monroe's sequence, demonstrates the topic's relevance to audience members.

As we'll see today, there is evidence to support the idea that consumers and companies share a responsibility to ensure safer conditions for factory workers. This is why I encourage all of you to become socially conscious consumers and help convince companies to adopt ethical manufacturing standards. Being a socially conscious consumer means being aware of the issues communities face worldwide and actively trying to correct them.

> Jacob states his thesis.

Why would companies do business with factories that allow dangerous working conditions? It's actually quite simple: Corporations want bigger profit margins. The cheaper the production costs, the more money they make when the product sells. And since consumers show more interest in buying lower-priced products than in thinking about how such items are produced, the pressure is on to provide inexpensive goods. The only way to do this and still make money is to make the goods at the lowest cost possible.

But there is a way to break this cycle of cheap labor and deadly working conditions. You, me, all of us as consumers, must be willing to step up and take an active role in the system.

> **Step 2**, the **need** step, shows listeners why they should listen to the speaker's propositions—in this case, to help factory workers obtain safer working conditions.

We can do this in two ways: First, we can pressure companies to improve working conditions for factory laborers, and second, we can pay fairer prices. Some consumer groups are now signaling their willingness to do this, and corporations are responding.

> **Step 3**, the **satisfaction** step, identifies how to meet the need.

The force behind this new kind of partnership is called *cause-related marketing.* According to the *Financial Times*, cause-related marketing is when a company and a charity (or a consumer group) tackle a social or an environmental problem and create business value for the company at the same time.

> Jacob clearly defines a potentially confusing term, offering an explanation from a credible source.

In March 2012, the global marketing firm Nielsen conducted a worldwide study on consumer responses to cause marketing. The poll found that two-thirds of consumers around the world say they prefer to buy products and services from companies that give back to society. Nearly 50 percent of consumers said that they were, and I'm quoting here, "willing to pay more for goods and services from companies that are giving back."

> Jacob provides convincing evidence from credible sources.

The fact that large numbers of consumers are concerned enough about fairness to pay more for products is key to solving the problems that surround the ethical manufacture of clothing. Corporations can appeal to this group of socially conscious consumers, as they are called, by addressing concerns about ethical manufacturing. What do corporations gain by meeting these concerns? It allows them to charge more for their products while also raising their profit margins and improving their brand image. This means that as socially conscious consumers, we can set the standards that corporations must meet if they wish to maximize their profit from our purchasing power.

You may find yourself asking, "Can this actually work?" The answer is a simple yes. In both the food and apparel industries, calls for changes in working conditions led to the now widely known nonprofit organization Fair Trade USA. According to its website, Fair Trade USA is an organization that seeks "to inspire the rise of the [socially] conscious consumer and eliminate exploitation" worldwide. If products are stamped with the Fair Trade logo, it means the farmers and workers who created those products were fairly treated and justly compensated through an internationally established price.

In **Step 4,** the **visualization** step, Jacob offers a vision of outcomes associated with the proposed solution.

Fair Trade USA made its mark in the food industry through its relationship to coffee production in third-world nations. Its success helped major companies such as Starbucks and Whole Foods recognize the strength of cause marketing: If you appeal to the high ethical standards of socially conscious consumers, they will pay more for your product.

Appealing to high ethical standards is often directly related to tragedies like the one that occurred in Bangladesh. After the factory collapsed, the major apparel sellers faced intense criticism over their lax labor practices. In response, these companies are now much more interested in establishing their products as Fair Trade to meet socially conscious consumer standards. For example, as Jason Burke, Saad Hammadi, and Simon Neville report in the May 13, 2013, edition of the *Guardian*, major fashion chains like H&M, Zara, C&A, Tesco, and Primark have pledged to help raise the standards for working conditions. According to the article, they will be helping to "finance fire safety and building improvements in the factories they use in Bangladesh."

Note that Jacob provides evidence in support of his claim.

So, what exactly can you do to help bring about ethical labor practices within the clothing industry?

The two steps I encourage you to take are these: Become informed, and ask questions about what you're buying—whether it's shoes, a t-shirt, or any other type of apparel.

> **Step 5** of Monroe's motivated sequence—the **action** step—is a direct request of listeners ("call to action") to act on the speaker's suggestions and concrete directions for doing so.

To be informed, go to web-sites such as fairtradeusa.org, thirdworldtraveler.com, and tenthousandvillages.com, which list and sell products from clothing manufacturers who have worked to meet the Fair Trade conditions. This list grows monthly, and by supporting these companies through your purchases, you can become a socially conscious consumer.

Additionally, ask questions of other retailers. Whether you shop online or at local retail stores, ask direct questions before purchasing clothes—for example: Where are your products made? Do you have proof of Fair Trade practices? Where can I find this information before I make my purchase? Such questions define the socially conscious consumer, and they ensure that you will not be directly contributing to unsafe and unfair labor practices.

Although several factors contributed to the tragedy in Bangladesh, there is one clear way to help prevent future disasters: Become a socially conscious consumer. By being informed and asking questions, you, too, can make a difference in the lives of workers around the world.

> Jacob concludes by reinforcing his call to action and leaves the audience with a new perspective to consider.

CHAPTER 25 ●●●●

Speaking on Special Occasions

Special occasions stand out from the ordinary rhythm of life, marking passages, celebrating life's highlights, and commemorating events. Such occasions often feature the observance of important ceremonies and rituals as well as speeches.

◉ Functions of Special Occasion Speeches

A **special occasion speech** is one that is prepared for a specific occasion and for a purpose dictated by that occasion. Awards ceremonies call for remarks that acknowledge accomplishments, for example, and acceptance speeches that display gratitude. Special occasion speeches can be either informative or persuasive or, often, a mix of both. However, neither of these functions is the main goal; the underlying function of a special occasion speech is to *entertain, celebrate, commemorate, inspire,* or *set a social agenda*:

- In speeches that *entertain,* listeners expect a lighthearted, amusing speech; they may also expect the speaker to offer a certain degree of insight into the topic at hand. Venues such as banquets, awards dinners, and roasts frequently feature speakers whose main purpose is to entertain.
- In speeches that *celebrate* a person, a place, or an event, listeners look to the speaker to praise the subject of the celebration; they also anticipate a degree of ceremony in accordance with the norms of the occasion. Weddings, anniversaries, retirement parties, and awards ceremonies call for speeches that celebrate.
- In speeches that *commemorate* an event or a person (at dedications of memorials or at gatherings held in someone's honor), listeners expect the speaker to offer remembrance and tribute.
- In speeches that *inspire* (including inaugural addresses, keynote speeches, and commencement speeches), listeners expect to be motivated by examples of achievement and heroism.
- In speeches that *set social agendas* (such as occur at gatherings of cause-oriented organizations, fund-raisers, campaign banquets, conferences, and conventions), listeners expect the articulation and reinforcement of the goals and values of the group.

◉ Types of Special Occasion Speeches

Special occasion speeches include (but are not limited to) introductions, speeches of acceptance, award presentations, roasts and toasts, eulogies and other speeches of tribute, after-dinner speeches, and speeches of inspiration.

Speeches of Introduction

A **speech of introduction** is a short speech with two goals: to prepare or "warm up" the audience for the speaker and to motivate audience members to listen to what the main speaker has to say. A good speech of introduction balances four elements: the speaker's background, the subject of the speaker's message, the occasion, and the audience.

- *Describe the speaker's background and qualifications for speaking.* Relate something about the speaker's achievements, offices held, and other facts to demonstrate why the speaker is relevant to the occasion. The object is to heighten audience interest and build the speaker's credibility.
- *Briefly preview the speaker's topic.* Give the audience a sense of why the subject is of interest, bearing in mind that it is not the introducer's job to evaluate the speech. The rule is: Get in and out quickly with a few well-chosen remarks.
- *Ask the audience to welcome the speaker.* This can be done simply by saying something like "Please welcome Cesar Cruz."
- *Be brief.* Speak just long enough to accomplish the goals of preparation and motivation. One well-known speaker recommends a two-minute maximum.[1]

✓ CHECKLIST
Guidelines for Introducing Other Speakers

- ❏ Identify the speaker correctly. Assign him or her the proper title, such as "vice president for public relations" or "professor emeritus."
- ❏ Practice a difficult-to-pronounce name beforehand.
- ❏ Contact the speaker ahead of time to verify any facts about him or her that you plan to cite.

Speeches of Acceptance

A **speech of acceptance** is made in response to receiving an award. Its purpose is to express gratitude for the honor bestowed on the speaker. The speech should reflect that gratitude.

- *Prepare in advance.* If you know or even suspect that you are to receive an award, decide before the event what you will say.
- *Express what the award means to you.* Convey to the audience the value you place on the award. Express yourself genuinely and with humility.
- *Express gratitude.* Thank by name each of the relevant persons or organizations involved in giving you the award. Acknowledge any team players or others who helped you attain the achievement for which you are being honored.

QUICK TIP

Respond to the Introduction

Whenever you are introduced by another speaker, acknowledge and thank him or her for the introduction. Common methods of responding include "I appreciate those kind words" and "Thank you for making me feel welcome." Accept praise with humility and perhaps even with humor: "Your description was so gracious that I did not realize you were speaking about me."

Speeches of Presentation

The goal of the **speech of presentation** is twofold: to communicate the meaning of the award and to explain why the recipient is receiving it.

- *Convey the meaning of the award.* Describe what the award is for and what it represents. Mention the sponsors and describe the link between the sponsors' goals and values and the award.
- *Explain why the recipient is receiving the award.* Describe the recipient's achievements and special attributes that qualify him or her as deserving of the award.

Roasts and Toasts

A **roast** is a humorous tribute to a person, one in which a series of speakers jokingly poke fun at him or her. A **toast** is a brief tribute to a person or an event being celebrated. Both roasts and toasts call for short speeches whose goal is to celebrate an individual and his or her achievements.

- *Prepare.* Impromptu though they might appear, the best roasts and toasts reflect time spent drafting and, importantly, rehearsing. As you practice, time the speech.
- *Highlight remarkable traits of the person being honored.* Restrict your remarks to one or two of the person's most unusual or recognizable attributes. Convey the qualities that have made him or her worthy of celebrating.
- *Be positive and be brief.* Even if the speech is poking fun at someone, as in a roast, keep the tone positive. Remember, your overall purpose is to pay tribute to the honoree. For example, at the 2015 annual White House Correspondents' Dinner roast, Saturday Night Live cast member Cecily Strong struck the right balance of humor and social satire when she joked to then-President Barack Obama: "Your hair is so white now, it can talk back to the police."[2]

Eulogies and Other Tributes

The word **eulogy** derives from the Greek word meaning "to praise." Those delivering eulogies, usually close friends or family members of the deceased, are charged with celebrating and commemorating the life of someone while consoling those who have been left behind.

- *Balance delivery and emotions.* The audience looks to the speaker for guidance in dealing with the loss and for a sense of closure, so stay in control. If you do feel that you are about to break down, pause, take a breath, and focus on your next thought.
- *Refer to the family of the deceased.* Families suffer the greatest loss, and a funeral is primarily for their benefit. Show respect for the family, mentioning each member by name.
- *Be positive but realistic.* Emphasize the deceased's positive qualities while avoiding excessive praise.

QUICK TIP

Commemorate Life—Not Death

A eulogy should pay tribute to the deceased as an individual and remind the audience that he or she is still alive, in a sense, in our memories. Rather than focus on the circumstances of death, focus on the life of the person. Talk about the person's contributions and achievements, and demonstrate the person's character. Consider telling an anecdote that illustrates the type of person you are eulogizing. Even humorous anecdotes may be appropriate if they effectively humanize the deceased.

After-Dinner Speeches

Its name notwithstanding, the contemporary **after-dinner speech** is just as likely to occur before, during, or after a lunch seminar or other type of business, professional, or civic meeting as it is to follow a formal dinner. In general, an after-dinner speech is expected to be lighthearted and entertaining. At the same time, listeners expect to gain insight into the topic at hand and/or to hear an outline of priorities and goals for the group. Thus social agenda-setting is a simultaneous goal of many after-dinner speeches.

- *Recognize the occasion.* Connect the speech with the occasion. Delivering remarks unrelated to the event may leave the impression that it is a **canned speech**—that is, one that the speaker uses again and again in different settings.

- *Balance seriousness with lightheartedness.* Even when charged with addressing a serious topic, the after-dinner speaker should make an effort to keep his or her remarks low-key enough to accompany the digestion of a meal.
- *Avoid stand-up comedy.* Many speakers treat the after-dinner speech as an opportunity to string together a series of jokes only loosely centered on a theme. However, the after-dinner speech is still a speech. If you are naturally very funny, use that skill, but in the context of a speech.

Speeches of Inspiration

While many special occasion speeches may well be inspiring, a **speech of inspiration** deliberately seeks to uplift members of the audience and to help them see things in a positive light. Sermons, commencement addresses, "pep talks," and nomination speeches are all inspirational in nature. Effective speeches of inspiration touch on deep feelings in the audience. Through emotional force, they urge us toward purer motives and harder effort and remind us of a common good.

- *Appeal to audience members' emotions (pathos).* Three means of evoking emotion are touching upon shared values, using vivid imagery, and telling stories (see p. 173). Techniques of language, such as repetition, alliteration, and parallelism can also help transport the audience from the mundane to a loftier level (see Chapter 15).
- *Use real-life stories.* Few things move us as much as the ordinary person who achieves the extraordinary, whose struggles result in triumph over adversity and the realization of a dream. Recognizing this, many U.S. presidents have taken to weaving stories about "ordinary American heroes" into their State of the Union addresses.
- *Be dynamic.* If it fits your personality, use a dynamic speaking style to inspire through delivery. Combining an energetic style with a powerful message can be one of the most successful strategies for inspirational speaking.
- *Make your goal clear.* Inspirational speeches run the risk of being vague, leaving the audience unsure what the message was. Whatever you are trying to motivate your listeners to do, let them know.
- *Close with a dramatic ending.* Use a dramatic ending to inspire your audience to feel or act. Recall from Chapter 14 the various methods of concluding a speech, including a quotation, story, or call to action.

SAMPLE SPECIAL OCCASION SPEECH

Following is a commencement speech delivered by actor and comedian Will Ferrell at his alma mater, *the University of Southern California. Ferrell weaves real-life anecdotes into his speech and uses self-deprecating humor to build common ground with the new graduates. As he shares his hard-won life lessons, he focuses on uplifting audience members and arousing their better instincts, and he ends with a uniquely memorable conclusion—all key components of a speech of inspiration.*

2017 University of Southern California Commencement Address

Will Ferrell

It is such an honor to deliver this year's commencement address to the University of Southern California's graduating class of 2017…

I graduated [from USC] in 1990 with a degree in Sports Information. Yes. You heard me, Sports Information. A program so difficult, so arduous, that they discontinued the major eight years after I left. Those of us with Sports Information degrees are an elite group. We are like the Navy Seals of USC graduates. There are very few of us and there was a high dropout rate.

> Humor can easily backfire, but Ferrell uses it effectively here and throughout his speech. His self-deprecating humor creates easy bonds of identification between himself and the graduates.

So I graduate and I immediately get a job right out of college working for ESPN, right? Wrong. No, I moved right back home. Back home to the mean streets of Irvine, California…Pretty great success story, right? Yeah, I moved back home for a solid two years, I might add. And I was lucky, actually. Lucky that I had a very supportive and understanding mother. And she recognized that while I had an interest in pursuing sportscasting, my gut was telling me that I really wanted to pursue something else. And that something else was comedy.

For you see, the seeds for this journey were planted right here on this campus. This campus was a theater or testing lab, if you will. I was always trying to make my friends laugh whenever I could find a moment. I had a work-study job at the humanities audiovisual department that would allow me to take off from time to time. By *allow me*, I mean I would just leave and they didn't notice. So I would literally leave my job if I knew friends were attending class close by and crash a lecture while in character. My good buddy Emil, who's also here today... told me one day that I should crash his Thematic Options literature class. So I cobbled together a janitor's outfit complete with work gloves, safety goggles, a dangling lit cigarette, and a bucket full of cleaning supplies. And then I proceeded to walk into the class, interrupting the lecture, informing the professor that I'd just been sent from Physical Plant to clean up a student's vomit. True story.

Ferrell paints a vivid picture with these specific, concrete details, allowing the audience to easily visualize the scene.

What Emil neglected to tell me was that the professor of his class was Ronald Gottesman, a professor who co-edited the *Norton Anthology of American Literature*. Needless to say, a big-time guy. A month after visiting my friend's class as a janitor, I was walking through the campus when someone grabbed me by the shoulder and it was Ron Gottesman. I thought for sure he was going to tell me to never do that again. Instead what he told me was that he loved my barging in on his class and that he thought it was one of the funniest things he'd ever seen and would I please do it again? So on invitation from Professor Gottesman, I would barge in on his lecture class from time to time as the guy from Physical Plant coming by to check on things, and the professor would joyfully play along.

One time I got my hands on a power drill and I just stood outside the classroom door operating the drill for a good minute. Unbeknownst to me, Professor Gottesman was wondering aloud to his class, "I wonder if we're about to get a visit from our Physical Plant guy?" I then walked in as if on cue and the whole class erupted in laughter. After leaving, Professor Gottesman then weaved the surprise visit into his lecture on Walt Whitman and *Leaves of Grass*. Moments like these encouraged me to think maybe I was funny to whole groups of people who didn't know me, and this wonderful professor had no idea how his encouragement of me—to come and interrupt his class no less— was enough to give myself permission to be silly and weird.

My senior year I would discover a comedy and improv troupe called the Groundlings located on Melrose Avenue. This was the theater company and school that gave the starts to Laraine Newman, Phil Hartman, John Lovitz, Pee-wee Herman, Conan O'Brien, and Lisa Kudrow, to name a few. Later it would become my home where I would meet the likes of Chris Kattan, Cheri O'Teri, Ana Gasteyer, Chris Parnell, Maya Rudolph, Will Forte, and Kristin Wiig. I went to one of their shows during the spring semester of my senior year and in fact got pulled up onstage during an audience participation sketch. I was so afraid and awestruck at what the actors were doing that I didn't utter a word. And even in this moment of abject fear and total failure I found it to be thrilling to be on that stage. I then knew I wanted to be a comedic actor.

> Ferrell's storytelling includes important points of identification with his audience, who are also discovering what they want to become.

So starting in the fall of 1991, for the next three and a half years I was taking classes and performing in various shows at the Groundlings and around Los Angeles. I was even trying my hand at stand-up comedy. Not great stand-up, mind you, but enough material to get myself up in front of strangers... My stand-up act was based mostly on material derived from watching old episodes of *Star Trek*. My opening joke was to sing the opening theme to *Star Trek*. Not even funny, just weird.

But I didn't care. I was just trying to throw as many darts at the dartboard, hoping that one would eventually stick. Now don't get me wrong, I wasn't extremely confident that I would succeed during this time period, and after moving back to LA there was many a night where in my LA apartment, I would sit down to a meal of spaghetti topped with mustard, with only $20 in my checking account and I would think to myself, "Oh well, I can always be a substitute schoolteacher." And yes, I was afraid. You're never not afraid. I'm still afraid. I was afraid to write this speech. And now, I'm just realizing how many people are watching me right now, and it's scary. Can you please look away while I deliver the rest of the speech?

But my fear of failure never approached in magnitude my fear of what if. What if I never tried at all?

> Everyone has speech anxiety, even famous comedians. Here again Ferrell creates identification with his audience.

By the spring of 1995 producers from *Saturday Night Live* had come to see the current show at the Groundlings. After two harrowing auditions and two meetings with executive producer Lorne Michaels, which all took place over the course of six weeks, I got the word I was hired to the cast of *Saturday Night Live* for the '95–'96 season.

I couldn't believe it. And even though I went on to enjoy seven seasons on the show, it was rocky beginning for me. After my first show, one reviewer referred to me as "the most annoying newcomer of the new cast." Someone showed this to me and I promptly put it up on the wall in my office, reminding myself that to some people I will be annoying. Some people will not think I'm funny, and that that's okay. One woman wrote to me and said she hated my portrayal of George W. Bush. It was mean-spirited, not funny and besides you have a fat face. I wrote her back and I said, I appreciate your letter and she was entitled to her opinion, but that my job as a comedian especially on a show like *Saturday Night Live* was to hold up a mirror to our political leaders and engage from time to time in satirical reflection. As for my fat face, you are 100% right. I'm trying to work on that. Please don't hesitate to write me again if you feel like I've lost some weight in my face…

Even as I left *SNL*, none of the studios were willing to take a chance on me as a comedy star. It took us three years of shopping *Anchorman* around before anyone would make it. When I left *SNL*, all I really had was a movie called *Old School* that wouldn't be released for another year, and a subpar script that needed a huge rewrite about a man raised by elves at the North Pole.

Now one may look at me as having great success, which I have in the strictest sense of the word, and don't get me wrong: I love what I do and I feel so fortunate to get to entertain people. But to me, my definition of success is my sixteen-and-a-half-year marriage to my beautiful and talented wife, Vivica. Success are my three amazing sons, Magnus, 13, Matthias, 10, and Axel, age 7. Right there, stand up guys, take a bow, there you go.

Success to me is my involvement in the charity Cancer for College, which gives college scholarships to cancer survivors, started by my great friend and SC alum Craig Pollard, a two-time cancer survivor himself, who thought of the charity while we were fraternity brothers at the Delt house, up on West Adams...

No matter how cliché it may sound, you will never truly be successful until you learn to give beyond yourself. Empathy and kindness are the true signs of emotional intelligence, and that's what Viv and I try to teach our boys. Hey Matthias, get your hands off Axel right now! Stop it. I can see you. Okay? Dr. Ferrell's watching you.

> A speech of inspiration urges the audience toward purer motives, as Ferrell does here with his emphasis on the values of love of family and generosity of spirit.

To those of you graduates sitting out there who have a pretty good idea of what you'd like to do with your life, congratulations. For many of you who maybe don't have it all figured out, it's okay. That's the same chair that I sat in. Enjoy the process of your search without succumbing to the pressure of the result. Trust your gut, keep throwing darts at the dartboard. Don't listen to the critics and you will figure it out.

Class of 2017, I just want you to know you will never be alone on whatever path you may choose. If you do have a moment where you feel a little down just think of the support you have from this great Trojan family and imagine me, literally picture my face, singing this song gently into your ear:

"If I should stay, I would only be in your way. So I'll go, but I know, I'll think of you every step of the way. And I will always love you, will always love you, will always love you, Class of 2017. And I will always love you."

> Who but Will Ferrell would end a speech by breaking into song? This conclusion is sure to create a lasting impression on his audience.

Thank you. Fight on!

part

8

Online, Group, and Business Contexts

● ● ● ● ● ● ● ● ● ● ● ● ●

LaunchPad
macmillan learning

VIDEO ACTIVITY
Go to LaunchPad to watch a video of a group that is disrupted by unproductive personal conflict. Visit **launchpadworks.com**

LaunchPad includes:

☑ **LearningCurve** adaptive quizzing

◎ A curated collection of video clips and full-length speeches

Additional resources, such as presentation software tutorials and documentation help.

CHAPTER 26 ●●●●

Preparing Online Presentations

The demand for people skilled in delivering presentations online continues to grow as use of digital media becomes routine. In this environment, competence in speaking online will help you to qualify for many work and civic roles.

◎ Apply Your Knowledge of Face-to-Face Speaking

Online presentations require the same basic elements of planning and delivery as in-person presentations. As in traditional public speaking, an online speaker will select among the three general speech purposes of informing, persuading, or marking a special occasion (see p. 50). Both traditional and online speaking call for careful audience analysis, credible supporting materials, a clear organizational structure, and a natural delivery style. And whether presenting online or in person, as a speaker you must continually engage the audience; when separated physically, this focus becomes all the more critical.

◎ Plan for the Unique Demands of Online Delivery

While much is similar, important differences exist between online and in-person speaking, in both the means of delivery and the nature of the audience. As you plan your presentations, follow the fundamental techniques of public speaking you already know while making the necessary adjustments to transmit your message effectively online.

📁 **LaunchPad** Go to LaunchPad to watch a video of the online speech *Preventing Cyberbullying* at launchpadworks.com

Know the Equipment

Online presentations require some familiarity with digital communication tools. Well before your actual delivery, review the equipment you'll be using and rehearse with it several times.

Tools used to produce and display online presentations include:

- Website or app for distribution to audience (e.g., Facebook Live, Google Meet, WebEx, GoToMeeting, Adobe Connect)
- Hardware for recording audio and video (webcam/video camera, microphone)
- Software for recording and editing audio and video (e.g., Adobe Audition)
- Video capture software (e.g., ScreenFlow, Camtasia)
- Web-based presentation software (e.g., Prezi)
- Podcasting software (e.g., GarageBand, Audacity)
- Popular commercial websites (e.g., YouTube)
- Online conferencing tools (e.g., Skype, Huddle, GoToMeeting)

Focus on Vocal Variety

In an online presentation, the audience cannot interact with your physical presence, making your voice an even more critical conduit of communication. In place of body movement, vocal variety—alterations in volume, pitch, speaking rate, pauses, and pronunciation and articulation—must hold audience interest. Especially important to eliminate are vocal fillers such as "umm" and "aah." Instead, strategically use pauses to help audience members process information.

QUICK TIP

Focus on Projecting Enthusiasm and Naturalness

Staring into a computer screen rather than listeners' eyes makes it difficult to infuse your voice with the enthusiasm and naturalness that eye contact encourages. But a lively conversational style is key for most online presentations. Consider delivering your first presentation with someone else in the room, talking to that person rather than to the screen. Alternatively, experiment with addressing your remarks to a picture, photograph, or even your own reflection in a mirror.[1]

Provide Superior Visual Aids

The audience might not see you in person, but with presentation aids you can still provide them with a compelling visual experience. Consider how you can illustrate talking points in eye-catching text form or with photos, animations, and video clips (see Chapters 19–21). Software and web platforms can help you easily create slides, screencasts, and video for online presentations (see later in this chapter).

◉ Plan the Delivery Mode

Online presentations can be streamed in real time or recorded for distribution later, whenever an audience wants to access them. Understanding the advantages and limitations of both delivery modes can help you plan more effectively.

Real-Time Presentations

Real-time presentations connect the presenter and audience in live, or **synchronous communication**. Interactivity is a chief advantage of this type of presentation: Speaker and audience can respond to one another in real time either orally or via chat or text. As in traditional speaking, audience feedback allows you to adapt topic coverage according to audience input and questions, for example, or adjust technical issues as they occur.

A chief limitation of real-time presentations is scheduling them around people's available time and conflicting time zones. The more geographically dispersed the audience, the greater the logistical challenge. As such, many speakers reserve real-time presentations for occasions when they are in time zones close to the audience.

Recorded Presentations

In a **recorded presentation**, transmission and reception occur at different times, in **asynchronous communication**. The audience can access the presentation at their convenience, such as listening to a podcast at night. Lack of direct interaction with the audience poses challenges, however. Without immediate feedback from the audience to enliven the presentation, you must work harder to create engagement by providing compelling content, delivery style, and presentation aids.

◉ Choose an Online Presentation Format

Online presentation formats include videos, podcasts, vodcasts, and webinars, any of which may be streamed in real time or recorded for later delivery.

Video

Many people use video to present online: from individuals using a smartphone camera or webcam, to professional companies sending out messages using high definition digital video cameras. With **video capture software**, such as Camtasia or Adobe Audition, you can seamlessly incorporate video clips into an online presentation. The "Record Slideshow" feature in the Tools menu of PowerPoint can serve a similar purpose.

You can also use video capture software or dedicated screen-casting software to create screencasts. A **screencast** captures whatever is displayed on your computer screen, from text to slides to streaming video. Screencasts can be streamed in real time, recorded for playback, or exported to a hosting website. The screencast format is especially useful for training purposes.

Podcasts and Vodcasts

A **podcast** is a digital audio recording of a presentation cap-tured and stored in a form that is accessible via the web or an app. A **vodcast** (also called *vidcast* and *video podcasting*) is a podcast containing video. Both podcasts and vodcasts can played on apps such as Audacity, Stitcher, iTunes, Google Play Music, and Soundcloud.

Recording, storing, and delivering a speech via podcast requires a microphone; simple, free digital audio recording

---

✓ CHECKLIST

Creating a Podcast

The basic equipment and software needed to create a podcast are included on most current personal computers, tablets, and smartphones. The only other pieces you may need are an external microphone and audio recording software such as Audacity. Then try these steps:

❑ Plan what you want to say.

❑ Seat yourself in an upright position directly facing your computer, with the microphone no more than 8 inches from your mouth.

❑ Make sure that your external microphone is plugged into your computer, or that your built-in microphone is operational.

❑ Open your audio recording software. Be familiar with how to start, pause, and stop a recording.

❑ Activate the recording software and begin speaking into the microphone. You're now making your presentation.

❑ At the conclusion of your presentation, stop the recording.

❑ Save the new recording as an audio file, such as .mp3.

❑ Close your audio recording software and disengage the microphone.

❑ Go to the new audio file saved to your computer, and open and play it. Now you are listening to your recorded presentation.

❑ Transfer the saved file to a website, blog, or podcast hosting site.

Figure 26.1 Podcast Offerings from the U.S. Centers for Disease Control and Prevention

software (e.g., Audacity); and a website to host the podcast. Using PowerPoint, you can use the "Record Audio" feature to produce a podcast-like presentation file; the file can be used and distributed as you would any PowerPoint file, even via email.

QUICK TIP

Put a Face to the Speaker(s)

To encourage a feeling of connection between yourself and the audience during a webinar, consider displaying a headshot of yourself, with your name and title. A second slide might announce start and finish times; a third, a list of speech objectives.[4] During the presentation, you can alternate displays of text and graphic slides with views of your photograph (and/or other presenters), or in some cases, place photographs side-by-side with the aids.

Webinars

Webinars are real-time seminars, meetings, training sessions, or other presentations that connect presenters and audiences from their computers or mobile devices.[2] Webinars typically include live video conversation; video capture and screencasting; and functions such as chat, instant messaging, and polling.

As in any presentation, planning a webinar starts with considering the audience. Many webinars are *team presentations*, so use the guidelines on p. 221 during the planning stages.[3]

1. Start with a title that indicates what the webinar will do for the audience (e.g., "How New Graduation Requirements Will Affect You").

2. Time each aspect of the webinar and distribute the following information to each presenter:

    Introduction of speaker(s) and purpose

    Length and order of each speaker's remarks

    Length of question-and-answer session, if separate

3. Rehearse the webinar (remotely if necessary).

4. Check meeting room for noise and visual distractions; check equipment.

5. Create a backup plan in case of technical problems.

✓ CHECKLIST

Online Presentation Planning

Keeping in mind both the fundamental guidelines for preparing and presenting an in-person speech as well as those unique considerations of online presentations, here are some additional tips to follow.[5]

❑ *Be well organized.* Offer a clear statement of purpose and preview of main points. Proceed with a solid structure that the audience can easily follow. Conclude by restating your purpose, reviewing the main points, and encouraging the audience to watch or listen for more.

❑ *Design powerful presentation aids.* For video and webcasts, plan for meaningful graphics and images that properly convey your ideas.

❑ *Keep your audience engaged.* In real-time presentations, encourage audience interaction by incorporating chat, instant messaging, or polling features. In recorded presentations, offer an email address, Twitter address, or URL where audience members can submit comments and questions. Use these tools to gather feedback, much the way you would use eye contact in a face-to-face presentation.

(continued)

❑ *Prepare a contingency plan in case of technology glitches.* For
example, have a backup computer running simultaneously
with the one used to deliver the presentation. Provide a
list of FAQs or a web page with instructions for audience
members to manage technology problems.

❑ *Maintain ethical standards.* Use the same degree of decorum
as you would in an in-person speech, bearing in mind that
online presentations have the potential to go viral.

❑ *Get in plenty of practice time.* Rehearse, record, and listen
to yourself as many times as needed.

CHAPTER 27 ●●●●

Communicating in Groups

Most of us will spend a substantial portion of our educational
and professional lives participating in **small groups** or teams
(usually between three and twenty people); and many of the
experiences we have as speakers, including preparing and delivering group presentations (see Chapter 28) occur in groups.
Thus, as with public speaking itself, understanding how to work
cooperatively within a group setting is an important life skill.

◉ Focus on Goals

How well or poorly you meet the objectives of the group—
whether to coordinate a team presentation or to accomplish
some other purpose—is largely a function of how closely you
keep sight of the group's goals and avoid behaviors that detract
from them. Setting an *agenda* can help participants stay on
track by identifying items to be accomplished during a meeting; often it will specify time limits for each item.

◉ Plan on Assuming Dual Roles

In a work group, you will generally assume a task role and a
social role, and sometimes both.[1] **Task roles** are the hands-on
roles that directly relate to the group's accomplishment of its
objectives. Examples include *recording secretary* (takes notes)
and *moderator* (facilitates discussion).

Members also adopt various **social roles** reflecting individual members' personality traits. Social roles function to help
facilitate effective group interaction, such as *the harmonizer*
(smoothes over tension by settling differences) and *gatekeeper*
(keeps the discussion moving and gets everyone's input).

Sometimes, group members focus on individual needs irrelevant to the task at hand. **Antigroup roles** such as *floor hogger* (not allowing others to speak), *blocker* (being overly negative about group ideas; raising issues that have been settled), and *recognition seeker* (calling attention to oneself rather than to group tasks) do not further the group's goals and should be avoided.

Center Disagreements around Issues

Whenever people come together to consider an important issue, conflict is inevitable. But conflict doesn't have to be destructive. In fact, the best decisions are usually those that emerge from productive conflict.[2] In *productive conflict*, group members clarify questions, challenge ideas, present counterexamples, consider worst-case scenarios, and reformulate proposals. Productive conflict centers disagreements around issues rather than personalities. Rather than wasting time arguing with one another over personal motives or perceived shortcomings, productive conflict encourages members to rigorously test and debate ideas and potential solutions.

Resist Groupthink

For groups to be truly effective, its members need to form a cohesive unit with a common goal. At the same time, they must avoid **groupthink**, the tendency to minimize conflict by refusing to examine ideas critically or test solutions.[3] Groups prone to groupthink typically exhibit these behaviors:

- Participants reach a consensus and avoid conflict in order not to hurt others' feelings, but without genuinely agreeing.
- Members who do not agree with the majority feel pressured to conform.
- Disagreement, tough questions, and counterproposals are discouraged.
- More effort is spent justifying the decision than testing it.

Adopt an Effective Leadership Style

When called upon to lead a group, bear in mind the four broad styles of leadership, and mix and match the leadership styles that best suit your group's needs.[4]

- *Directive*: Leader controls group communication by conveying specific instructions to members
- *Supportive*: Leader attends to group members' emotional needs, stressing positive relationships
- *Achievement-oriented*: Leader sets challenging goals and high standards
- *Participative*: Leader views members as equals, welcoming their opinions, summarizing points, and identifying problems that must be solved rather than dictating solutions

Whatever style or styles of leadership you adopt, remember that the most effective leaders (1) remain focused on their group's goals; (2) hold themselves and the group accountable for achieving results; (3) treat all group members in an ethical manner; and (4) inspire members to contribute their best.[5]

Set Goals

As a leader, aim to be a catalyst in setting and reaching goals in collaboration with other group members. It is the leader's responsibility to ensure that each group member can clearly identify the group's purpose(s) and goal(s).

QUICK TIP

Optimize Decision Making in Groups

Research suggests that groups can reach the best decisions by adopting two methods of argument: *devil's advocacy* (arguing for the sake of raising issues or concerns about the idea under discussion) and *dialectical inquiry* (devil's advocacy that goes a step further by proposing a countersolution to the idea).[6] Both approaches help expose underlying assumptions that may be preventing participants from making the best decision. As you lead a group, consider how you can encourage both methods of argument.

Encourage Active Participation

Groups tend to adopt solutions that receive the largest number of favorable comments, whether these comments emanate from one individual or many. If only one or two members participate, it is their input that sets the agenda, whether or not their solution is optimal.[7]

When you lead a group, take these steps to encourage group participation:

- *Directly ask members to contribute.* Sometimes one person, or a few people, dominate the discussion. Encourage others to contribute by redirecting the discussion in their direction ("Patrice, we haven't heard from you yet" or "Juan, what do you think about this?").
- *Set a positive tone.* Some people are reluctant to express their views because they fear ridicule or attack. Minimize such fears by setting a positive tone, stressing fairness, and encouraging politeness and active listening.
- *Make use of devil's advocacy and dialectical inquiry* (*see Quick Tip above*). Raise pertinent issues or concerns, and entertain solutions other than the one under consideration.

Use Reflective Thinking

To reach a decision or solution that all participants under-stand and are committed to, guide participants through the six-step process of reflective thinking shown in Figure 27.1, which is based on the work of educator John Dewey.[8]

Step 1   Identify the problem
- What is being decided upon?

Group leader summarizes problem, ensures that all group members understand problem, and gains agreement from all members.

↓

Step 2   Conduct research and analysis
- What information is needed to solve the problem?
  Conduct research to gather relevant information.
  Ensure that all members have relevant information.

↓

Step 3   Establish guidelines and criteria
- Establish criteria by which proposed solutions will be judged.
  Reach criteria through consensus and record criteria.

↓

Step 4   Generate solutions
- Conduct brainstorming session.
  Don't debate ideas; simply gather and record all ideas.

↓

Step 5   Select the best solution
- Weigh the relative merits of each idea against criteria. Select one alternative that can best fulfill criteria.
  If more than one solution survives, select solution that best meets criteria.
  Consider merging two solutions if both meet criteria.
  If no solution survives, return to problem identification step.

↓

Step 6   Evaluate solution
- Does the solution have any weaknesses or disadvantages?
- Does the solution resemble the criteria that were developed?
- What other criteria would have been helpful in arriving at a better solution?

FIGURE 27.1 Making Decisions in Groups: John Dewey's Six-Step Process of Reflective Thinking

CHAPTER 28

Delivering Group Presentations

Group presentations are oral presentations prepared and delivered by a group of three or more individuals. Regularly assigned in the classroom and frequently delivered in the workplace, successful group presentations of the types described in Chapters 29–36 require close cooperation and planning.

◉ Use Group Communication Guidelines

Preparing and delivering a successful group presentation depends on effective communication among members. Use the guidelines in Chapter 27 on collaborating in groups to set goals, assign roles and tasks, and manage conflict.

Analyze the Audience and Set Goals

Even if the topic is assigned and the audience consists solely of the instructor and classmates (perhaps in an online setting), consider the audience's interests and needs with respect to the topic and how you can meet them. For example, if the presentation is a business report or proposal, be certain to address the specific concerns of the employees, clients, customers, or others the presentation is meant for. Just as you would prepare an individual speech, brainstorm and set down in writing the central idea and goals for the presentation.

Assign Roles and Tasks

Start by designating a *group leader* to help guide coordination among members, beginning with the selection of roles and tasks. Decide what parts of the presentation team members will present and set firm time limits for each portion.

Establish Information Needs

Establish the scope and type of research needed—for example, surveys your team does itself, scholarly articles, government data, or other sources? Assign members to various aspects of the research.

Establish Transitions between Speakers

Work out transitions between speakers ahead of time—for example, whether a designated group member will introduce every speaker or whether each speaker will introduce the next speaker upon the close of his or her presentation. The quality of the presentation will depend in large part on smooth transitions between speakers.

Consider the Presenters' Strengths

Audiences become distracted by marked differences in style, such as hearing a captivating speaker followed by an extremely dull one. If you are concerned about an uneven delivery, consider choosing the person with the strongest presentation style and credibility level for the opening. Put the more cautious presenters in the middle of the presentation. Select another strong speaker to conclude the presentation.[1]

QUICK TIP

Be Mindful of Your Nonverbal Behavior

During a team presentation, the audience's eyes will fall on everyone involved, not just the person speaking. Thus any signs of disinterest or boredom by a team member will be easily noticed. Give your full attention to the other speakers on the team, and project an attitude of interest toward audience members.

Coordinate the Presentation Aids

To ensure design consistency, consider assigning one person the job of coordinating templates for slides, video, and/or audio (see Chapter 20). The team can also assign a single individual the task of presenting the aids as the other team members speak. If this is done, be sure to position the person presenting the aids unobtrusively so as not to distract the audience from the speaker.

Rehearse the Presentation Several Times

Together with the whole group, members should practice their portions of the presentation, with any presentation aids they will use, in the order they will be given in the final form. Rehearse with all members several times, until the presentation proceeds smoothly. Assign at least one member to set up and check any equipment needed to display the aids.

◉ Presenting in Panels, Symposia, and Forums

Panels, symposia, and forums are group discussions in which multiple speakers share their expertise with an audience; forums are convened specifically to discuss issues of public interest. Members of panels, symposia, and forums often may not meet beforehand to coordinate their remarks.

Panel Discussions

In a **panel discussion**, a group of people (at least three, and generally not more than nine) discusses a topic in the presence of an audience. Panel discussions do not feature formally prepared speeches. Instead, a skilled chairperson or **moderator** directs a discussion. The moderator begins by describing the purpose of the panel and introducing panel members, then launches the discussion by directing a question to one or more of the participants. At the conclusion of the panel, the moderator summarizes the discussion and directs questions from the audience.

If serving as a moderator, plan on circulating an agenda and list of ground rules to the participants ahead of the presentation. When preparing remarks for a panel discussion, either as the moderator or as a discussant, gather the following information:

- Who is your audience, and what do they know about the topic? What ideas can be emphasized to encourage greater understanding?
- What aspects of the topic will the other participants address? What are their areas of expertise?
- How much time is allotted for the question-and-answer session? You will need to plan accordingly.
- Which key points should be reviewed in conclusion?

Symposia

A **symposium** is a meeting or conference at which several speakers deliver prepared remarks on different aspects of the same topic. Symposia provide audiences with in-depth and varied perspectives on a topic. Sometimes the symposium concludes with a question-and-answer period; at other times, it is followed by a panel discussion among symposium participants. Following symposia, the presentations may be published.

When preparing a presentation for a symposium, consider the following:

- Who is your audience?
- What aspects of the topic will the other participants address?
- In what order will the speakers address the audience?
- What are your time constraints for your prepared remarks?
- Will you engage in questions and answers with the other speakers, or just with the audience?

Public Forums

A **forum** is an assembly for the discussion of issues of public interest. Public forums often are convened to help policymakers and voters alike deliberate about key policy issues. These forums can take place in a physical space, such as a town hall, on television, or online.

Forums may feature a panel or a symposium, followed by an extensive question-and-answer period with the audience. One well-known forum is the *town hall meeting*, in which citizens deliberate on issues of importance to the community. City and state governments sponsor town hall meetings to gather citizen input about issues that affect them, using this input to formulate policy.

When participating in public forums as a member of the audience, consider the following:

- Organize your thoughts as much as possible in advance by jotting down your question or comment on a piece of paper. Use the guidelines for impromptu speaking described in Chapter 16.
- Do not duplicate someone else's questions or comments unless it adds to the discussion.
- Use no more time than necessary to make your points.
- If appropriate, include a *call to action* at the conclusion of your comments (see p. 183).

✓ CHECKLIST
Group Presentation Tips

- ❏ Establish in writing the specific purpose and goals of the presentation.
- ❏ Decide on the scope and types of research needed.
- ❏ Specify each team member's responsibilities regarding content and presentation aids.
- ❏ Determine how introductions will be made—all at once at the beginning or by having each speaker introduce the next one.
- ❏ Practice introductions and transitions to create a seamless presentation.
- ❏ Assign someone to manage the question-and-answer session.
- ❏ Rehearse the presentation with all group members and with presentation aids several times from start to finish.

CHAPTER 29

Business and Professional Presentations

In many business and professional positions, delivering presentations is part of the job. Whether pitching a service to customers or informing managers of a project's progress, your skill as a speaker will get you noticed and, often, promoted.

Rather than being formal public speeches, business and professional presentations are forms of **presentational speaking**—oral presentations delivered by individuals or teams addressing people in the classroom, workplace, or other group settings. Presentational speaking has much in common with formal public speaking, yet important differences exist:[1]

- *Degree of formality.* Presentational speaking is *less formal* than public speaking; on a continuum, it would lie midway between public speaking at one end and conversational speaking at the other.
- *Audience factors.* Public-speaking audiences tend to be self-selected or voluntary participants, and they regard the speech as a onetime event. Attendees of oral presentations are more likely to be part of a captive audience, as in the workplace or classroom, and may be required to attend frequent presentations. Due to the ongoing relationship among the participants, attendees also share more information with one another than those who attend a public speech and thus can be considered to have a common knowledge base.
- *Speaker expertise.* Listeners generally assume that a public speaker has more expertise or firsthand knowledge than they do on a topic. Presentational speakers, by contrast, are more properly thought of as "first among equals."

Apart from these differences, the guidelines described throughout this *Pocket Guide* apply equally to oral presentations and public speeches.

◉ Become Familiar with Reports and Proposals

The majority of business and professional presentations (both oral and written) take the form of *reports* or *proposals*. Corporations and nonprofit, educational, and government organizations alike depend on reports and proposals, both formal and informal, to supply information and shape decisions.

A **report** is a systematic and objective description of facts and observations related to business or professional interests; it may or may not contain recommendations. Reports without recommendations are strictly informative; those that offer analysis and recommendations combine both informative and persuasive intent.

Reports address literally thousands of different topics, audiences, and objectives; some require extensive research and offer lengthy analyses while others may simply summarize weekly changes in personnel or projects. Formats for reports vary accordingly, but many reports include the following:

1. Preview/summary of reasons for the report; including its scope, methods, and limitations; and main conclusions and recommendations
2. Discussion of the findings/presentation of evidence
3. Key conclusions drawn from evidence
4. Recommendations based on evidence

A **proposal** recommends a product, procedure, or policy to a client or company. Organizations must constantly make decisions such as whether to switch to a new health plan or implement a new employee grievance procedure, and proposals offer a plan on how to proceed. Usually, proposals advocate for a specific solution. Careful adaptation to the audience is therefore critical to an effective presentation (see Chapter 6).

Proposals may be assigned by a superior, solicited by a potential client (by a written *request for proposal* or *"RFP"*), or offered unsolicited to either superiors or clients. Frequently, proposals incorporate or respond to information communicated in reports. The audience for a proposal can be a single individual or a group; in either event the audience will have primary or sole responsibility for evaluating the proposal.

Proposals can be quite lengthy and formally organized or relatively brief and loosely structured. As in reports, individual organizations have their own templates for organizing proposals, but many proposals follow these general steps:

1. Introduce the issue.
2. State the problem.
3. Describe the method by which the problem was investigated.
4. Describe the facts learned.
5. Offer explanations and an interpretation of the findings.
6. Offer recommendations, including time lines and budgets.
7. End with a *call to action*, reiterating your recommendation persuasively.

Sample Types of Reports and Proposals in Business and the Professions	
Reports	Proposals
• Progress report	• Sales proposal
• Audit report	• Business plan proposal
• Market research report	• Request for funding (see p. 239)
• Quality testing report	• Research proposal
• Staff report	• Quality improvement proposal (see p. 249)
• Committee report	• Policy proposal (see p. 242)

The table above lists some of the many types of reports and proposals. Following are guidelines for preparing the *sales proposal, staff report*, and *progress report*.

The Sales Proposal

A **sales proposal** or **sales pitch** attempts to lead a potential buyer to purchase a service or a product. Successful sales pitches, which are persuasive by nature, clearly show how the product or service meets the needs of the potential buyer and demonstrate how it surpasses other options available. In fact, studies have shown that exceptional salespeople uncover and expose unrecognized needs and help customers pinpoint solutions.[2]

AUDIENCE   The target audience for a sales proposal depends on who has the authority to make the purchase. Some proposals are invited by the potential buyer; others are "cold sales" in which the presenter approaches a potential buyer with a product or a service. In some cases, the audience might be an intermediary—a firm's office manager, for example, who then makes a recommendation to the company's director.

ORGANIZATION   Plan on organizing a sales proposal as you would a persuasive speech, selecting among the motivated sequence, problem-solution, problem-cause-solution, or comparative advantage patterns (see Chapter 24). The *comparative advantage pattern* works well when the buyer must choose between competing products and seeks reassurance that the product being presented is indeed superior. The *problem-solution* or *problem-cause-solution pattern* is especially effective when selling to a buyer who needs a product to solve a problem.

Sometimes called the *basic sales technique*, the *motivated sequence*, with its focus on audience needs, offers an excellent

✅ CHECKLIST

Using Monroe's Motivated Sequence in a Sales Proposal

- ❑ Identify the potential buyer's needs and wants and appeal to them.
- ❑ Using the product's features, match its benefits to the customer's needs and wants.
- ❑ Stress what the product can do for the customer.
- ❑ Engage the customer's senses, using sight, sound, smell, and touch.
- ❑ Do not leave the sales encounter without making the ask.[2]
- ❑ Get the buyer to do something (look something up, promise to call someone, or schedule a meeting). Buyers who invest their time are more likely to invest in what you are selling.[3]

means of appealing to buyer psychology. To use it to organize a sales proposal, do the following:

1. Draw the potential buyer's attention to the product.
2. Isolate and clarify the buyer's need for the product.
3. Describe how the product will satisfy the buyer's need.
4. Illustrate the beneficial effects that will result from buying the product.
5. Invite the buyer to purchase the product.

The Staff Report

A **staff report** informs managers and other employees of new developments that affect them and their work, or reports on the completion of a project or task.

AUDIENCE   The audience for a staff report is usually a group, but it can be an individual. The recipients of a staff report then use the information to implement new policy, to coordinate other plans, or to make other reports to other groups.

ORGANIZATION   Organize a formal staff report as follows:

1. State the problem or question under consideration (sometimes called a *charge* to a committee or a subcommittee).
2. Provide a description of procedures and facts used to address the issue.
3. Discuss and analyze the facts that are most pertinent to the issue.

4. Provide a concluding statement.

5. Offer recommendations.

The Progress Report

A **progress report** updates clients or principals on developments in an ongoing project. It is similar to a staff report, with the exception that the audience can include people *outside* the organization as well as within it. Progress reports help managers determine the value of employees and uncover hidden costs of doing business.[4] On long-term projects, progress reports may be given at designated intervals or at the time of specific task completions. On short-term projects, reports can occur daily.

AUDIENCE   The audience for a progress report might be supervisors, clients, or customers; developers and investors; company officers; media representatives; or same-level co-workers. Progress reports are commonplace in staff and committee meetings in which subcommittees report on their designated tasks.

ORGANIZATION   Different audiences may want different kinds of reports, so establish the expectations of your intended audience, then modify the following accordingly:

1. Briefly review progress made up to the time of the previous report.

2. Describe new developments since the previous report.

3. Describe the personnel involved and their activities.

4. Detail the time spent on tasks.

5. Explain supplies used and costs incurred.

6. Explain any problems and make recommendations for their resolution.

7. Provide an estimate of tasks to be completed for the next reporting period.

part

⑨

Speaking in Other College Courses

● ● ● ● ● ● ● ● ● ● ● ● ● ●

CHAPTER 30

Presentations Assigned across the Curriculum

No matter which major you select, oral presentations will be part of your academic career. Chapters 31–36 describe various course-specific presentations, from the *scientific talk* to the *design review*. This chapter contains guidelines for preparing five types of presentations frequently assigned across the curriculum, including the *journal article review*, *service learning presentation*, *poster presentation*, *debate*, and *case study*.

◉ Journal Article Review

A frequent speaking assignment in many courses is the **journal article review**. A biology instructor might ask you to provide an overview of a peer-reviewed study on cell regulation, for example, or a psychology teacher might require that you talk about a study on fetal alcohol syndrome. Typically, when delivering a presentation on a journal article, your instructor will expect you to do the following, in this order.

1. Identify the author's thesis or hypothesis.
2. Explain the methods by which the author arrived at the conclusions.
3. Explain the results of the study.
4. Identify the author's methods and, if applicable, theoretical perspective.
5. Evaluate the study's quality, originality, and validity.
6. Describe the author's sources, and evaluate their credibility.
7. Show how the findings advance knowledge in the field.

◉ The Service Learning Presentation

Many courses offer the opportunity to engage in service learning projects, in which students learn about and help address a need or problem in a community agency or nonprofit organization, such as may exist in a mental-health facility, an economic development agency, or antipoverty organization. Typically, the **service learning presentation** describes your participation in the project and includes the following information.

1. Description of the service task
    a. What organization, group, or agency did your project serve?
    b. What is the problem or issue, and how did you address it?
2. Description of what the service task taught you about those you served
    a. How were they affected by the problem or issue?
    b. How did your solution help them? What differences did you observe?
3. Explanation of how the service task and outcome related to your service learning course
    a. What course concepts, principles, or theory relate to your service project, and how?
    b. What observations give you evidence that the principles apply to your project?
4. Application of what was learned to future understanding and practice
    a. How was your understanding of the course subject improved or expanded?
    b. How was your interest in or motivation for working in this capacity affected by the project?
    c. What do you most want to tell others about the experience and how it could affect them?

◉ The Poster Presentation

Another common speaking assignment across the curriculum is the **poster presentation**, which displays information about a study, an issue, or a concept on a large (usually roughly 4′ × 3′ or 4′ × 6′) poster. Poster presentations typically follow the structure of a scientific journal article, including an *abstract, introduction, description of methods, results, conclusion*, and *references*. Presenters display their key findings on posters, arranged so session participants can examine them freely; on hand are copies of the written report, with full details of the study. The presenter is prepared to answer questions as they arise.

A good poster presenter considers his or her audience, understanding that with so much competing information, the poster must be concise, visually appealing, and focused on the most important points of the study.

When preparing the poster, follow these guidelines.

• Select a succinct and informative title; make it 84-point type or larger.

- Arrange blocks of text in columns beginning from the upper left to lower right side of the poster.
- Include an *abstract* (a brief summary of the study) describing the essence of the report and how it relates to other research in the field. Offer compelling and "must know" points to hook viewers, and summarize information for those who will only read the abstract.
- Ensure a logical and easy-to-follow flow from one part of the poster to another.
- Edit text to a minimum, using clear graphics wherever possible.
- Select a muted color for the poster itself, such as gray, beige, light blue, or white, and use a contrasting, clear font color (usually black).
- Make sure your font size is large enough to be read comfortably from at least three feet away.
- Design figures and diagrams to be viewed from a distance, and label each one.
- Label and include a concise summary of each figure in a legend below each one.
- Be prepared to provide brief descriptions of your poster and to answer questions; keep your explanations short.[1]

Address your audience while presenting and explain your research without reading verbatim from the poster; if needed, prepare a speaking outline (see Chapter 13). Rehearse your poster presentation as you would any other speech.

The Debate

Debates are a popular oral presentation format in many college courses, calling upon skills in persuasion (especially the reasoned use of evidence; see Chapter 24) and the ability to think quickly and critically. In a **debate**, opposing sides alternate turns at presenting arguments affirming or negating a claim or proposition. Careful research of the topic under consideration is paramount.

Debate Sides, Resolutions, and Formats

Classroom debates may be either individual debates, in which one person takes a side against another person, or team debates in which each side consists of two or more debaters. In either case, the *affirmative* ("*pro*") *side* supports a proposition with a *resolution*—a statement asking for change or consideration of a controversial issue (for example, "Resolved, that colleges should abolish the SAT and the ACT"). The *negative* ("*con*") *side* opposes the resolution.

Depending on the type of debate selected, resolutions can address propositions of *fact*, of *value*, and of *policy* (see p. 180). For example, in the *Lincoln-Douglas (L-D)* format, two individuals argue the resolution as a proposition of value ("Resolved, euthanasia should be legalized"). In the *team policy debate* format, opposing teams argue resolutions as *propositions of policy* (as in the whether or not colleges should use standardized tests).

Many classroom debates follow a sequence similar to this: The first speech introduces the argument of each team. The second speech, or "rebuttal," critically analyzes the opposing team's argument. The third speech summarizes the strongest arguments for the audience.

Advance Strong Arguments

Whether you take the affirmative or negative side, you must advance strong arguments in support of your position. Credible evidence and reasoning are key to arguing for or against a debate proposition (see Chapter 24). Equally important is using this evidence and reasoning to refute weaknesses in these elements put forth by your opponents.

When constructing your response to the resolution, be sure to formulate a *pro* or *con* thesis that does not merely agree or disagree but includes concrete reasons for your position. For example, a *pro* side thesis for the resolution that colleges should abolish the SAT and the ACT might be: "Colleges should abolish the SAT and the ACT *because grades and extracurricular activities provide a better, and fairer, student profile.*" A *con* side thesis might be: "Colleges should use the SAT and ACT *because the tests accurately reflect the knowledge the student has mastered.*" In the debate, offer strong evidence in support of these reasons.

QUICK TIP

Flowing the Debate

In a formal debate, debaters must attack and defend each argument. Even in a less formal classroom debate, "dropping" or ignoring an argument can seriously compromise your credibility. To keep track of your opposition's claims, try using a note-taking method called "flowing the debate." On a sheet of paper or spreadsheet, note points that you want to challenge and why. Write checkmarks next to points you have addressed.

◉ The Case Study

A **case study** documents a real (or realistic) situation, relating to business, law, medicine, science, or another discipline, which poses difficult problems requiring solutions. Students read a detailed account and then apply what they have studied to analyze and resolve the problems. Instructors typically ask students to report orally on the case study, either alone or in teams. Students are expected to consider the case carefully and then report on the following items.

1. Description/overview of the major issues involved in the case
2. Statement of the major problems and issues involved
3. Identification of any relevant alternatives to the case
4. Presentation of the best solutions to the case, with a brief explanation of the logic behind them
5. Recommendations for implementing the solutions, along with acknowledgment of any impediments

◉ Prepare for Different Types of Audiences

In the workplace, presentations may be delivered to fellow workers, colleagues, managers, clients, or others. Knowing this, instructors may ask that you tailor your oral presentations to a mock (practice) on-the-job audience, with your classmates serving as stand-ins. As seen in the table below, audiences include the **expert or insider audience**, **colleagues within the field**, the **lay audience**, and the **mixed audience**.

Types of Audiences in the Working World	
Type of Audience	Characteristics
Expert or insider audience	People who have intimate knowledge of the topic, issue, product, or idea being discussed (e.g., an investment analyst presents a financial plan to a group of portfolio managers)
Colleagues within the field	People who share the speaker's knowledge of the general field under question (e.g., psychology or computer science), but who may not be familiar with the specific topic under discussion (e.g., short-term memory or voice recognition systems, respectively)

Type of Audience	Characteristics
Lay audience	People who have no specialized knowledge of the field related to the speaker's topic or of the topic itself (e.g., a city engineer describes failure of water treatment system to the finance department)
Mixed audience	An audience composed of a combination of people—some with expert knowledge of the field and topic and others with no specialized knowledge. This is perhaps the most difficult audience to satisfy (e.g., an attending surgeon describes experimental cancer treatment to a hospital board comprised of medical professionals, financial supporters, and administrative personnel).

✓ CHECKLIST

Tips on Presenting to a Mixed Audience

- ❑ Research the audience and gear your talk to the appropriate level of knowledge and interests.
- ❑ Avoid technical or specialized terms and explain any that you must use.
- ❑ Carefully construct the introduction and clearly identify the central idea and main points of the talk. If possible, present a compelling "story" listeners can learn about if they stay the course.
- ❑ Alert the audience to the order of your coverage: "I will first focus on the big picture and on marketing/sales issues. I will then present design specifications and data analysis." In this way, each audience segment will know what to expect and when.
- ❑ Devote half to two-thirds of your time to an introduction or overview of your subject and save the highly technical material for the remaining time.[2]
- ❑ Include everyone. Try to address different levels of knowledge and different perspectives in turn.

❑ Be clear about the level at which you are speaking: "I am going to present the primary results of this project with minimal detailed information, but I'm happy to review the statistics or experimental results in more detail following the presentation."

❑ Be alert to audience reactions. If you notice that your listeners are experiencing discomfort, consider stopping and asking for feedback about what they want. You might then change course and opt for a more in-depth, high-level approach, depending on what they say.

CHAPTER 31 ●●●●

Science and Mathematics Courses

The purpose of many science and math presentations is to inform the audience of the results of original or replicated research or problem solving. Instructors and classmates want to know the processes by which you arrived at your experimental results or how you solved a particular problem. For example, your biology instructor may assign an oral report on the extent to which you were able to replicate an experiment on cell mitosis. A math instructor may ask you to apply a concept to an experiment or an issue facing the field. A key challenge of these presentations is clearly and accurately communicating complex information to audiences with varying levels of knowledge.

QUICK TIP

What Do Science-Related Courses Include?

Known for their focus on exacting processes, science-related disciplines include the physical sciences (e.g., chemistry and physics), the natural sciences (e.g., biology and medicine), and the earth sciences (e.g., geology, meteorology, and oceanography). Fields related to mathematics include accounting, statistics, and applied mathematics subfields.

Preparing Effective Presentations in Science and Mathematics

Presentations in the sciences and mathematics must first of all be grounded in the scientific method. Presentations must clearly illustrate the nature of the research question, describe the methods used in gathering and analyzing data, and explain the results. However, presentations need not be—nor should they be—dry and merely factual. Experimentation is a process of discovery, and the fits and starts that often accompany its completion can make for compelling stories during your talk.

Typically, instructors will expect you to do the following in a scientific or mathematics presentation:

- Use observation, proofs, theorems, and experiments as support for your points.
- Clearly explain scientific or mathematical terms at a level appropriate to the audience.
- Be selective in your focus on details, highlighting critical information but not overwhelming listeners with information they can refer to in the written paper.
- Use analogies to build on prior knowledge and demonstrate underlying causes (see p. 163 for guidelines on explaining difficult concepts).
- Use well-executed aids, from slides to equations drawn on a whiteboard, to illustrate important concepts (see Chapters 19–21 for detailed guidelines).

Research Presentation

In the **research presentation** (also called the **scientific talk** or *oral scientific presentation*), you describe research you conducted, either alone or as part of agroup. You may deliver this information as a stand-alone oral presentation or as a poster session (see p. 236).

A research presentation usually follows the standard model used in scientific investigation and includes the following elements:

1. *An introduction* that includes the research question, the hypothesis, the scope of the study, and the objective
2. *A description of methods* used to investigate the research question, including where the study took place and the conditions under which it was carried out
3. *The results of the study*, summarizing key findings and highlighting insights regarding the questions/hypotheses investigated; this is the body of the presentation.

4. *Discussion and conclusions,* in which the speaker interprets the data or results and discusses their significance. As in any speech, the conclusion should link back to the introduction, reiterating the research question and highlighting the key findings.

◉ Process Analysis Presentation

A **process analysis presentation** explains how an experimental or a mathematical process works and under what conditions it can be used. This is generally a ten- to fifteen-minute individual presentation. In a theoretical math class, for example, your assignment might be to describe an approach to solving a problem, such as the Baum–Welch algorithm, including examples of how this approach has been used, either inappropriately or appropriately. This type of presentation generally does the following:

1. Identifies the conditions under which the process should be used
2. Offers a detailed description of the process (at times including a demonstration)
3. Discusses the benefits and shortcomings of the process

QUICK TIP

Get to the Point

If you lose the audience at the beginning of your scientific talk, chances are slim that you'll regain their attention. Listeners want to know what the talk is about—that is, what key question you investigated—so make certain that you communicate the research question in the first few minutes of your scientific talk. Follow this by stating why you believe the question is important and why addressing it is relevant.

◉ Field Study Presentation

A **field study presentation** describes research conducted in natural settings, using methods such as direct observation, surveys, and interviews. For example, a biology major might research links between soil erosion and hiking activity in a public park, or an environmental studies major might describe animal behavior in an oil spill. Field study presentations may be assigned as individual, team, or poster-session presentations. Whatever the topic under investigation and methods of data collection, field study presentations address the following:

1. Overview and scope of the field research (e.g., if explaining animal behavior in an oil spill, describe the prevalence of oil spills and the effects on environment and wildlife)

2. Description of the site (e.g., describe the habitat before and after the spill, noting ecological interactions)

3. Methods used in the research (e.g., participant observation, type of sample collection, measurement techniques; how were the behaviors observed? Who provided the observations? When and for how long?)[1]

4. Interpretation/analysis of the data

5. Future directions for the research

✓ CHECKLIST

Steps in Preparing a Focused Scientific Presentation

❏ Create an informative title that describes the research.

❏ Place your presentation in the context of a major scientific principle.

❏ Focus on a single issue and adjust it to the interests and knowledge level of your audience.

❏ Identify the underlying question you will address, divide it into subquestions, and answer each question.

❏ Follow a logical line of thought.

❏ Explain scientific concepts unambiguously, with a minimum of jargon.

❏ Use analogies to increase understanding.

❏ End with a clearly formulated conclusion related to your chosen scientific principle.[2]

CHAPTER 32 ●●●●

Technical Courses

Oral presentations in technical courses often focus on the design of a product or system—whether it is a set of plans for a building, a prototype robot, or an innovative computer circuit design. Technical presentations include reports and proposals that provide instructions, advocate a product or service, update progress, make recommendations, or request funding. (See Chapter 29 on reports and proposals and the *progress report*; see this chapter for *requests for funding*.) Assignments in engineering, architecture, and other technical courses also typically include the *design review*, described below.

QUICK TIP

What Are the Technical Disciplines?

Technical disciplines include, but are not limited to, the STEM fields (science, technology, engineering, and mathematics) as well as the design-oriented disciplines of graphic design, architecture, and industrial design.

Preparing Effective Technical Presentations

The technical presenter faces the challenge of scaling complex information and processes to audience members with differing levels of technical expertise. Carefully conceived presentation aids—including diagrams, prototypes, drawings, computer simulations, design specifications, and spreadsheets—are key to the technical presentation, yet the aids must not overwhelm the presentation itself. Presentations are often delivered in teams, so close coordination among members is essential (see Chapter 28).

Typically, people who attend technical presentations possess a range of technical knowledge, and effective technical speakers gear the presentation to the appropriate level for the audience, using accessible language, avoiding jargon (see Chapter 15), and offering analogies to clarify hard-to-understand concepts and processes (see Chapter 22).

Both informative and persuasive strategies come into play in technical presentations, and the best technical presenters know how to appeal to their audiences' needs and motivations to gain agreement for a proposal or design[1] (see p. 175).

Effective technical presentations sell ideas. The technical presenter must persuade clients, managers, or classmates that a design, an idea, or a product is a good one. As one instructor notes, "You can never assume that your product or design will just sell—*you* have to do that."[2]

Effective technical presentations are also detailed and specific and use numbers as evidence. Instead of offering general, sweeping statements, they provide hard data and clearly stated experimental results.

Engineering Design Review

The **engineering design review** explains problem-solving steps in devising a product or system in response to an identified need. Virtually all capstone engineering courses require that students prepare design reviews, which are generally informative in nature, although their purpose may include convincing the audience that the design decisions are sound. (In varying formats, design reviews are also assigned in basic science and mathematics courses.) Design reviews may incorporate a **prototype** (model) demonstration and are usually delivered as team presentations. Design reviews typically include the following:

1. Identification of the problem to be solved/need to be met and overview of objectives
2. Description of the design concept and specifications
3. Discussion of why the proposed design will solve the problem
4. Discussion of any experimental testing that has been completed on the design
5. Discussion of future plans and unresolved problems
6. Discussion of schedule, budget, and marketing issues

Architecture Design Review

The **architecture design review** combines two functions: It enables the audience to visualize the design, and it sells the design. Using a narrative structure, in which you tell the "story" of the design, combined in places with a *spatial organizational pattern*, in which you arrange main points in order of physical proximity of the design (see Chapter 12), can help you do this. At a minimum, architecture design reviews typically cover:

1. Background on the site
2. Discussion of the design concept
3. Description and interpretation of the design

Request for Funding

In the **request for funding presentation**, a team member or the entire team provides evidence that a project, a proposal, or a design idea is worth funding. Requests for funding, which are persuasive in nature, cover the following ground:

1. Overview of customer specifications and needs
2. Analysis of the market and its needs
3. Overview of the design idea or project and how it meets those needs
4. Projected costs for the project
5. Specific reasons why the project should be funded

QUICK TIP

Avoid These Technical Presentation Pitfalls

Professionals working in technical fields point to three major obstacles to designing and delivering a successful technical presentation: (1) too much information crammed into aids and failure to construct and practice with them early in the process, (2) insufficient preparation and practice with fellow team members, and (3) failure to select an appropriate organization and structure for the presentation.[3] Bearing these pitfalls in mind during preparation will set you on a winning path.

CHAPTER 33 ●●●●●

Social Science Courses

Students taking social science courses (including psychology, sociology, political science, economics, and anthropology) learn to evaluate and conduct both *qualitative research*, in which the emphasis is on observing, describing, and interpreting behavior, as well as *quantitative research*, in which the emphasis is on statistical measurement. Often the focus of inquiry is explaining or predicting human behavior or social forces, answering questions such as what, how, and why?[1]

Oral presentation assignments in social science courses frequently include the *literature review presentation, theoretical research presentation, program evaluation presentation,* and *policy proposal* (see this chapter). Other commonly assigned presentations are described elsewhere in this guide: see the *poster presentation* (p. 229), *case study presentation* (p. 232), *scientific research ("scientific talk") presentation* (p. 235), *process analysis presentation* (p. 236), *field study presentation* (p. 236), and *evidence-based practice presentation* (p. 248).

◉ Preparing Effective Presentations in the Social Sciences

Good social scientific presentations clearly explain the research question, refer to current research, support arguments with evidence, use theory to build explanations, and use timely data.

- *Illustrate the research question.* Pay special attention to illustrating the nature of the research question and the methods used to investigate it.
- *Refer to current research.* Credible social scientific presentations refer to recent findings in the field. Instructors are more likely to accept experimental evidence if it is replicable over time and is supported by current research.
- *Use theory to build explanations.* Theory is central to social scientific research, informing the types of questions asked, the research methods used, and means by which evidence is interpreted. Thus your discussion of the research should reflect the theoretical framework within which the research was conducted.[2]
- *Support arguments with evidence.* Each of your assertions or claims must be accompanied by evidence for or against it and which can be used by others to evaluate the claims.

◉ Literature Review Presentation

Frequently, instructors ask students to summarize and evaluate the existing research related to a given topic. A communications student, for example, might review the literature on gender bias in the promotion of newspaper reporters into management. After considering the key studies related to the topic, the student would describe the conclusions uncovered by the research and suggest directions for future work. A **literature review presentation** typically includes the following:

1. Statement of the topic under review
2. Description of the available research, including specific points of agreement and disagreement among sources
3. Evaluation of the strengths and weaknesses of the research, including the methodology used and whether findings can be generalized to other studies
4. Conclusions that can be drawn from the research
5. Suggested directions for future study

When including a literature review in conjunction *with your own research study*, follow these broad guidelines:

1. Introduce your topic.
2. Review the literature pertinent to your topic.

3. State your research question or hypothesis and describe how it relates to the literature.

4. Discuss your research methods.

5. Discuss your results, including shortcomings and implications for future research.

QUICK TIP

Narrow Your Topic

Since most of your social scientific presentations will be relatively brief, make sure to sufficiently narrow your topic or research question and scale your findings to fit the time allotted (see Chapter 7). For example, rather than selecting an overly broad topic such as "substance abuse," consider "frequency of alcohol-related deaths among U.S. college students in year X."

Program Evaluation Presentation

In addition to explaining social phenomena, social scientists often measure the effectiveness of programs developed to address these issues. Instructors may ask you to evaluate a program or policy, perhaps one you observed in a service learning assignment. Typically, the **program evaluation presentation** includes the following:

1. Explanation of the program's mission

2. Description of the program's accomplishments

3. Discussion of how the accomplishments were measured (e.g., the evaluation methods and questions), including any problems in collecting and/or assessing the evaluation research

4. Conclusions regarding how well or poorly the program has met its stated objectives

Policy Proposal Presentation

As well as evaluating programs and policies, you may be asked to recommend a course of action on an issue or a problem. A **policy proposal presentation** typically includes the following:

1. Definition and background review of the current policy and its shortcomings

2. Discussion of alternatives to policy, including the pros and cons of each

3. Recommendation of a specific policy with clear argument for why this option is better than each of the alternatives

4. Application of forecasting methods to show likely results of the recommended policy

5. Plan for implementation of the recommendations

6. Discussion of future needs or parameters to monitor and evaluate the policy option.

CHAPTER 34 ●●●●

Arts and Humanities Courses

Speaking assignments in arts and humanities courses often require that you analyze and interpret the meaning of a particular idea, event, person, story, or artifact. Instructors expect that these interpretations will be grounded in the conventions of the field and build on the research within it. An instructor of literature may ask you to explain the theme of a novel or a poem, for example, or an art history professor may ask you to identify the various artistic and historical influences on a sculpture or a painting. Some presentations may be performative in nature, with students expressing artistic content. Assignments include summaries of works; presentations of interpretation and analysis; presentations that compare and contrast an idea, an event, or a work; and individual and team debates (see pp. 230–231).

QUICK TIP

Disciplines in the Arts and Humanities

What fields are included in the arts and humanities? Typically included are English, literature, history, religion, philosophy, foreign languages, art history, theater, and music.

◎ Preparing Effective Arts and Humanities Presentations

Good presentations in the arts and humanities help audiences understand and put into context the meaning of original works or scholarship. Working from within the conventions of the discipline, the presenter identifies the work's key themes and the means by which the author or creator communicates them. Instructors will expect you to investigate the following:

- What is the thesis or central message in the text or work?
- What questions/issues/themes does the author address?
- How does the author or creator organize or structure the work?
- Who is the audience for the work?
- What influences or sources inform the work?

◉ Presentations of Interpretation and Analysis

Often in the arts and humanities, instructors assign presentations requiring students to interpret the relevance of a historical or a contemporary person or event; a genre or school of philosophical thought; or a piece of literature, music, or art. Instructors look to students to think of topics in new ways by providing original interpretations. A presentation on the historical significance of Reconstruction after the Civil War of 1861–1865, for example, will be more effective if you offer a new way of viewing the topic rather than reiterating what other people have said or what is already generally accepted knowledge. A debate on two philosophical ideas will be most effective when you assert issues and arguments that are different from those that the audience has thought of before. The more original the interpretation (while remaining logical and supported by evidence), the more compelling the presentation will be for the audience.

◉ Presentations That Compare and Contrast

A common assignment in the arts and humanities is to *compare and contrast* events, stories, people, or artifacts in order to highlight similarities or differences. For example, you might compare two works of literature from different time periods or two historical figures or works of art. These presentations may be informative or persuasive; if the latter, the student will argue in favor of one figure or period over another. Presentations that compare and contrast include the following elements:

1. *Thesis statement* outlining the connection between the events, stories, people, or artifacts
2. *Discussion of main points*, including several examples that highlight similarities and differences

3. *Concluding evaluative statement* about the comparison (e.g., if the presentation is persuasive, why one piece of literature was more effective than another; if informative, a restatement of similarities and differences)

◉ Debates

Often, students will engage in debates on opposing ideas, historical figures, or philosophical positions. In a history class, students might argue whether women in sixteenth-century Western Europe experienced a Renaissance. The speaker must present a brief argument (two to three minutes) about the topic; the opposing speaker then responds with another point of view. Whatever side of an issue you address, prepare a well-composed argument with strong supporting evidence (see pp. 230–231).

QUICK TIP

Be Prepared to Lead a Discussion

Many students taking arts and humanities courses will research a question and then lead a classroom discussion on it. For example, a student of literature may lead a discussion on Anton Chekhov's play *The Cherry Orchard*. The speaker would be expected to provide a synopsis of the plot, theme, and characters and offer an analysis of the play's meaning. For directions on leading a discussion, see p. 247.

CHAPTER 35 ●●●●

Education Courses

In education courses, the most common speaking assignments focus on teaching and related instructional tasks, such as giving a lecture or demonstrating an activity. In a mathematics education course, you may give a mini-lecture on a particular geometric theorem. In a learning-styles course, you may tailor an activity to a variety of different learners.

Education courses include subfields such as curriculum and instruction, physical education, secondary and elementary education, and education administration.

Preparing Effective Education Presentations

Good presentations in education are marked by clear organization, integration of the material into the broader course content, two-way communication, and student-friendly supporting material. Above all, effective educational presentations succeed in fostering understanding. Follow these strategies as you prepare your presentations.

- *Use a learning framework.* Select one or more cognitive learning frameworks, such as the Bloom or Marazano taxonomy, and frame the information accordingly.
- *Organize material logically.* Presentations in education must be tightly organized so that the audience can easily access information. The simpler the organizational structure, the better (see Chapters 12 and 24). Use organizing devices such as preview statements, internal summaries, and transitions to help listeners follow ideas in a lecture, for example (see Chapter 11).
- *Integrate discussion into overall course content.* Describe how the lecture for the day relates to the previous day's lecture, and articulate learning objectives for the presentation. In a discussion or group activity, make clear connections between students' comments and other topics that have been raised or will be raised later in the course.
- *Tailor examples and evidence to the audience.* Use familiar examples and evidence that the audience can grasp easily. Using familiar examples will enhance learning; try to choose ones that are close to the students' experiences.

Delivering a Lecture

A **lecture** is an informational speech for an audience of student learners. Standard lectures range from thirty minutes to one hour in length; a *mini-lecture* generally lasts about ten to fifteen minutes. Typically, lectures include the following:

1. A clear introduction of the topic (see Chapter 14)
2. Statement of the central idea of the lecture
3. Statement of the connection to previous topics covered
4. Discussion of the main points
5. Summary of the lecture and preview of the next assigned topic
6. Question-and-answer period

QUICK TIP

Focus on Interactive Learning

Good lecturers actively engage students in the learning process, pausing to pose questions about the topic, allowing time for discussion, and incorporating short activities into the mix.[1] Rather than delivering a monologue, they encourage student participation.

Facilitating a Group Activity

In the **group activity presentation**, you describe an activity to be completed following a lecture. Typically this short presentation includes the following:

1. A brief review of the main idea of the lecture
2. An explanation of the goal of the activity
3. Directions on carrying out the activity
4. A preview of what students will gain from the activity and what the discussion following it will cover

Facilitating a Classroom Discussion

In a **classroom discussion**, you will lead a discussion following a lecture, offering brief remarks and then guiding the discussion as it proceeds.

1. Begin by outlining critical points to be covered.
2. Prepare several general guiding questions to launch the discussion.
3. Prepare relevant questions and examples for use during the discussion.

CHAPTER 36 ●●●●

Nursing and Allied Health Courses

Speaking assignments in nursing and allied health courses (including physical therapy, occupational therapy, radiology, pharmacy, and other areas of health care) range from the *service learning presentation, poster presentation,* and *journal article review* (see Chapter 30) to those described in this chapter.[1] Students are assigned a mix of individual and group presentations.

◉ Preparing Effective Presentations in Nursing and Allied Health Courses

Good presentations in health-related courses accurately communicate scientific knowledge while reviewing the patient's clinical status and potential treatment options. The presenter will support any assertions and recommendations with relevant scientific literature supporting evidence-based clinical practice. Instructors will expect you to do the following:

1. Use evidence-based guidelines.
2. Demonstrate a solid grasp of the relevant scientific data.
3. Organize the presentation in order of severity of patient problems.
4. Present the patient as well as the illness—that is, remember that the patient is not merely a collection of symptoms, but a human being, so present him or her as such.
5. Include only essential facts, but be prepared to answer any questions about all aspects of the patient and care.

◉ Evidence-Based Practice Presentation

The **evidence-based practice (EBP) presentation** reviews scientific literature on a clinical problem, critically evaluates the findings, and suggests best practices for standards of care. To fulfill these criteria, EBP presentations do the following:

1. Define the research problem (e.g., the clinical issue).
2. Critically review the scientific literature on a practice related to the clinical issue, describing method/design, sample size, and reliability.
3. Discuss the strength of the evidence and indicate whether or not the practice should be adopted into clinical practice.[2]

◉ Clinical Case Study Presentation

A **clinical case study** is a detailed analysis of a person or group with a particular disease or condition. Clinical case studies inform medical teams or other audiences about the following:

1. Overview of patient information (presentation and background)
2. Description of pre-treatment workup, including results
3. Review of treatment options/plan of care
4. Outcome of treatment plan
5. Surveillance plan (follow-up patient care based on evidence-based practice)

◉ Quality Improvement Proposal

In the **quality improvement proposal**, the speaker recommends the adoption of a new (or modified) health practice or policy, such as introducing an improved treatment regimen at a burn center. This report (sometimes assigned as part of a capstone course) addresses the following:

1. Review of existing practice
2. Description of proposed quality improvement
3. Review of the scientific literature on the proposed practice
4. Plan of action for implementation

◉ Treatment Plan Report

The ability to communicate information about patients or clients is important for all health care providers. Either individually or as part of a health care team, people in the helping professions routinely report patients' conditions and outline plans of treatment to other health care providers. One form of treatment plan report, called the **case conference**, includes the following:

1. Description of patient status
2. Explanation of the disease process
3. Steps in the treatment regimen
4. Goals for patient and family
5. Plans for patient's care at home
6. Review of financial needs
7. Assessment of resources available

The **shift report** is a concise overview of the patient's status and needs, delivered to the oncoming caregiver. It includes the following information:

1. Patient name, location, and reason for care
2. Current physical status
3. Day on clinical pathway for particular diagnosis
4. Pertinent psychosocial data, including plans for discharge and involvement of caregivers
5. Care needs (physical, hygiene, activity, medication, nutritional).

Appendices

APPENDIX A ●●●●

Citation Guidelines

Instructors will often require that you include a bibliography of sources with your speech (see Chapters 4 and 9). You can document sources by following documentation systems such as *Chicago*, APA, MLA, CSE, and IEEE.

◉ *Chicago* Documentation

Two widely used systems of documentation are outlined in *The Chicago Manual of Style*, Seventeenth Edition (2017). The first provides for bibliographic citations in endnotes or footnotes. The second form, typically used by public speakers in a variety of disciplines, employs an author-date system: Sources are cited in the text, with full bibliographic information given in a concluding list of references. This method is illustrated below. The author-date method is also used in works cited lists in both the sample working outline in Chapter 13 (p. 98) and the informative speech in Chapter 22 (p. 166). For information about the author-date system—and more general information about *Chicago*-style documentation—consult the *Chicago Manual*, Chapters 14 and 15.

1. BOOK BY A SINGLE AUTHOR Give the author's last name, followed by a comma and the author's first name. Then give the year of publication; the book's title, in italics; and the city of publication followed by a colon and the publisher's name.

Alterman, Eric. 2003. *What Liberal Media? The Truth about Bias and the News.* New York: Basic Books.

2. BOOK BY TWO OR MORE AUTHORS Give the first author's last name followed by a comma and his or her first name. Insert the word "and" followed by the rest of the authors, with first name(s) listed before last name(s).

Kovach, Bill, and Tom Rosenstiel. 2014. *The Elements of Journalism: What Newspeople Should Know and the Public Should Expect.* 3rd ed. New York: Three Rivers Press.

3. EDITED WORK Follow the guidelines in Examples 1 and 2 above, except add a comma and "ed." (or "eds." if the work cited has more than one editor) after the last editor's name, before the year of publication.

Atkins, Joseph B., ed. 2002. *The Mission: Journalism, Ethics, and the World.* Ames: Iowa State University Press.

4. WORK WITHIN AN EDITED COLLECTION Give the author of the work you are citing, last name first. Then give the year of publication; and the title of the work cited, in quotation marks. Next, insert the word "In" followed by the name of the edited collection, in italics, ending with a comma. Insert "edited by," followed by the editor's name. Finally, list the city of publication followed by a colon and the publisher's name.

Dube, Jonathan. 2003. "Writing News Online." In *The Making of the American Essay*, edited by Jan Winburn. Boston: Bedford/St. Martin's.

5. ENTRY IN A REFERENCE WORK Use this format when you need to cite, for example, an entry in a dictionary or encyclopedia, either in print or online. List the title of the reference work, followed by "s.v." (Latin *sub verbo*, "under the word") and the term you looked up. If the citation is from an online reference work, add the URL (internet address) and the publication date or date of last revision; if neither is available, use your access date.

Encyclopedia Britannica Online, s.v. "Yellow Journalism." Accessed October 17, 2007. http://www.britannica.com /eb/article-9077903/yellow-journalism.

6. ARTICLE IN A MAGAZINE List the author, last name first; the year of publication; the article title, in quotation marks; the name of the publication, in italics; and the full publication date or, if no date is given, the full date on which you accessed the material. If you are citing a print article, give the page number. If you are citing an online article, give the URL.

Foer, Franklin. 2017. "When Silicon Valley Took Over Journalism." *The Atlantic*, September 2017. https://www. theatlantic.com/magazine/archive/2017/09/when -silicon-valley-took-over-journalism/534195/.

7. ARTICLE IN A JOURNAL Give the first author's last name, followed by his or her first name. If there is an additional author or authors, list them with first name(s) followed by last name(s). If you are citing a journal article with more than ten authors, list only the first seven authors followed by "et al." ("and others").

Next, list the year of publication; the title of the article, in quotation marks; the title of the journal, in italics; the volume and issue numbers; and the pages cited, if applicable. If the journal article was found online, list the DOI (digital object identifier). If no DOI is available, you may list the complete URL.

Goldstein, Tom. 2001. "Wanted: More Outspoken Views; Coverage of the Press Is Up, but Criticism Is Down." *Columbia Journalism Review* 40, no. 4: 144–45.

Lowrey, Wilson, and Zhou Shan. 2016. "Journalism's Fortune Tellers: Constructing the Future of News." *Journalism* 19, no. 2: 129–45. https://doi.org/10.1177 /1464884916670931.

8. ARTICLE IN A NEWSPAPER Follow the guidelines in Example 6, "Article in a Magazine."

Wampole, Christy. 2018. "What Is the Future of Speculative Journalism?" *New York Times*, January 22, 2018. https://www.nytimes.com/2018/01/22/opinion /speculative-journalism-future.html.

9. ARTICLE IN AN ELECTRONIC DATABASE Follow the guidelines in Example 7 above. Provide the DOI, if available (see the second model in Example 7). If no DOI is available, it is acceptable to simply list the name of the database in which you found the article.

Martin, William C. 2004. "People of Faith: Religious Conviction in American Journalism and Higher Education." *Social Forces* 82, no. 3: 1214–16, Project MUSE.

10. WEBSITE Give the author's last name, followed by his or her first name. If the author's name is not listed on the website, use the name of the site sponsor instead. Next, list the date of publication or modification; if no date is listed on the website, write "n.d." Give the title of the page or section of the website that you are citing. Give the full publication date; if no date is listed on the website, give the full date on which you accessed the material. Finally, give the complete URL.

Johnson, Adam. 2018. "WaPo Editor Blames Lack of US Leadership for Famine Caused by US Leadership." January 23, 2018. https://fair.org/home/wapo-editor-blames-lack-of-us-leadership-for-famine-caused-by-us-leadership/.

11. BLOG POST Follow the guidelines in Examples 6 and 8 above. Give the name of the blog in place of the publication's name.

Flynn, Kerry. 2018. "As Billionaires Call for Regulation, Facebook Throws Money at Journalism Scholarships," Mashable, accessed January 29, 2018. https://mashable .com/2018/01/26/facebook-journalism-scholarships -billionaires-regulation-news/#C_Jlsb74kOqh

12. ONLINE VIDEO OR AUDIO Give the last name of the author, uploader, or creator, followed by his or her first name. List the year in which the video or audio was recorded or the year in which the material was uploaded to the web; if unknown, write "n.d." Next, list the work's title in quotation marks. List the full original filming date, if given on the website; otherwise, include the full date on which the video or audio was uploaded. If no date is given, include the date on which you accessed the material. If applicable, you may also list the location where the material was originally recorded. Write "Video" or "Audio," followed by the length of the video or audio clip in minutes and seconds. Finally, include the complete URL.

Maza, Carlos. 2017. "The 'This Is Fine' Bias in Cable News." August 4, 2017. Video, 5:02. https://www.vox .com/videos/2017/8/4/16089558/strikethrough -this-is-fine-bias-cable-news

13. INTERVIEW Include the first name of the person being interviewed, followed by his or her last name, a comma, the words "interview by," and the interviewer's name. If the interview aired as part of a television or radio program, include the name of the program and the network. If the interview aired online—for example, in a podcast or simply as a text interview in an online article—include the name of the program and the website (if applicable) and the complete URL. When possible, include the format (e.g., "Audio" or "Video") and the length of the interview in minutes and seconds.

Cronkite, Walter. 1996. Interview by Daniel Schorr. *Frontline*, PBS, April 2, 1996.

Schlichtman, John. 2018. Interview by Lulu Garcia-Navarro. *Weekend Edition Sunday*, NPR, January 28, 2018. Audio, 11:01. https://www.npr.org/2018/01/28/581280992 /there-isn-t-a-just-housing-choice-how-we-ve-enabled -the-pains-of-gentrification.

14. GOVERNMENT DOCUMENT List the name of the government body or agency that produced the document. If applicable, also list the name of the specific committee that produced the document. Next, give the document's title, in italics. If you are citing a United States Congressional hearing or testimony, include the number of the Congress, abbreviated "Cong."; and the number of the session, abbreviated "sess." Finally, include the city of publication, followed by a colon and the publisher's name.

United States Senate. Committee on Foreign Relations. 2015. *The U.S. Role in the Middle East: Hearing before the Committee on Foreign Relations, United States Senate.* 114th Cong., 1st sess. Washington, D.C.: GPO, 2015.

15. PERSONAL COMMUNICATION In most cases, personal communication—which includes emails, text messages, posts on social media, and handwritten letters—are cited in the text only. They are not typically included in the works cited list.

⦿ APA Documentation

Most disciplines in the social sciences—psychology, anthropology, sociology, political science, education, and economics—use the author-date system of documentation established by the American Psychological Association (APA). This citation style highlights dates of publication because the currency of published material is of primary importance in these fields.

In the author-date system, use an author or organization's name in a signal phrase or parenthetical reference within the main text to cite a source.

For example, you could cite Example 1 in this section with the author's name in a signal phrase as follows:

> Nakazawa (2009) states that stress hormones like cortisol can dramatically alter how immune cells work.

or with a parenthetical reference as follows:

> Stress hormones such as cortisol travel to the immune system and can dramatically alter how immune cells work (Nakazawa, 2009).

Each in-text citation refers to an alphabetical references list that you must create.

For more information about APA format, see the *Publication Manual of the American Psychological Association*, Seventh Edition (2019). The manual advises users to omit retrieval dates for content that is unlikely to change, such as published journal articles, and to omit the database from which material is retrieved as long as an identifier such as a DOI (digital object identifier) or, if no DOI is available, the URL where you found the material.

The numbered entries that follow introduce and explain some conventions of this citation style using examples related to the topic of stress management. Note that in the titles of books and articles, only the first word of the title and subtitle and proper nouns are capitalized.

1. BOOK BY A SINGLE AUTHOR Begin with the author's last name and initials, followed by the date of publication in parentheses. Next, italicize the book's title, and end with the publisher.

Nakazawa, D. J. (2009). *The autoimmune epidemic*. Simon & Schuster.

2. BOOK BY MULTIPLE AUTHORS OR EDITORS

Williams, S., & Cooper, L. (2002). *Managing workplace stress: A best practice blueprint.* Wiley.

3. ARTICLE IN A REFERENCE WORK If an online edition of the reference work is cited, give the retrieval date and the URL. Omit end punctuation after the URL.

Beins, B. C. (2010). Barnum effect. In I. B. Weiner & W. E. Craighead (Eds.), *The Corsini encyclopedia of psychology* (4th ed., Vol. 4, pp. 203–204). Wiley.

Biofeedback. (2007). In *Encyclopaedia Britannica online.* Retrieved January 29, 2020 from http://www.britannica.com /EBchecked/topic/65856/biofeedback

4. GOVERNMENT DOCUMENT

U.S. Department of Health and Human Services. (1997). *Violence in the workplace: Guidelines for understanding and response.* Government Printing Office.

5. JOURNAL ARTICLE Begin with the author's last name and initials followed by the date of publication in parentheses. Next, list the title of the article and italicize the title of the journal in which it is printed. Then give the volume number, italicized, and the issue number in parentheses. End with the inclusive page numbers of the article. For an article found online, if a DOI number is given, include it in the format *https://doi.org/xxxxx.* Otherwise, include the URL where you found the article. Omit the end period after a DOI or URL.

Dollard, M. F., & Metzer, J. C. (1999). Psychological research, practice, and production: The occupational stress problem. *International Journal of Stress Management, 6*(4), 241–253.

Christian, M. S., Bradley, J. C., Wallace, J. C., & Burke, M. J. (2009, September). Workplace safety: A meta-analysis of the roles of person and situation factors. *Journal of Applied Psychology, 94*(5), 1103–1127. https://doi.org/10.1037/a0016172

6. MAGAZINE ARTICLE

Cobb, K. (2002, July 20). Sleepy heads: Low fuel may drive brain's need to sleep. *Science News, 162*, 38.

7. NEWSPAPER ARTICLE

Zimmerman, E. (2010, December 19). Learning to tame your office anxiety. *The New York Times*, BU8.

Zimmerman, E. (2010, December 19). Learning to tame your office anxiety. *The New York Times.* https://www.nytimes.com/2010/12/19/jobs/19career.html

8. UNSIGNED NEWSPAPER ARTICLE

Stress less: It's time to wrap it up. (2002, December 18). *Houston Chronicle*, A1.

9. DOCUMENT FROM A WEBSITE List the author, the date of publication (use "n.d." if there is no date), the title of the document, italicized, and the URL for the document. If there is no author, begin the entry with the document title. Do not include a retrieval date unless the content is likely to change. Omit punctuation at the end of the URL.

Centers for Disease Control and Prevention. (1999). *Stress . . . at work* (NIOSH Publication No. 99–101). http://www.cdc.gov/niosh/docs/99–101

10. PERSONAL WEBSITE Simply note the site in your speech:

Dr. Wesley Sime's stress management page is an excellent resource (http://www.unl.edu/stress/mgmt/).

11. BLOG POST

Lippin, R. (2007, July 31). US corporate EAP programs: Oversight, Orwellian or Soviet psychiatry redux? [Blog post]. http://medicalcrises.blogspot.com/2007/07/us-corporate-eap-programs-oversight.html

12. EMAIL Simply note the message in your speech:

An email message from the staff of AltaVista clarifies this point (D. Emanuel, personal communication, May 12, 2005).

13. MATERIAL FROM AN ONLINE DATABASE

MacKay, D. G. (1971). Stress pre-entry in motor systems. *The American Journal of Psychology, 84*(1), 35–51. https://doi.org/10.2307/1421223

14. ABSTRACT FROM AN INFORMATION SERVICE OR ONLINE DATABASE Cite as you would for a full article, but include [Abstract] after the article title.

Viswesvaran, C., Sanchez, J., & Fisher, J. (1999). The role of social support in the process of work stress: A meta-analysis [Abstract]. *Journal of Vocational Behavior, 54*(2), 314–334. https://doi.org/10.1006/jvbe.1998.1661

15. **PERSONAL INTERVIEW** Simply note the interview in your speech:

> During her interview, Senator Cole revealed her enthusiasm for the new state-funded stress management center (M. Cole, personal communication, October 7, 2005).

◉ MLA Documentation

Created by the Modern Language Association, MLA documentation style is fully outlined in the *MLA Handbook for Writers of Research Papers*, Eighth Edition (2016). Disciplines that use MLA style include English literature, the humanities, and various foreign languages.

In MLA format, you document materials from other sources with in-text citations that incorporate signal phrases and parenthetical references. For example, you could cite Example 1 in this section with the author's name in a signal phrase as follows:

> Berg notes that " 'Chicano' is the term made popular by the Mexican American civil rights movement in the 1960s and 1970s" (6).

Or with a parenthetical reference as follows:

> The term "Chicano" was "made popular by the Mexican American civil rights movement in the 1960s and 1970s" (Berg 6).

Each in-text citation refers to an alphabetical works-cited list that you must create.

The sample citations given here all relate to a single topic: film appreciation and criticism.

1. **BOOK BY A SINGLE AUTHOR OR A SINGLE EDITOR** Citations for most books are arranged as follows: (1) the author's name, last name first; (2) the title and subtitle, italicized; and (3) the city of publication, an abbreviated form of the publisher's name, and the date of publication. Each of these three pieces of information is followed by a period and one space.

For a book with a single editor, follow the same guidelines, but add a comma and "ed." after the editor's name.

Berg, Charles Ramírez. *Latino Images in Film: Stereotypes, Subversion, and Resistance.* Austin: U of Texas P, 2002.

2. **BOOK BY MULTIPLE AUTHORS OR EDITORS** Give the first author's name, last name first; then list the name(s) of the other author(s) in regular order with a comma between authors and the word "and" before the last one.

For a book with multiple editors (or a book with one author and one editor), follow the same guidelines, but add a comma and "ed." or "eds." after the final editor's name.

Grieveson, Lee, and Haidee Wasson, eds. *Inventing Film Studies*. Durham: Duke UP, 2008.

3. ARTICLE IN A REFERENCE WORK If you are citing an online version of a reference work, give the author (if there is one), title of the entry, name of the publication, date of publication (if available), and the URL.

If you are citing a print version of a reference work, include the publisher's name.

"Auteur Theory." *Encyclopaedia Britannica*, 27 Dec. 2017, https://www.britannica.com/art/auteur-theory.

Katz, Ephraim. "Film Noir." *The Film Encyclopedia*, 7th ed., HarperCollins, 2012.

4. GOVERNMENT DOCUMENT

United States, House Committee on the Judiciary. *National Film Preservation Act of 1996*. 104th Cong., 2nd sess. H. Rept. 104–558. Washington: GPO, 1996.

United States, House Committee on House Administration. *Library of Congress Sound Recording and Film Preservation Programs Reauthorization Act of 2008*. 110th Cong., 2nd sess. H. Rept. 110–683. *GPO*, 2 Oct. 2008, https://www.congress.gov/110/plaws/publ336/PLAW-110publ336.pdf.

5. MAGAZINE ARTICLE List the author, last name first; the title of the article, in quotation marks; the title of the publication, in italics; and the publication date. If you are citing an online article, include the URL. If you are citing a print article, include the page number(s) on which the article appears.

Horn, Robert. "From Bangkok to Cannes, Thai Political Tensions Remain." *Time*, 24 May 2010, http://content.time.com/time/world/article/0,8599,1991310,00.html.

Ansen, David. "Shock and Yawn." *Newsweek*, 26 Oct. 2009, p. 48.

6. JOURNAL ARTICLE If an article is accessed online through a database service, after the publication information, add the name of the database in italics, followed by the DOI.

Skrebels, Paul. "*All Night Long*: Jazzing around with Othello." *Literature/Film Quarterly*, vol. 36, no. 2, 2008, pp. 147–56.

Holcomb, Mark. "A Classic Revisited: *To Kill a Mockingbird*." *Film Quarterly*, vol. 55, no. 4, summer 2002, pp. 34–40. *JSTOR*, doi:10.1525/fq.2002.55.4.34.

7. NEWSPAPER ARTICLE If you are citing a newspaper article found online, include the complete URL. If you are citing a print newspaper article, include the page number(s). If the article is an editorial, insert the word "Editorial" after the URL or page number.

Dargis, Manohla. "Unblinking Eye, Visual Diary: Warhol's Films." *New York Times*, 21 Oct. 2007, http://www.nytimes.com/2007/10/21/movies/21darg.html.

Peers, Martin. "HBO Could Draw True Blood Online." *Wall Street Journal*, 23 Oct. 2010, pp. B16+.

"Avatars Don't Smoke." *New York Times*, 8 Jan. 2010, p. A26. Editorial.

8. ENTIRE WEBSITE

Railton, Stephen. *Mark Twain in His Times.* Stephen Railton / U of Virginia Library, 2012, twain.lib.virginia.edu/.

9. ARTICLE OR OTHER SHORT WORK ON A WEBSITE

Gallagher, Sean. "The Last Nomads of the Tibetan Plateau." *Pulitzer Center on Crisis Reporting*, 25 Oct. 2012, pulitzercenter .org/reporting/china-glaciers-global-warming-climate-change-ecosystem-tibetan-plateau-grasslands-nomads.

10. BLOG POST Give the author's name; the title of the post or comment in quotation marks (if there is no title, use the description "Blog post" or "Blog comment"); the title of the blog, italicized; the date of the post or comment; and the complete URL.

Scola, Nancy. "And the White House Tweets Back." *TechPresident*, Personal Democracy Media, 5 May 2009, http://tech-president.com/blog-entry/and-white-house-tweets-back.

mitchellfreedman. Comment on "Cloud Atlas's Theory of Everything," by Emily Eakin. *NYR Daily*, NYREV, 3 Nov. 2012, www.nybooks.com/daily/2012/11/02/ken-wilber-cloud -atlas/.

11. EMAIL MESSAGE

Boothe, Jeanna. "Re: Top 100 Movies." Received by Will Hurst, 16 Feb. 2012.

12. PODCAST

Accomando, Beth. "Horror Movies As Spiritual Practice." *Cinema Junkie*, NPR, 22 Dec. 2017, https://www.npr.org/podcasts/442951456/cinema-junkie.

13. WORK OF ART OR PHOTOGRAPH

Christenberry, William. *Coleman's Café*. 1971, Hunter Museum of Art, Chattanooga. Ektacolor Brownie Print.

14. INTERVIEW

Sanderson, Andrew. Personal interview. 12 June 2011.

◎ CSE Documentation

The CSE (Council of Science Editors) style is most frequently used in the fields of biology and environmental science. The current CSE style guide is *Scientific Style and Format: The CSE Manual for Authors, Editors, and Publishers*, Eighth Edition (2014). Publishers and instructors who require the CSE style do so in three possible formats: a citation-sequence superscript format, a name-year format, or a citation-name format, which combines aspects of the other two systems.

- Citation-sequence superscript format: Use superscript numbers for in-text references. In the references list, number and arrange the references in the sequence in which they are first cited in the speech.

- Name-year format: Use the name and year, in parentheses, for the in-text reference. In the references list, give the references, unnumbered, in alphabetical order.

- Citation-name format: Use superscript numbers for in-text references. In the references list, arrange the references in alphabetical order and number the list sequentially.

In the following examples, all of which refer to environmental issues, you will see that the citation-sequence format calls for listing the date after the publisher's name in references for books and after the name of the periodical in references for articles. The name-year format calls for listing the date immediately after the author's name in any kind of reference. Notice also the absence of a comma after the author's last name, the absence of a period after an initial, and the absence of italics in titles of books or journals.

1. BOOK BY ONE AUTHOR Be sure to list the total number of pages in the book.

Citation-Sequence and Citation-Name

[1] Houghton JT. Global warming: the complete briefing. 4th ed. Cambridge (UK): Cambridge University Press; 2009. 456 p.

Name-Year

Houghton JT. 2009. Global warming: the complete briefing. 4th ed. Cambridge (UK): Cambridge University Press. 456 p.

2. BOOK BY TWO OR MORE AUTHORS

Citation-Sequence and Citation-Name

[2] Harf JE, Lombardi MO. Taking sides: clashing views on global issues. 6th ed. New York: McGraw-Hill; 2010. 432 p.

Name-Year

Harf JE, Lombardi MO. 2010. Taking sides: clashing views on global issues. 6th ed. New York: McGraw-Hill. 432 p.

3. JOURNAL ARTICLE If citing a journal on the internet, add the medium, date cited, and the URL. Also give the DOI code if available. Omit end punctuation after a URL or DOI.

Citation-Sequence and Citation-Name

[3] Brussard PF, Tull JC. Conservation biology and four types of advocacy. Conserv Biol. 2007; 21(1):21–24.

[3] Brussard PF, Tull JC. Conservation biology and four types of advocacy. Conserv Biol [Internet]. 2007 [cited 2010 Oct 22]; 21(1):21–24. Available from: http://www.blackwell-synergy.com/toc/cbi/21/1 doi:10.1111/j.1523-1739.2006.00640.x

Name-Year

Brussard PF, Tull JC. 2007. Conservation biology and four types of advocacy. Conserv Biol. 21(1):21–24.

Brussard PF, Tull JC. 2007. Conservation biology and four types of advocacy. Conserv Biol [Internet]. [cited 2010 Oct 22]; 21(1):21–24. Available from: http://www.blackwell-synergy.com/toc/cbi/21/1 doi:10.1111/ j.1523-1739.2006.00640.x

4. MAGAZINE ARTICLE

Citation-Sequence and Citation-Name

[4] Sheppard K. Bad breakup: why BP doesn't have to tell the EPA—or the public—what's in its toxic dispersants. Mother Jones. 2010 Sep-Oct:41.

Name-Year

Sheppard K. 2010 Sep-Oct. Bad breakup: why BP doesn't have to tell the EPA—or the public—what's in its toxic dispersants. Mother Jones. 41.

5. NEWSPAPER ARTICLE

Citation-Sequence and Citation-Name

[5] Zeller T Jr. Negotiators at climate talks face deep set of fault lines. New York Times. 2009 Dec 6; Sect. WK:3 (col. 1).

Name-Year

Zeller T Jr. 2009 Dec 6. Negotiators at climate talks face deep set of fault lines. New York Times. Sect. WK:3 (col. 1).

6. WEBSITE For material found on a website, give the author's name (if any) and the title of the material, followed by "Internet" in brackets. Add the place of publication, the publisher, date of publication, followed by the date of citation in brackets. Add "Available from:" and the URL.

Citation-Sequence and Citation-Name

[6] Coastal Programs: The Barnegat Bay Estuary Program [Internet]. Trenton (NJ): Department of Environmental Protection, Division of Watershed Management. c1996-2004 [updated 2010 Feb 18; cited 2011 Oct 23]. Available from: http://www.nj.gov/dep/watershedmgt/bbep.htm

Name-Year

Coastal Programs: The Barnegat Bay Estuary Program [Internet]. c1996-2004. Trenton (NJ): Department of Environmental Protection, Division of Watershed Management. [updated 2010 Feb 18; cited 2011 Oct 23]. Available from: http://www.nj.gov/dep/watershedmgt/bbep.htm

7. EMAIL MESSAGE CSE recommends mentioning personal communications in text, but not listing them in the list of references. An explanation of the material should go in the "Notes."

. . . (2012 email from Maura O'Brien to me; unreferenced, see "Notes").

8. EMAIL DISCUSSION LIST OR NEWSGROUP MESSAGE

[8] Affleck-Asch W. Lawncare methods causing heavy damage to environment [discussion list on the Internet]. 2004 Aug 17, 2:30 pm [cited 2011 Dec 2]. [about 10 paragraphs]. Available from: http://www.mail-archive.com/ecofem%40csf.colorado.edu

◎ IEEE Documentation

The Institute of Electrical and Electronics Engineers (IEEE) style requires that references appear at the end of the text, not in alphabetical order but in the order in which the references are cited in the text or speech. A bracketed reference number precedes each entry. For more information on IEEE documentation, check the *IEEE Standards Style Manual* online at **https://www.ieee.org/documents/style_manual.pdf**.

1. BOOK

[1] Thomas, R. E., Albert, R. J., and Toussaint G. J., *The Analysis and Design of Linear Circuits*, 6th ed. Hoboken, NJ: Wiley, 2009, p. 652.

2. PERIODICAL

[2] Melfi, M., Evon, S., and McElveen R., "Induction versus permanent magnet motors," *IEEE Industry Applications Magazine*, vol. 15, no. 6, pp. 28–35, Nov./Dec. 2009. doi: 10.1109/MIAS.2009.934443

3. WEB PAGE

[3] National Academy of Engineering, "Lasers and fiber optics timeline," *Greatest Engineering Achievements of the 20th Century*, n.d. [Online]. Available: http://www.greatachievements.org/?id=3706

APPENDIX B ●●●●

Question-and-Answer Sessions

Deftly fielding questions is a final critical component of making a speech or a presentation. As the last step in preparing your speech, anticipate and prepare for questions the audience is likely to pose to you. Write these questions down, and practice answering them. Spend time preparing an answer to the most difficult question that you are likely to face. The confidence you will gain from smoothly handling a difficult question should spill over to other questions.[1]

◉ Protocol during the Session

As a matter of courtesy, call on audience members in the order in which they raise their hands. Consider the following guidelines:

- *Repeat or paraphrase the question* ("The question is 'Did the mayor really vote against . . . '"). This will ensure that you've heard it correctly, that others in the audience know what you are responding to, and that you have time to reflect upon and formulate an answer. Note that there are a few exceptions to repeating the question, especially when the question is hostile. One expert suggests that you should always repeat the question when speaking to a large group; when you're in a small group or a training seminar, however, doing so isn't necessary.[2]

- *Initially make eye contact with the questioner; then move your gaze to other audience members.* This makes all audience members feel as though you are responding not only to the questioner but to them as well.

- *Remember your listening skills.* Give questioners your full attention, and don't interrupt them.

- *Don't be afraid to pause while formulating an answer.* Many speakers feel they must feed the audience instantaneous responses; this belief sometimes causes them to say things that they later regret. This is especially the case in media interviews (see Appendix C). Pauses that seem long to you may not appear lengthy to listeners.

- *Keep answers concise.* The question-and-answer session is not the time to launch into a lengthy treatise on your favorite aspect of a topic.

Handling Hostile and Otherwise Troubling Questions

When handling hostile questions, do not get defensive. Doing so will only damage your credibility and encourage the other person. Maintain an attitude of respect, and stay cool and in control. Attempt to defuse the hostile questioner with respect and goodwill. Similarly, never give the impression that you think a question is stupid or irrelevant.

- *Do not repeat or paraphrase a hostile question.* This only lends the question more credibility than it is worth. Instead, try to rephrase it more positively[3] (e.g., in response to the question "Didn't your department botch the launch of product X?," you might respond, "The question was 'Why did product X experience a difficult market entry?' To that I would say that . . .").

- *If someone asks you a seemingly stupid question, do not point that out.* Instead, respond graciously.[4]

Ending the Session

Never end a question-and-answer session abruptly. As time runs out, alert the audience that you will take one or two more questions and then must end. The session represents one final opportunity to reinforce your message, so take the opportunity to do so. As you summarize your message, thank your listeners for their time. Leave an air of goodwill behind you.

Preparing for TV and Radio Communication

The underlying principles described throughout this guide will stand you in good stead as you prepare to communicate online, as discussed in Chapter 26, or on television or radio. These latter speaking situations do present some unique challenges, however.

◉ Speaking on Television

On television, you are at the mercy of reporters and producers who will edit your remarks to fit their time frame. Therefore, before your televised appearance, find out as much as you can about the speech situation—for example, how long you will be on camera and whether the show will be aired live or taped. You may need to convey your message in *sound bite* form—succinct statements that summarize your key points in twenty seconds or less.

Eye Contact, Body Movements, and Voice

Knowing where to direct your gaze is critical in televised appearances, as is controlling body movement and voice. The following are some guidelines:

- Don't play to the camera. In a one-on-one interview, focus on the interviewer. Do not look up or down or tilt your head sideways; these movements will make you look uncertain or evasive.[1]

- If there is an audience, treat the camera as just another audience member, glancing at it only as often as you would at any other individual during your remarks.

- If there is only the camera, direct your gaze at it as you speak.

- Keep your posture erect.

- Exaggerate your gestures slightly.

- Project your voice, and avoid speaking in a monotone.

◉ Dress and Makeup

To compensate for the glare of studio lights and distortions caused by the camera, give careful consideration to dress and grooming:

- Choose dark rather than light-colored clothing. Dark colors such as blue, gray, green, and brown photograph better than lighter shades.

- Avoid stark white, because it produces glare.

- Avoid plaids, dots, and other busy patterns because they tend to jump around on the screen.

- Avoid glittering jewelry, including tie bars.

- If you use makeup, wear a little more makeup than usual because bright studio lights tend to make you look washed out.

◉ Speaking on Radio: The Media Interview

The following are guidelines for preparing for media interviews on the radio. These same guidelines can be applied to the television interview.

- Know the audience and the focus of the program. What subjects does the broadcast cover? How long will the interview be? Will it be aired in real-time or recorded?

- Brush up on background information, and have your facts ready. Assume that the audience knows little or nothing about the subject matter.

- Use the interviewer's name during the interview.

- Prepare a speaking outline on notecards for the interview. Remember that the microphone will pick up the sound of papers being shuffled.

- Remember that taped interviews may be edited. Make key points in short sentences, and repeat them using different words.[2] Think in terms of sound bites.

- Anticipate questions that might arise, and decide how you will answer them.

- Use transition points to acknowledge the interviewer's questions and to bridge your key message points, such as "I am not familiar with that, but what I can tell you is . . ."; "You raise an interesting question, but I think the more important matter is. . . ."[3]

- Avoid the phrase "No comment." It will only exaggerate a point you are trying to minimize. Instead, say, "I am not at liberty to comment/discuss. . . ."

APPENDIX D ●●●●

Tips for Non-Native Speakers of English

In addition to the normal fear of speaking in front of a group, non-native English speakers face the added challenges of giving a presentation in a language that is not their own. To help reduce your anxiety if English is not your native language, preparation and practice are extremely valuable. There are several helpful and effective steps you can take to minimize fear and to produce a high-quality presentation.

◉ Think Positively

Research shows that thinking positively about preparing and delivering an oral presentation actually decreases your anxiety and helps you prepare more effectively. Public speaking will provide many opportunities to improve your English and to help you become a more proficient communicator in English. As you listen to your classmates' speeches, you will gain valuable exposure to spoken English. You can also learn what to do and what *not* to do from the positive— and negative—features of your classmates' presentations. In addition, by spending time writing and outlining your speech, you will gain confidence in your organizational and written language skills. Finally, the extra motivation of speaking in front of a group will encourage you to focus on some language skills that may need improvement, such as pronunciation.

◉ Consider Your Context and Audience

As you are preparing your presentation, be aware that presentation styles differ greatly from one country to another. Therefore, it is very important that you consider the cultural context of your presentation as well as the expectations of your audience. An American academic audience expects the main points to be presented clearly in the introduction and then explained in more detail throughout the presentation. This differs from some cultures in which the support or evidence is presented first, and sometimes the audience is expected to draw their own conclusions. An unfamiliar presentation style or organization may confuse and distract an American audience, and they may be trying to figure out your main points instead of paying attention to what you are saying.[1]

◉ Capitalize on Your Language Uniqueness

It will probably be clear to your audience that you are not a native English speaker, but apologizing for your English ability will only result in negative attention. However, instead of ignoring this obvious fact, take advantage of your uniqueness. When appropriate, explain and use words from your native language to emphasize your points. This will help the audience better appreciate your native language and accent. For example, the Spanish word *corazón* has a lyrical quality that makes it sound much better than its English counterpart, "heart." Take advantage of the beauty of your native language.

If appropriate, consider sharing a personal experience with the audience. Stories from other countries and cultures often fascinate listeners. Unique cultural traditions, eyewitness accounts of newsworthy events, or stories passed down orally from one generation to the next are just some of the possibilities. Depending on the goal of your speech, you may be able to use your experiences as supporting material for a related topic or even as the topic itself.

◉ Practice, Practice, Practice

There is no substitute for preparation and practice. Whether you are a native or non-native English speaker, you should prepare your presentation early so that you have plenty of time to practice, get feedback, and work on your organization and pronunciation. Of course, you should make both a working outline and a speaking outline to make sure you present all of the important and necessary information (see Chapter 13). In addition, you can practice with a friend or make a video and watch it with a friend who will give you good, honest advice. A native speaker or your instructor can probably give the best feedback. Practice will give you a chance to develop comfort and confidence with your information and organization, to figure out the best way to put your information into sentences, and to work on the length and timing of the presentation. When you are practicing, take your time and speak slowly. Speaking slowly during your presentation will give your listeners time to get used to your voice and to be able to focus on your message.

◉ Focus on Your Pronunciation

Because languages vary in the speech sounds they use, virtually everyone who learns to speak another language will speak that language with an accent. Even native speakers have different accents, so you should not be overly concerned about having an accent. However, it is important to determine whether specific features of your pronunciation significantly interfere with your ability to be understood. There are several ways that you can improve your pronunciation.

First, from your own experience or through a little research, you can learn about the types of challenges that English presents to speakers of your home language. You may have difficulty recognizing and producing certain sounds in English. For example, if your first language doesn't differentiate between the /sh/ sound and the /ch/ sound, you may say *share* instead of *chair* or *shoes* instead of *choose*.[2] More importantly, pronunciation involves more than just the sounds of the vowels and consonants; correct pronunciation also requires that you pay attention to word and syllable stress, rhythm, and intonation.[3] Some sounds or syllables are emphasized more than others by making them longer or louder, and the meaning of a sentence is communicated not just with words, but by raising and lowering the pitch of your voice. Inaccurate stress, rhythm, and intonation may actually be more confusing than the incorrect pronunciation of vowels and consonants, so it is vital to pay attention to all of these speech factors.

As mentioned above, recording your presentation and listening to it in the presence of a native speaker, a friend, or even your instructor can be helpful. Once you have identified which words you have difficulty pronouncing, you can work to improve your pronunciation. Many online dictionary tools provide audio recordings of words, so you can hear how they should be pronounced. Listen and repeat difficult words several times. Take a break and then repeat them several more times. Even with this practice, you may forget the correct pronunciation when you are nervous and in front of your classmates. To remind yourself of the correct pronunciation during your presentation, you can include the pronunciations of difficult words as part of your speaking outline.

Finally, if you have significant difficulty with the pronunciation of a specific word, you can use a thesaurus to find a synonym that is simpler and easier to pronounce. Again, check with a friend or your instructor to make sure that you are using the correct meaning of the words you have selected for your speech.

◉ Final Suggestions

In the long term, interacting with native English speakers in everyday life will help enormously. Making friends with native speakers outside the classroom will give you examples of correct pronunciation and ways of communicating and help you to start thinking in English rather than translating in your mind from one language to the other. If your experience with English is limited and you must give an oral presentation, Robert Anholt, a scientist and the author of *Dazzle 'Em with Style: The Art of Oral Scientific Presentation*, suggests the following:

- Practice the presentation often, preferably with a friend who is a native English speaker.

- Learn the presentation almost by heart.

- Create strong presentation visual aids that will convey most of the story by themselves.[4]

Glossary ●●●●

abstract language Language that is general or non-specific. See also *concrete language*.

active listening A multistep, focused, and purposeful process of gathering and evaluating information.

ad hominem fallacy A fallacy of reasoning in which a speaker targets a person instead of the issue at hand.

after-dinner speech A speech that is likely to occur before, after, or during a formal dinner, a breakfast or lunch seminar, or a business, professional, or civic meeting.

agora In ancient Greece, a public square or marketplace. See also *forum* and *public forum*.

alliteration The repetition of the same sounds, usually initial consonants, in two or more neighboring words or syllables.

analogy An extended *metaphor* or *simile* that compares an unfamiliar concept or process with a more familiar one in order to help the listener understand the one that is unfamiliar.

anaphora A *rhetorical device* in which a speaker repeats a word or phrase at the beginning of successive phrases or sentences.

anecdote A brief story, often humorous, of a real-life incident that links back to the speaker's theme.

antigroup role A disruptive role, such as "floor hogger" and "blocker," that detracts from a group's purpose and so should be avoided.

antithesis A rhetorical device in which two ideas are set off in balanced (parallel) opposition to each other.

architecture design review An oral presentation that enables the audience to visualize and judge the feasibility and appeal of an architectural design.

argument A stated position with support, for or against an idea or issue; contains the core elements of claim, evidence, and warrants.

articulation The clarity or forcefulness with which sounds are made, regardless of whether they are pronounced correctly.

asynchronous communication Communication in which interaction between speaker and receiver does not occur simultaneously. See also *recorded presentation* and *synchronous communication*.

attitudes Our general evaluations of people, ideas, objects, or events.

audience analysis The process of gathering and analyzing demographic and psychological information about audience members.

audience-centered perspective An approach to speech preparation in which each phase of the speech preparation process—from selection and treatment of the topic to deciding about organization, language, and method of delivery—is geared toward communicating a message the audience will find meaningful.

authoritative warrant A warrant that appeals to the credibility (ethos) that the audience assigns to the source of the evidence. See also *warrant*.

bandwagoning A fallacy of reasoning in which the speaker offers an argument as true because general opinion supports it.

begging the question A fallacy of reasoning in which an argument is presented as necessarily true, even though no evidence is offered in support of it.

beliefs The ways in which people perceive reality or determine the very existence or validity of something.

body (of speech) The part of the speech in which the speaker develops the main points intended to fulfill the speech purpose.

body language Facial expressions, eye behavior, gestures, and general body movements. Audiences are sensitive to a speaker's body language.

brainstorming A problem-solving technique, useful for developing speech topics, that involves the spontaneous generation of ideas through word association, topic mapping, and other techniques.

brief example A single illustration of a point.

call to action A challenge to audience members to act in response to a speech—see the problem in a new way, change their beliefs about the problem, or change both their actions and their beliefs with respect to the problem. Placed at the conclusion of a speech.

canned speech A speech used repeatedly and without sufficient adaptation to the rhetorical situation.

canons of rhetoric A classical approach to speechmaking in which the speaker divides a speechmaking process into five parts: invention, arrangement, style, memory, and delivery.

captive audience An audience required to attend a speech. See also *voluntary audience*.

case conference An oral report prepared by health care professionals evaluating a patient's condition and outlining a treatment plan.

case study A detailed illustration of a real (or realistic) situation, relating to business, law, or other disciplines, which poses dilemmas or problems requiring solutions.

categorical pattern See *topical pattern of arrangement.*

causal (cause-effect) pattern A pattern of organizing speech points in order of causes and then of effects, or vice versa.

causal reasoning A line of reasoning ("warrant") offering a cause-and-effect relationship as proof of a claim.

central processing A mode of processing a persuasive message that involves thinking critically about the contents of the message and the strength and quality of the speaker's arguments; described in the *elaboration likelihood model of persuasion (ELM).* See also *peripheral processing.*

channel The medium through which the speaker sends a message (e.g., sound or air waves, and electronic transmission).

chart A visual representation of data and its relationship to other data in compact form. Charts useful for speakers include flow charts, organization charts, and tables.

cherry-picking Selectively presenting only those facts and statistics that buttress one point of view while ignoring competing data.

chronological pattern of arrangement A pattern of organizing speech points in a natural sequential order; used when describing a series of events in time or when the topic develops in line with a set pattern of actions or tasks.

civic-mindedness A ground rule of ethical public speaking in which the speaker demonstrates caring about his or her community, as expressed in the speech.

claim (proposition) The declaration of a state of affairs, in which a speaker attempts to prove something by providing *evidence* and reasons (*warrants*).

claim of fact An argument that focuses on whether something is or is not true or whether something will or will not happen.

claim of policy An argument that recommends that a specific course of action be taken, or approved, by an audience.

claim of value An argument that addresses issues of judgment.

classroom discussion presentation A presentation in which the speaker provides a brief overview of the topic under discussion and introduces a series of questions to guide students through the topic.

cliché An overused phrase such as "works like a dog."

clinical case study A presentation that provides medical personnel with a detailed analysis of a person or group with a particular disease or condition and reviews plans for treatment.

closed-ended question Question designed to elicit a small range of specific answers. See also *open-ended question*.

co-culture A community of people whose perceptions and beliefs differ significantly from those of other groups within the larger culture.

cognitive restructuring A speech anxiety-reduction technique in which you train your mind to think about something that makes you anxious (such as public speaking) in a more positive way.

colleagues within the field An audience of persons who share the speaker's knowledge of the general field under discussion but who may not be familiar with the specific topic.

colloquial expression An informal expression, often with regional variations of speech.

common knowledge Information that is likely to be known by many people and is therefore in the public domain and does not need attribution.

communication ethics Our ethical responsibilities when seeking influence over other people and for which there are positive and negative, or "right" or "wrong," choices of action.

comparative advantage pattern A pattern of organizing speech points so that the speaker's viewpoint or proposal is shown to be superior to one or more alternative viewpoints or proposals.

conclusion (of speech) The part of the speech in which the speaker reiterates the speech thesis, summarizes main points, and leaves the audience with something to think about or act upon.

concrete language Nouns and verbs that convey specific and tangible (as opposed to abstract) meaning. See also *abstract language*.

connotative meaning The individual associations that different people bring to bear on a word. See also *denotative meaning.*

coordinate points Ideas that are given the same weight in an outline and are aligned with one another; thus Main Point II is coordinate with Main Point I. See also *subordinate points.*

coordination and subordination The logical placement of ideas (speech points) in an outline relative to their importance to one another. Ideas that are coordinate are given equal weight; an idea that is subordinate to another is given relatively less weight.

copyright A legal protection afforded original creators of literary or artistic works.

critical thinking The ability to evaluate claims on the basis of well-supported reasons.

cultural values The dominant values in a given culture. See also *values.*

debate An oral presentation in which two individuals or groups argue an issue from opposing viewpoints.

decoding The process of interpreting a message. See also *encoding.*

deep web The large portion of the web that general search engines cannot access because the information is licensed and/or fee-based.

defensive listening A poor listening behavior in which the listener reacts defensively to a speaker's message.

delivery The vocal and nonverbal behavior that a speaker uses in a public speech; one of the five *canons of rhetoric.*

delivery cue A brief reminder note or prompt placed in the speaking outline that can refer to transitions, timing, speaking rate and volume, presentation aids, quotations, statistics, and difficult-to-pronounce or remember names or words.

demographics The statistical characteristics of a given population considered in analysis of audience members; typically includes age, gender, ethnic or cultural background, socioeconomic status (including income, occupation, and education), and religious and political affiliation; other factors such as group membership, geographic location, and disability may also be important to consider.

denotative meaning The literal or dictionary definition of a word. See also *connotative meaning.*

derived credibility A stage of *speaker credibility* in which audience members assign the speaker credibility based on the actual message, including the quality of evidence and the skill with which the speech is delivered. See also *initial credibility* and *terminal credibility*.

dialect A distinctive way of speaking associated with a particular region or social group.

dialogic communication The sharing of ideas and open discussion through civil discourse.

dignity The feeling that one is worthy, honored, or respected as a person; audience members want to feel that the speaker accords them dignity.

direct quotation A statement made verbatim, or word for word, from a source. Direct quotations should always be acknowledged in a speech. See also *paraphrase* and *summary.*

disinformation The deliberate falsification of information.

dyadic communication Communication between two people, as in a conversation.

effective delivery Skillful application of natural conversational behavior to a speech in a way that is relaxed, enthusiastic, and direct.

either-or fallacy A fallacy of reasoning in which the speaker offers only two alternatives, even though there are multiple ways of viewing the issue.

elaboration likelihood model of persuasion (ELM) A model of persuasion that states that people process persuasive messages by one of two routes—either *central processing* or *peripheral processing*—depending on their degree of involvement in the message.

encoding The process of organizing a message, choosing words and sentence structure, and verbalizing the message. See also *decoding.*

engineering design review An oral presentation on the results of a design project.

epiphora A rhetorical device in which the speaker repeats a word or phrase at the end of successive statements.

ethnocentrism The belief that the ways of one's own culture are superior to those of other cultures.

ethos The Greek word for "character." According to classical rhetoricians such as Aristotle, audiences listen to and trust speakers if they exhibit competence (as demonstrated by the speaker's grasp of the subject matter) and good moral character. See also *logos* and *pathos.*

eulogy A speech whose purpose is to celebrate and commemorate the life of someone while consoling those who are left behind.

evidence Supporting material that provides grounds for belief. See also *claim* and *warrant.*

evidence-based practice (EBP) presentation A presentation that reviews the scientific literature on a clinical problem, critically evaluates the findings, and suggests best practices for standards of care.

example (as form of support) An illustration of a speech point whose purpose is to aid understanding by making ideas more concrete and by clarifying and amplifying meaning. See also *extended example* and *hypothetical example.*

expert audience (also called *insider audience*) An audience of persons with an intimate knowledge of the topic, issue, product, or idea being discussed.

expert testimony Any findings, eyewitness accounts, or opinions by professionals who are trained to evaluate or report on a given topic; a form of supporting material.

extended example A multifaceted illustration of the idea, item, or event being described, thereby getting the point across and reiterating it effectively. See also *example* and *hypothetical example.*

fact A documented occurrence, including actual events, dates, times, places, and people involved; a form of supporting material in a speech.

fair use doctrine The legal guidelines permitting the limited use of copyrighted works without permission for the purposes of scholarship and research.

fairness A ground rule of ethical public speaking; the act on the part of the speaker to make a genuine effort to see all sides of an issue and to be open-minded.

faulty analogy An inaccurate or misleading comparison suggesting that because two things are similar in some ways, they are necessarily similar in others. See also *logical fallacy.*

feedback Audience response to a message, which can be conveyed both verbally and nonverbally. Feedback from the audience often indicates whether a speaker's message has been understood and well or poorly received.

field study presentation An oral presentation typically delivered in the context of science-related disciplines, in which the speaker provides (1) an overview of the field research, (2) methods used in the research, (3) analysis of results of the research, (4) time line indicated how results will be used going forward.

"fighting words" Speech that provokes people to violence; not protected under the First Amendment.

"fight-or-flight" response The body's automatic physiological reaction in response to threatening or fear-inducing events, including public speaking.

figure of speech An expression, such as a *metaphor, simile,* or *analogy,* in which words are used in a nonliteral fashion.

First Amendment The amendment to the U.S. Constitution that guarantees freedom of speech ("Congress shall make no law abridging the freedom of speech . . .").

fixed-alternative question A *closed-ended question* that contains a limited choice of answers, such as "Yes," "No," or "Sometimes."

flip chart A large (27–34 inch) pad of paper on which a speaker can illustrate speech points.

flowchart A diagram that shows the step-by-step progression through a procedure, relationship, or process.

forum In ancient Rome, a public space in which people gathered to deliberate about the issues of the day. See also *agora* and *public forum.*

free speech The right to be free from unreasonable constraints on expression.

gender Social or psychological sense of self as corresponding with societal norms associated with masculine or feminine traits.

general speech purpose A statement of the broad speech purpose that answers the question, "Why am I speaking on this topic for this particular audience and occasion?" Usually the general speech purpose is to inform, to persuade, or to celebrate or commemorate a special occasion. See also *specific speech purpose.*

generational identity The collective cultural identity of a generation or cohort.

graph A visual representation of numerical data. Speakers use graphs to illustrate relationships among components or units and to demonstrate trends. Four major types of graphs are line graphs, bar graphs, pie graphs, and pictograms.

group activity presentation An oral presentation that introduces students to an activity and provides them with clear directions for its completion.

group presentation A type of oral presentation prepared and delivered by a group of three or more people.

groupthink The tendency of a group to accept information and ideas without subjecting them to critical analysis.

handout Printed material that conveys information that is either impractical to give to the audience in another manner or intended to be kept by audience members after a presentation.

hasty generalization A fallacy of reasoning in which a speaker attempts to support a claim by asserting that a particular piece of evidence (an isolated instance) is true for all conditions concerned.

hate speech Any offensive communication—verbal or nonverbal—directed against people's race, ethnicity, religion, gender, disability, or other characteristics.

hearing The physiological, largely passive process of perceiving sound. See also *listening*.

heckler's veto Speech meant to drown out a speaker's message; such speech silences freedom of expression.

hierarchy of needs A classic model of human action developed by Abraham Maslow built on the principle that people are motivated to act first on the basis of their elemental needs.

hypothetical example An illustration of something that could happen in the future if certain events were to occur. See also *example* and *extended example*.

identification A feeling of commonality with another; when appropriate, speakers attempt to foster a sense of identification between themselves and audience members.

imagery Colorful and concrete words that appeal to the senses. See also *analogy, metaphor*, and *simile*.

indentation In an outline, the plotting of speech points to indicate their weight relative to one another; subordinate points are placed underneath and to the right of higher-order points.

information Data set in a context for relevance.

informative speaking See *informative speech.*

informative speech A speech providing new information, new insights, or new ways of thinking about a topic. The general purpose of informative speaking is to increase the audience's understanding and awareness of a topic.

initial credibility A stage of *speaker credibility* in which audience members assign credibility to a speaker based on initial impressions, formed by such factors as the speaker's reputation, physical appearance, and non-verbal behavior. See also *derived credibility* and *terminal credibility*.

insider audience See *expert audience.*

integrity The quality of being incorruptible; the unwillingness to compromise for the sake of personal expediency; a component of *ethos* or *speaker credibility*.

internal preview An extended transition that alerts audience members to ensuing speech content.

internal summary An extended transition that draws together important ideas before proceeding to the next speech point.

intonation The rising and falling of voice pitch across phrases and sentences.

introduction (of speech) The first part of a speech, in which the speaker establishes the speech purpose and its relevance to the audience and previews the topic and main points.

invective Abusive speech: accusatory and attacking speech.

jargon Specialized terminology developed within a given endeavor or field of study and which must be translated for lay audiences.

journal article review A presentation (or written report) that reviews and critically assesses the article's ideas for an audience of knowledgeable persons in the discipline.

key-word outline The briefest form of outline; uses the smallest possible units of understanding associated with a specific point to outline the main and supporting points.

lay audience An audience of persons lacking specialized knowledge of the general field related to the speaker's topic and of the topic itself.

lay testimony Firsthand findings, accounts, or opinions from nonexperts such as eyewitnesses.

lazy speech A poor speech habit in which the speaker fails to properly articulate words.

learning style A preferred way of processing information; one learning theory model suggests that there are visual, aural, read/write, and kinesthetic modes of learning.

lecture An informational speech to an audience of student learners.

listening The conscious act of receiving, comprehending, interpreting, and responding to messages. See also *hearing.*

listening distraction Anything that competes for a listener's attention; the source of the distraction may be internal or external. See also *noise.*

literature review presentation An oral presentation in which the speaker reviews the body of research related to a given topic or issue and offers conclusions about the topic based on this research.

logical fallacy A statement that is based on an invalid or a deceptive line of reasoning. See also *ad hominem fallacy*, *bandwagoning*, *begging the question*, *either-or fallacy*, *faulty analogy*, *hasty generalization*, *non sequitur*, and *slippery slope*.

logos The Greek rhetorician Aristotle used this term to refer to persuasive appeals to reason and logic. See also *ethos* and *pathos*.

main points Statements that express the key ideas and major themes of a speech. Their function is to make claims in support of the thesis statement. See also *supporting points*.

malapropism The inadvertent use of a word or phrase in place of one that sounds like it.

mass communication Communication that occurs between a speaker and a large audience of unknown people. The receivers of the message are not present with the speaker or are part of such an immense crowd that there can be little or no interaction between speaker and listener. Television, radio news broadcasts, and mass rallies are examples of mass communication.

message The content of the communication process—thoughts and ideas put into meaningful expressions.

metaphor A figure of speech used to make implicit comparisons without the use of "like" or "as" (e.g., "Love is a rose"). See also *analogy* and *simile*.

misinformation Information that is false.

mixed audience An audience composed of a combination of persons—some with expert knowledge of the field and topic and others with no specialized knowledge.

mixed metaphor A comparison that juxtaposes two unlike, often clichéd, expressions, such as "He went off the deep end like a bull in a china shop."

model A three-dimensional, scale-size representation of an object such as a building.

moderator A person who presides over a discussion or meeting.

motivated sequence pattern An organizational pattern for a persuasive speech based on a five-step process developed by Alan Monroe that begins with arousing attention and ends with calling for action.

motivational warrant A line of reasoning that appeals to the needs, desires, emotions, and values of audience members as the basis for accepting evidence in support of a claim.

motive A predisposition to behave in certain ways.

multimedia effect A learning principle that suggests that we learn better from words and pictures than from words alone, provided that the aids complement, or add to, the information rather than simply match the spoken point.

mumbling Slurring words together at low volume and pitch so they are barely audible.

narrative A story based on personal experiences or imaginary incidents. See also *story*.

narrative pattern A pattern of organizing speech points so that the speech unfolds as a story, with characters, plot, and setting. In practice, this pattern often is combined with other organizational patterns.

noise Anything that interferes with the communication process between a speaker and an audience so that the message cannot be understood; the source may be external (in the environment) or internal (psychological or physical factors).

non sequitur An argument in which the conclusion does not connect to the reasoning.

nonverbal communication Communication other than the spoken word, including body language, voice, and appearance.

nonverbal immediacy Acts that create the perception of psychological closeness between the speaker and audience members.

one-sided message In persuasive speaking, a message that does not mention opposing claims. See also *two-sided message*.

online presentation A presentation delivered over any distance via the internet; can include both real-time and recorded presentations.

open-ended question A survey or interview question designed to allow respondents to elaborate as much as they want. See also *closed-ended question*.

oral citation A speaker's oral acknowledgement of the source of speech material that is derived from other people's ideas.

oral style The specific word choice, sentence structure, and rhetorical devices (techniques of language) that speakers use to express their ideas.

oratory In classical terms, the art of public speaking.

organizational pattern A structure used to organize main points to obtain the speaker's intended purpose. Patterns described in this guide include topical, causal, chronological, spatial, problem-solution, narrative, Monroe's Motivated Sequence, refutation, and comparative advantage.

outline An organizing device that separates main and supporting points—the major speech claims and the evidence to support them—into larger and smaller divisions and subdivisions.

panel discussion A type of oral presentation in which a group of persons (at least three, and generally not more than nine) discusses a topic in the presence of an audience and under the direction of a moderator.

parallelism The arrangement of words, phrases, or sentences in similar grammatical and stylistic form. Parallel structure can help the speaker emphasize important ideas in the speech.

paraphrase A restatement of someone else's statements or written work that alters the form or phrasing but not the substance of that person's ideas. See also *direct quotation* and *summary*.

pathos The Greek rhetoritician used this term to refer to persuasive appeals based on emotion. See also *ethos* and *logos*.

pause A strategic element of a speech used to enhance meaning by providing a type of punctuation, emphasizing a point, drawing attention to a key thought, or just allowing listeners a moment to contemplate what is being said.

performance anxiety A feeling of anxiety that occurs the moment one begins to perform.

peripheral processing A mode of processing a persuasive message that does not consider the quality of the speaker's message but is influenced by such non-content issues as the speaker's appearance or reputation, certain slogans or one-liners, or obvious attempts to manipulate emotions. Peripheral processing of messages occurs when people lack the motivation or the ability to pay close attention to the issues. See also *elaboration likelihood model of persuasion (ELM)* and *central processing*.

persuasive speech A speech whose general purpose is to effect some degree of change in the audience's beliefs, attitudes, values, or behavior.

phrase outline A delivery outline that uses a partial construction of the sentence form of each point, instead of using complete sentences that present the precise wording for each point.

pitch The range of sounds from high to low (or vice versa) determined by the number of vibrations per unit of time; the more vibrations per unit (also called "frequency"), the higher the pitch, and vice versa.

plagiarism The act of using other people's ideas or words without acknowledging the source.

podcast A digital audio recording of a presentation captured and stored in a form accessible via the internet.

policy proposal presentation An oral presentation that offers recommendations for solving a problem or addressing an issue.

positive self-talk A speech anxiety reduction technique of turning negative thoughts to positive ones.

poster presentation A visual presentation on a poster, arranged on a freestanding board, containing a display summarizing a study or an issue for viewing by participants at professional conferences. The speaker prepares brief remarks and remains on hand to answer questions as needed.

preparation anxiety A form of *public speaking anxiety (PSA)* that arises when the speaker begins to prepare for a speech, at which point he or she might feel overwhelmed at the amount of time and planning required. See also *performance anxiety*.

pre-performance anxiety A form of *public speaking anxiety (PSA)* that occurs when a speaker begins to rehearse a speech.

pre-preparation anxiety A form of *public speaking anxiety (PSA)* that arises when a speaker learns he or she must give a speech.

presentation aid A *prop, model, picture, graph, chart, video, audio,* or *multimedia* used alone or in combination to illustrate speech points.

presentational speaking A form of speaking in which individuals or groups deliver reports addressing colleagues, clients, or customers within a business or professional environment.

preview A statement included in the introduction of a speech in which the speaker identifies the main speech points.

primary source Firsthand account or direct evidence of the information involved. See also *secondary source*.

problem-cause-solution pattern A pattern of organizing speech points so that they demonstrate (1) the nature of the problem, (2) reasons for the problem, and (3) proposed solution(s).

problem-solution pattern A pattern of organizing speech points so that they demonstrate the nature and significance of a problem first, and then provide justification for a proposed solution.

process analysis presentation A presentation that describes how an experimental or a mathematical process works and under what conditions it can be used.

program evaluation presentation A report on a program's mission with a description of its accomplishments and how they were measured, and conclusions on how well or poorly the program has met its stated objectives.

progress report A report that updates clients or principals on developments in an ongoing project.

pronunciation The correct formation of word sounds.

prop Any live or inanimate object used by a speaker as a presentation aid.

propaganda Information represented in such a way as to provoke a desired response.

proposal A type of business or professional presentation in which the speaker provides information needed for decisions related to modifying or adopting a product, procedure, or policy.

proposition See *claim.*

prototype A model of a design.

psychographics The study and analysis of audience members' attitudes, beliefs, values, and behavior as they relate to a topic.

public discourse Open conversation or discussion in a public forum.

public domain Bodies of work, including publications and processes, available for public use without permission; not protected by copyright or patent.

public forum Any space (physical or virtual) in which people gather to voice their ideas about public issues.

public speaking A type of communication in which a speaker delivers a message with a specific purpose to an audience of people who are present during the delivery of the speech. Public speaking always includes a speaker who has a reason for speaking, an audience that gives the speaker its attention, and a message that is meant to accomplish a purpose.

public-speaking anxiety (PSA) Fear or anxiety associated with a speaker's actual or anticipated communication to an audience.

quality improvement proposal A report that recommends the adoption of a new (or modified) health practice or policy.

questionnaire A written survey designed to gather information from a large pool of respondents. See also *open-ended question* and *closed-ended question*.

real-time presentation A presentation broadcast at the time of delivery; real-time presentations connect the presenter and the audience live and at the same time. See also *synchronous communication*.

reasoning by analogy Comparing two similar cases to imply that what is true in one case is true in the other. See also *warrant by analogy*.

receiver The recipient(s) of a source's message.

reckless disregard for the truth A quality of statements made with the awareness that they are false; this form of speech is illegal. See also *slander*.

recorded presentation A presentation in which speaker and audience are separated by time and space and the presentation is stored and played back from a digital medium. See also *asynchronous communication*.

refutation pattern A pattern of organizing speech points in which each main point addresses and then refutes an opposing claim to a speaker's position.

report A presentation that includes a systematic and objective description of facts and observations related to business or professional interests.

request for funding presentation An oral presentation providing evidence that a project, proposal, or design idea is worth funding; frequently delivered in technical fields such as engineering, computer science, and architecture.

research presentation A type of oral presentation following the model used in scientific investigations, including an introduction, description of methods, results, and conclusion.

respect To feel or show deferential regard; one of five "ethical ground rules" in public speaking.

responsibility A charge, trust, or duty for which one is accountable.

rhetoric The practice of oratory, or public speaking. More broadly, a term with multiple meanings, all of which relate to aspects of human communication.

rhetorical device A technique of language to achieve a desired effect.

rhetorical question A question that does not invite an actual response but is used to make the audience think.

rhetorical situation The circumstances that call for a public response and for the speech itself; in broad terms, consideration of the audience, occasion, and overall speech context when planning a speech.

roast A humorous tribute to a person; one in which a series of speakers jokingly poke fun at the individual being honored.

roman numeral outline An outline format in which main points are enumerated with roman numerals (I, II, III); supporting points with capital letters (A, B, C); third-level points with Arabic numerals (1, 2, 3); and fourth-level points with lowercase letters (a, b, c).

sales proposal (sales pitch) A type of oral presentation that attempts to lead a potential buyer to purchase a service or product described by the presenter.

scale question A closed-ended question that measures the respondent's level of agreement or disagreement with specific issues. See also *closed-ended question*.

scanning A technique for creating eye contact with audiences; the speaker moves his or her gaze across an audience from one listener to another and from one section to another, pausing to gaze briefly at individual listeners.

screencast (also called "video screen capture") An online presentation that relies on software that captures whatever is displayed on a computer, from text to slides to streaming video.

secondary source Analysis or commentary about things not directly observed or created; news, commentary, and scholarship found in books, articles, and a myriad of sources other than the original. See also *primary source*.

selective perception A psychological principle that posits that listeners pay attention selectively to certain messages and ignore others.

sentence outline An outline in which each main and supporting point is stated in sentence form and in precisely the way the speaker wants to express the idea; generally used for working outlines.

service learning presentation A presentation in which students report on how, as part of their coursework, they helped to address a need or problem in a community agency or nonprofit organization.

shared meaning The mutual understanding of a message between speaker and audience.

shift report An oral report by a health care worker that concisely relays patient status and needs to incoming caregivers.

simile A figure of speech used to compare one thing with another by using the words "like" or "as" (e.g., "He works like a dog"). See also *figure of speech*.

six-by-six rule A rule of design that suggests using no more than six words per line and six lines or bullet points per slide or other visual aid.

slander Defamatory speech.

slippery slope A fallacy of reasoning in which one instance of an event or one small step will necessarily lead to a series of unwanted events or actions.

small group A collection of between three and twenty people.

small group communication Communication involving a small number of people who can see and speak directly with one another, as in a business meeting.

social role In groups, a role that helps facilitate effective group interaction, such as the "harmonizer" or the "gatekeeper." See also *task role*.

socioeconomic status (SES) A cluster of demographic characteristics of audience members, including income, occupation, and education.

source The source, or sender, is the person who creates the message.

source credibility A contemporary term for *ethos*; refers to our level of belief in a source's credentials and track record for providing accurate information.

source qualifier A brief description of the source's qualifications to address the topic (e.g., "Pulitzer-Prize-winning author," "researcher at the Mayo Clinic").

spatial pattern of arrangement A pattern of organizing main points in order of their physical proximity or direction relative to each other; used when the purpose of a speech is to describe or explain the physical arrangement of a place, a scene, or an object.

speaker credibility A modern version of *ethos*; the quality that reveals that a speaker has a good grasp of the subject, displays sound reasoning skills, is honest and non-manipulative, and is genuinely interested in the welfare of audience members. See also *derived credibility, initial credibility* and *terminal credibility*.

speaking extemporaneously A type of delivery that falls somewhere between impromptu and written or memorized delivery. Speakers delivering an extemporaneous speech prepare well and practice in advance, giving full attention to all facets of the speech—content, arrangement, and delivery. Instead of memorizing or writing the speech word for word, they speak from a *key-word outline* or *phrase outline*.

speaking from manuscript A type of delivery in which the speaker reads the speech verbatim—that is, from prepared written text that contains the entire speech, word for word.

speaking from memory A type of delivery in which the speaker puts the entire speech, word for word, into writing and then commits it to memory.

speaking impromptu A type of delivery that is unpracticed, spontaneous, or improvised.

speaking outline A delivery outline to be used when practicing and actually presenting a speech.

speaking rate The pace at which a speech is delivered. The typical public speech occurs at a rate slightly less than between 120–170 words per minute.

special occasion speech A speech whose general purpose is to entertain, celebrate, commemorate, inspire, or set a social agenda.

specific speech purpose A statement of precisely what you want the audience to gain from the speech: "To inform (or persuade) my audience about the factors to consider when purchasing an electric car." See also *general speech purpose*.

speech of acceptance A *special occasion speech* made in response to receiving an award with the purpose of expressing gratitude for the honor bestowed on the speaker.

speech of inspiration A *special occasion speech* whose purpose is to inspire or motivate the audience to consider positively, reflect on, and sometimes even to act on the speaker's words.

speech of introduction A short *special occasion speech* defined by two goals: to prepare or "warm up" audience members for the main speaker and to motivate them to listen to what the speaker has to say.

speech of presentation A *special occasion speech* whose purpose is twofold: to communicate the meaning of the award and to explain why the recipient is receiving it.

staff report A presentation that informs managers and other employees of new developments relating to personnel that affect them and their work.

statistic Quantified evidence; data that measure the size or magnitude of something, demonstrate trends, or show relationships with the purpose of summarizing information, demonstrating proof, and making points memorable.

stereotyping The act of generalizing about an apparent characteristic of a person or a group's culture or ethnicity that falsely claims to define all of its members.

story An account of events. See also *narrative*.

subordinate points Speech points subordinate to others are given relatively less weight. In an outline, they are indicated by their indentation below the more important points. See also *coordinate points* and *supporting points*.

substantive warrant A warrant that relies on factual evidence to link a claim to evidence. See also *warrant by analogy* and *warrant by cause*.

summary (of supporting material) A brief overview of someone else's ideas, opinions, or theories. See also *direct quotation* and *paraphrase*.

supporting material Examples, narratives, testimony, facts, and statistics that support the speech thesis and form the speech.

supporting points Subordinate speech points which elaborate on and verify the speaker's main points.

symposium A formal meeting at which several speakers deliver short speeches on different aspects of the same topic.

synchronous communication Communication in which interaction between speaker and receiver occurs simultaneously. See also *asynchronous communication*.

table A systematic grouping of data or other information in column form.

talking head A speaker who remains static, standing stiffly behind a podium, and so resembles a televised shot of a speaker's head and shoulders.

target audience Those individuals within the broader audience who are most likely to be influenced in the direction the speaker seeks.

task role A type of role that directly relates to the accomplishment of the objectives and missions of a group. Examples include "recording secretary" and "moderator." See also *social role*.

terminal credibility A stage of *speaker credibility* in which the audience assigns the speaker credibility based on the totality of the audience's impressions of the speaker's performance, from start to finish. See also *derived credibility* and *initial credibility*.

testimony Firsthand findings, eyewitness accounts, and opinions by people, both lay (nonexpert) and expert.

thesis statement The theme, or central idea, of a speech that serves to connect all the parts of the speech in a single line. The main points, supporting material, and conclusion all bear upon the thesis.

toast A brief tribute to a person or an event being celebrated.

topic (mind) mapping A brainstorming technique in which you lay out words in diagram form to show categorical relationships among them; useful for selecting and narrowing a speech topic.

topical pattern of arrangement (also called *categorical pattern*) A pattern of organizing main points as subtopics or categories of the speech topic.

town hall meeting A *public forum* in which citizens deliberate on issues of importance to the community.

transition A word, phrase, or sentence that ties speech ideas together and enables a speaker to move smoothly from one point to the next.

trustworthiness The quality in public speaking of displaying both honesty and dependability.

two-sided message An argument in which the speaker mentions opposing points of view and sometimes refutes them. See also *one-sided message*.

values Our most enduring judgments or standards about what is good and bad in life, as shaped by our culture and our unique experiences within it.

vernacular language Language specific to particular regions of a country.

video capture software Software used to incorporate video clips into an online presentation.

visualization The practice of summoning feelings and actions consistent with successful performance; useful for speakers in overcoming speech anxiety.

vocal filler Unnecessary and undesirable sound or word used by a speaker to cover pauses in a speech or conversation, such as "uh," "hmm," "you know," "I mean," and "it's like."

vocal variety The variation of volume, pitch, rate, and pauses to create an effective vocal delivery.

vodcast (also called "vidcast" and "video podcasting") A podcast containing video clips.

voice A feature of verbs in written and spoken text indicating the subject's relationship to the action; verbs can be in either active voice or passive voice.

volume The relative loudness of a speaker's voice while giving a speech.

voluntary audience As opposed to a *captive audience,* an audience whose members have chosen to attend.

warrant A line of reasoning that justifies the link between a *claim* and *evidence* in the minds of the audience. See also *authoritative warrant* and *reasoning.*

warrant by analogy (also called *reasoning by analogy*) A means of justifying the link between claim and evidence by comparing two similar cases and implying that what is true for one case is true for the other.

warrant by cause (also called *causal reasoning*) A means of justifying the link between claim and evidence by providing a cause-effect relationship as proof of the claim.

webinar A real-time presentation, including training sessions, seminars, and other presentations that connect presenters and audiences from their desktops, regardless of where they are in the world.

word association A brainstorming technique used to generate and narrow speech topics in which one writes down ideas as they come to mind, beginning with a single word.

working outline A preparation or rough outline, often using full sentences, in which the speaker firms up and organizes speech points and incorporates material to support them.

Notes ●●●●

CHAPTER 1

1. "Why Warren Buffett's Most Valuable Skill Wasn't from a Diploma," Fox on Stocks, December 19, 2012, www.foxonstocks.com/why-warrenbuffetts-most -valuable0skill-wasn't-from-a-diploma/.

2. "Youth Voting," Center for Information and Research on Civic Learning and Engagement (CIRCLE), accessed November 8, 2017, civicyouth.org /quick-facts/youth-voting.

3. For a discussion of Daniel Yankelovich's three-step process by which public judgments occur, see Yankelovich, *Coming to Public Judgment: Making Democracy Work in a Complex World* (Syracuse, NY: Syracuse University Press, 1991).

4. For a discussion of conversation stoppers and rules of engagement, see W. Barnett Pearce, "Toward a National Conversation about Public Issues," in *The Changing Conversation in America: Lectures from the Smithsonian,* eds. William F. Eadie and Paul E. Nelson (Thousand Oaks, CA: Sage, 2002), 16.

5. Robert Perrin, "The Speaking-Writing Connection: Enhancing the Symbiotic Relationship," *Contemporary Education* 65 (1994): 62–64.

6. Kristine Bruss, "Writing for the Ear: Strengthening Oral Style in Manuscript Speeches," *Communication Teacher* 26, no. 2 (April 2012): 76–81.

7. Lloyd F. Bitzer, "The Rhetorical Situation," *Philosophy and Rhetoric* (Winter 1968): 1–14.

CHAPTER 3

1. Michael J. Beatty, "Situational and Predispositional Correlates of Public Speaking Anxiety," *Communication Education* 37 (1988): 28–39; Ralph Behnke and Chris R. Sawyer, "Milestones of Anticipatory Public Speaking Anxiety," *Communication Education* 48 (1999): 165–72; Graham D. Bodie, "A Racing Heart, Rattling Knees, and Ruminative Thoughts: Defining, Explaining, and Treating Public Speaking Anxiety," *Communication Education* 59 (2010): 70–105.

2. Behnke and Sawyer, "Milestones of Anticipatory Public Speaking Anxiety."

3. Behnke and Sawyer, "Milestones of Anticipatory Public Speaking Anxiety."

4. David-Paul Pertaub, Mel Slater, and Chris Barker, "An Experiment on Public Speaking Anxiety in Response to Three Different Types of Virtual Audience," *Presence: Teleoperators and Virtual Environments* 11 (2002): 670–78.

5. Joe Ayres, "Coping with Speech Anxiety: The Power of Positive Thinking," *Communication Education* 37 (1988): 289–96; Joe Ayres, "An Examination of the Impact of Anticipated Communication and Communication Apprehension on Negative Thinking, Task-Relevant Thinking, and Recall," *Communication Research Reports* 9 (1992): 3–11.

6. Pamela J. Feldman, Sheldon Cohen, Natalie Hamrick, and Stephen J. Lepore, "Psychological Stress, Appraisal, Emotion, and Cardiovascular Response in a Public Speaking Task," *Psychology and Health* 19 (2004): 353–68; Senqi Hu and Juong-Min Romans-Kroll, "Effects of Positive Attitude toward Giving a Speech on Cardiovascular and Subjective Fear Responses during Speech on Anxious Subjects," *Perceptual and Motor Skills* 81 (1995): 609–10.

7. Richard Branson, "Richard Branson on How to Calm Public Speaking Jitters," *Fortune,* January 12, 2015, fortune.com/2015/01/12/richard-branson-on-how -to-calm-public-speaking-jitters/.

8. Joe Ayres and Tim Hopf, "Visualization: Is It More Than Extra Attention?" *Communication Education* 38 (1989): 1–5; Joe Ayers and Tim Hopf, *Coping with Speech Anxiety* (Norwood, NJ: Ablex, 1993); Joe Ayres, Chia-Fang "Sandy" Hsu, and Tim Hopf, "Does Exposure to Visualization Alter Speech Preparation Processes?" *Communication Research Reports* 17 (2000): 366–74.

9. Ayres and Hopf, "Visualization," 2–3.

10. Herbert Benson and Miriam Z. Klipper, *The Relaxation Response* (New York: HarperCollins, 2000).

11. Laurie Schloff and Marcia Yudkin, *Smart Speaking* (New York: Plume, 1991), 91–92.

12. Lars-Gunnar Lundh, Britta Berg, Helena Johansson, Linda Kjellén Nilsson, Jenny Sandberg, and Anna Segerstedt, "Social Anxiety Is Associated with a Negatively Distorted Perception of One's Own Voice," *Cognitive Behavior Therapy* 31 (2002): 25–30.

CHAPTER 4

1. *Oxford English Dictionary*, s. v. "responsibility," accessed September 26, 2017, www.oed.com/view/Entry/163862?redirectedFrom=responsibility.
2. Richard L. Johannesen, Kathleen S. Valde, and Karen E. Whedbee, *Ethics in Human Communication*, 6th ed. (Long Grove, IL: Waveland Press, 2007).
3. Edward P. J. Corbett, *Classical Rhetoric for the Modern Student* (New York: Oxford University Press, 1990).
4. Shalom H. Schwartz, "An Overview of the Schwartz Theory of Basic Values," *Online Readings in Psychology and Culture* 2, no. 1 (2012), dx.doi .org/10.9707/2307-0919.1116.
5. Betsy Cooper et al., "How Americans View Immigrants and What They Want from Immigration Reform: Findings from the 2015 American Values Atlas," *Public Religion Research Institute*, March 29, 2016, www.prri.org/research/poll -immigration-reform-views-on-immigrants/.
6. Douglas M. Fraleigh and Joseph S. Tuman, *Freedom of Speech in the Marketplace of Ideas* (New York: Bedford/St. Martin's, 1997).
7. Newseum Institute, "First Amendment FAQ," www.newseuminstitute .org/first-amendment-center/first-amendment-faq/#speech.
8. William B. Gudykunst et al., *Building Bridges: Interpersonal Skills for a Changing World* (Boston: Houghton Mifflin, 1995), 92.
9. Michael Josephson, *Making Ethical Decisions: The Six Pillars of Character* (Josephson Institute of Ethics, 2002).
10. Josephson, *Making Ethical Decisions*.
11. Josephson, *Making Ethical Decisions*.
12. U.S. Copyright Office, accessed September 26, 2017, www.copyright.gov.
13. U.S. Copyright Office, "Fair Use," accessed September 26, 2017, www .copyright.gov/fair-use/more-info.html.

CHAPTER 5

1. Andrew D. Wolvin and Carolyn G. Coakley, "A Listening Taxonomy," in *Perspectives on Listening*, eds. Andrew D. Wolvin and Carolyn G. Coakley (Norwood, NJ: Ablex, 1993), 15–22.
2. "An ILA Definition of Listening," *Listening Post* 53, no. 1 (1995): 4–5.
3. Ethel Glenn, "A Content Analysis of Fifty Definitions of Listening," *Journal of the International Listening Association* 3 (1989): 21–31.
4. Laura A. Janusik and Andrew D. Wolvin, "24 Hours in a Day: Listening Update to the Time Studies," *International Journal of Listening* 23 (2009): 104–20; see also Richard Emanuel et al., "How College Students Spend Their Time Communicating," *International Journal of Listening* 22 (2008): 13–28.
5. Janusik and Wolvin, "24 Hours in a Day."
6. Avraham N. Kluger and Keren Zaidel, "Are Listeners Perceived as Leaders?" *International Journal of Listening* 27, no. 2 (2013): 73–84; S. A. Welch and William T. Mickelson, "A Listening Competence Comparison of Working Professionals," *International Journal of Listening* 27, no. 2 (2013): 85–99.
7. Albert H. Hastorf and Hadley Cantril, "They Saw a Game: A Case Study," *Journal of Abnormal and Social Psychology* 49, no. 1 (1954): 129–34; Gordon W. Allport and Lee J. Postman, "The Basic Psychology of Rumor," *Transactions of the New York Academy of Sciences* 8 (1945): 61–81.
8. Thomas E. Anastasi Jr., *Listen! Techniques for Improving Communication Skills* (Boston: CBI Publishing, 1982).
9. Christian Kiewitz et al., "Cultural Differences in Listening Style Preferences: A Comparison of Young Adults in Germany, Israel, and the United States," *International Journal of Public Opinion Research* 9, no. 3 (1997): 233–47, search .proquest.com/docview/60068159?accountid=10965; M. Imhof and L. A. Janusik, "Development and Validation of the Imhof Janusik Listening Concepts

Inventory to Measure Listening Conceptualization Differences between Cultures," *Journal of Intercultural Communication Research* 35, no. 2 (2006): 79–98.

10. Ronald D. Gordon, "Communication, Dialogue, and Transformation," *Human Communication* 9, no. 1 (2006): 17–30.

11. James Floyd, "Provocation: Dialogic Listening as Reachable Goal," *International Journal of Listening* 24 (2010): 170–73.

CHAPTER 6

1. Pablo Briñol and Richard E. Petty, "The History of Attitudes and Persuasion Research," *Handbook of the History of Social Psychology,* eds. Arie Kruglanski and Wolfgang Stroebe (New York: Psychology Press, 2011).

2. Richard E. Petty and John T. Cacioppo, *Attitudes and Persuasion: Classic and Contemporary Approaches* (Dubuque, IA: Wm. C. Brown, 1981); M. Fishbein and I. Ajzen, *Belief, Attitude, Intention, and Behavior: An Introduction to Theory and Research* (Reading, MA: Addison-Wesley, 1975); I. Ajzen and M. Fishbein, "The Influence of Attitudes on Behavior," *The Handbook of Attitudes,* eds. Dolores Albarracín, Blair T. Johnson, and Mark P. Zanna (Mahwah, NJ: Erlbaum, 2005), 173–221.

3. Richard E. Petty, S. Christian Wheeler, and Zakary L. Tormala, "Persuasion and Attitude Change," *Handbook of Psychology, Personality, and Social Psychology,* Vol. 5, eds. Theodore Millon, Melvin Lerner, and Irving B. Weiner (New York: John Wiley & Sons, 2003).

4. *The Stanford Encyclopedia of Philosophy,* s.v. "Belief," Winter 2011 edition, plato.stanford.edu/archives/win2011/entries/belief/.

5. N. Belden, J. Russonello, and V. Breglio, "Human Values and Nature's Future: Americans' Attitudes on Biological Diversity," 1995, public opinion survey analysis conducted for the Communications Consortium Media Center.

6. Herbert Simon, *Persuasion in Society,* 2nd ed. (New York: Routledge, 2011).

7. Simon, *Persuasion in Society.*

8. Kenneth Burke, *A Rhetoric of Motives* (Berkeley, CA: University of California Press, 1969).

9. See, for example, "Millennials, Gen X and Baby Boomers: Who's Working at Your Company and What Do They Think about Ethics?" Ethics Resource Center, 2009 National Business Ethics Survey Supplemental Research Brief, http://observgo.uquebec.ca/observgo/fichiers/53123_DAEPI%202.pdf; Dennis McCafferty, "Workforce Preview: What to Expect from Gen Z," *Baseline Magazine,* April 4, 2013, www.baselinemag.com/it-management/slideshows/workforce-preview-what-to-expect-from-gen-z; "Generations: Demographic Trends in Population and Workforce," Catalyst, May 1, 2012, www.catalyst.org/knowledge/generations-demographic-trends-population-and-workforce.

10. Jere R. Behrman and Nevzer Stacey, eds., *The Social Benefits of Education* (Ann Arbor, MI: University of Michigan Press, 2000).

11. "America's Changing Religious Landscape," Pew Research Center, May 12, 2015, www.pewforum.org/2015/05/12/americas-changing-religious-landscape/.

12. Daniel Canary and Kathryn Dindia, eds., *Sex Differences and Similarities in Communication,* 2nd ed. (Mahwah, NJ: Erlbaum, 2006).

13. U.S. Census Bureau Newsroom, June 2, 2016, accessed September 6, 2016, www.census.gov/newsroom/facts-for-features/2016/cb16-ff12.html.

14. U.S. Department of Education, National Center for Education Statistics, April 2016, "Digest of Education Statistics, 2014," nces.ed.gov/pubs2016/2016006.pdf.

15. U.S. Census Bureau, June 2, 2016, accessed January 25, 2018, www.census.gov/quickfacts/fact/table/US/PST045217.

16. "Facts on U.S. Immigrants, 2015," Pew Research Center, May 3, 2017, www.pewhispanic.org/2017/05/03/facts-on-u-s-immigrants/.

17. Steven A. Camarota and Karen Zeigler, "Nearly 65 Million U.S. Residents Spoke a Foreign Language at Home in 2015," Center for Immigration Studies, October 18, 2016, https://cis.org/Report/Nearly-65-Million-US-Residents-Spoke-Foreign-Language-Home-2015.

18. Edward D. Steele and W. Charles Redding, "The American Value System: Premises for Persuasion," *Western Speech* 26 (1962): 83–91; Robin M. Williams

Jr., *American Society: A Sociological Interpretation,* 3rd ed. (New York: Alfred A. Knopf, 1970).

19. World Values Survey Wave 2 1990-1994 OFFICIAL AGGREGATE v.20140429. World Values Survey Association (www.worldvaluessurvey.org). Aggregate File Producer: Asep/JDS, Madrid SPAIN.

20. Rushworth M. Kidder, *Shared Values for a Troubled World: Conversations with Men and Women of Conscience* (San Francisco: Jossey-Bass Publishers, 1994).

CHAPTER 8

1. Ian McEwan, "Freedom of Expression Sustains All Other Freedoms We Enjoy," *Vital Speeches of the Day,* Vol. XXXI, No. 8, August 2015, pp. 245–47.

2. Jonathan Drori, "Every Pollen Grain Has a Story," TED Talks, February 2010, www.ted.com/talks/jonathan_drori_every_pollen_grain_has_a_story.html.

3. Quoted in Katharine Q. Seelye, "Congressman Offers Bill to Ban Cloning of Humans," *New York Times,* March 6, 1997, sec. A.

4. Mark Turner, *The Literary Mind* (New York: Oxford University Press, 1996).

5. Melinda French Gates, "Raising the Bar on College Completion," Keynote Address, American Association of Community Colleges, April 20, 2010, www.gatesfoundation.org/media-center/speeches/2010/04/raising-the-bar-on-college-completion.

6. Steven D. Cohen, "The Art of Public Narrative: Teaching Students How to Construct Memorable Anecdotes," *Communication Teacher* 25, no. 4, (2011): 197–204, doi: 10.1080/17404622.2011.601726.

7. Jim Carrey, Commencement Address, Maharishi University of Management, May 24, 2014, www.mum.cdu/whats-happcning/graduation-2014/full-jim-carrey-address-video-and-transcript/.

8. Nick Morgan, "Why You Must Tell Stories, Not Dump Information, in Your Presentations," *Forbes,* May 9, 2013, www.forbes.com/sites/nickmorgan/2013/05/09/why-you-must-tell-stories-not-dump-information-in-your-presentations/#426926dd78bb; Kurt Braddock and James Price Dillard, "Meta-analytic Evidence for the Persuasive Effect of Narratives on Beliefs, Attitudes, Intentions, and Behaviors," *Communication Monographs,* 2016, doi:10.1080/03637.

9. Yaacov Schul and Ruth Mayo, "Two Sources Are Better Than One: The Effects of Ignoring One Message on Using a Different Message from the Same Source," *Journal of Experimental Social Psychology* 35 (1999): 327–45; Mike Allen et al., "Testing the Persuasiveness of Evidence: Combining Narrative and Statistical Forms," *Communication Research Reports* 17 (2000): 331–36, cited in Rodney A. Reynolds and J. Lynn Reynolds, "Evidence," in *The Persuasion Handbook: Developments in Theory and Practice,* eds. James Price Dillard and Michael Pfau (Thousand Oaks, CA: Sage, 2002), 427–44, doi: 10.4135/9781412976046.n22.

10. Reynolds and Reynolds, "Evidence."

11. "Airbus delivers 110th A380," Airbus, March 14, 2013, http://www.airbus.com/newsroom/press-releases/en/2013/03/airbus-delivers-100th-a380.html.

12. Josh Katz, "Drug Deaths in America Are Rising Faster Than Ever," *New York Times,* June 5, 2017, www.nytimes.com/interactive/2017/06/05/upshot/opioid-epidemic-drug-overdose-deaths-are-rising-faster-than-ever.html.

13. "State and County QuickFacts," U.S. Census Bureau, accessed October 3, 2017, https://www.census.gov/quickfacts/fact/table/CO/PST045217# viewtop.

14. Katz, "Drug Deaths in America Are Rising Faster Than Ever."

15. Bureau of Labor Statistics, "State Employment and Unemployment Summary," Sept. 15, 2017, www.bls.gov/news.release/laus.nr0.htm.

16. Maddy Osman, "18 Instagram Stats Every Marketer Should Know for 2017," Sprout Social, August 2, 2017, sproutsocial.com/insights/instagram-stats/.

17. Roger Pielke Jr., "The Cherry Pick," *Ogmius: Newsletter for the Center for Science and Technology Research* 8 (2004), sciencepolicy.colorado.edu/ogmius/archives/issue_8/intro.html.

CHAPTER 9

1. Elizabeth Kirk (original author), "Information and Its Counterfeits," Sheridan Libraries of Johns Hopkins University, August 10, 2017, guides .library.jhu.edu/c.php?g=202581&p=1334961; Man-pui Sally Chan et al., "Debunking: A Meta-Analysis of the Psychological Efficacy of Messages Countering Misinformation," *Psychological Science,* September 2017, doi:10.1177/0956797617714579.

CHAPTER 10

1. Ralph Underwager and Hollida Wakefield, "The Taint Hearing," paper presented at the 13th Annual Symposium in Forensic Psychology, Vancouver, BC, April 17, 1997, www.ipt-forensics.com/journal/volume10/j10_7.htm#en0.
2. Institute for Writing and Rhetoric, "Sources and Citation at Dartmouth College," produced by the Committee on Sources, May 2008, writing-speech .dartmouth.edu/learning/materials/sources-and-citations-dartmouth#3A.

CHAPTER 11

1. Gordon H. Bower, "Organizational Factors in Memory," *Cognitive Psychology* 1 (1970): 18–46.
2. Ian McEwan, "Freedom of Expression Sustains All the Other Freedoms We Enjoy," *Vital Speeches of the Day,* Vol. LXXXI, No. 8, August 2015.
3. Hermann Ebbinghaus, *On Memory: A Contribution to Experimental Psychology* (New York: Teachers College, 1813); Murray Glanzer and Anita R. Cunitz, "Two Storage Mechanisms in Free Recall," *Journal of Verbal Learning and Verbal Behavior* 5 (1966): 351–60.

CHAPTER 12

1. Raymond G. Smith, "Effects of Speech Organization upon Attitudes of College Students," *Speech Monographs* 18 (1951): 547–49; Ernest Thompson, "An Experimental Investigation of the Relative Effectiveness of Organizational Structure in Oral Communication," *Southern Speech Journal* 26 (1960): 59–69.
2. Melissa Del Bosque, "Beyond the Border: Into the Wilderness," *The Guardian,* August 6, 2014, www.theguardian.com/world/ng-interactive/2014 /aug/06/-sp-texas-border-deadliest-state-undocumented-migrants.
3. Randy Capps, Michael Fix, and Jie Zong, "A Profile of U.S. Children with Unauthorized Immigrant Parents," Migration Policy Institute Fact Sheet, January, 2016, www.migrationpolicy.org/research/profile-us-children-unauthorized -immigrant-parents.
4. Capps, Fix, and Zong, "A Profile of U.S. Children with Unauthorized Immigrant Parents."
5. Capps, Fix, and Zong, "A Profile of U.S. Children with Unauthorized Immigrant Parents."
6. Brian Eakin, "Homeland Security Grilled on Visa Overstays," Courthouse News Service, June 14, 2016, www.courthousenews.com/2016/06/14 /homeland-security-grilled-on-visa-overstays.htm.
7. Eakin, "Homeland Security Grilled on Visa Overstays."
8. Joe Davidson, "Visa Overstays a Security Risk When 99% of Foreigners Leave U.S. on Time?" *Washington Post,* June 15, 2016, www.washingtonpost .com/news/powerpost/wp/2016/06/15/visa-overstays-a-security-risk -when-99-of-foreigners-leave-u-s-on-time/.
9. Jie Zong and Jeanne Batalova, "Frequently Requested Statistics on Immigrants and Immigration in the United States," Migration Policy Institute, March 8, 2017, www.migrationpolicy.org/article/frequently-requested-statistics -immigrants-and-immigration-united-states.
10. "How the United States Immigration System Works: A Fact Sheet," American Immigration Council, August 12, 2016, www.immigrationpolicy.org/just-facts /how-united-states-immigration-system-works-fact-sheet.
11. Guillermo Cantor, Mark Noferi, and Daniel E. Martinez, "Enforcement Overdrive: A Comprehensive Assessment of ICE's Criminal Alien Program,"

American Immigration Council, November 1, 2015, www.immigrationpolicy .org/special-reports/enforcement-overdrive-comprehensive-assessment -criminal-alien-program.

12. "Life on the Internet Timeline," Public Broadcasting System, accessed April 3, 2000, www.pbs.org/internet/timeline/index.html.

CHAPTER 13

1. Mark B. McClellan, fifth annual David A. Winston lecture, National Press Club, Washington, DC, October 20, 2003, www.fda.gov/newsevents/speeches /speecharchives/ucm053609.htm.

CHAPTER 14

1. Jeremey Donovan, *How to Deliver a TED Talk* (CreateSpace Independent Publishing Platform, 2012).

2. Laurie Loisel, "Twitter Exec tells UMASS Amherst Grads to 'Hack the System,'" *Boston Globe*, May 6, 2016, www.bostonglobe.com/metro/2016/05/06/twitter -exec-tells-umass-amherst-grads-hack-system/uAYypkmN3v1QlHMSsaIyaJ /story.html.

3. William Safire, *Lend Me Your Ears: Great Speeches in History* (New York: Norton, 1992), 676.

4. Bas Andeweg and Jap de Jong, "May I Have Your Attention? Exordial Techniques in Informative Oral Presentations," *Technical Communication Quarterly* 7, no. 3 (Summer 1998): 271–84.

5. Nancy Duarte, *Harvard Business Review Guide to Persuasive Presentations* (Boston: Harvard Business Review Press, 2012).

6. Phillip Connor and Jens Manuel Krogstad, "Key Facts About the World's Refugees," Pew Research Center FactTank, October 5, 2016, www.pewresearch .org/fact-tank/2016/10/05/key-facts-about-the-worlds-refugees/.

7. Jamie Oliver, "Teach Every Child about Food," filmed February 2010, TED video, www.ted.com/talks/jamie_oliver.

8. Marvin Runyon, "No One Moves the Mail Like the U.S. Postal Service," *Vital Speeches of the Day* 61, no. 2 (1994): 52–55.

9. Robert L. Darbelnet, "U.S. Roads and Bridges: Highway Funding at a Crossroads," *Vital Speeches of the Day* 63, no. 12 (1997): 379.

10. Holger Kluge, "Reflections on Diversity," *Vital Speeches of the Day* 63, no. 6 (1997): 171–72.

11. Elpidio Villarreal, "Choosing the Right Path," *Vital Speeches of the Day* 72, no. 26 (2007): 784–86.

12. Emma Watson, "Gender Equality Is Your Issue Too," UN Women, September 20, 2014, www.unwomen.org/en/news/stories/2014/9/emma-watson-gender -equality-is-your-issue-too.

CHAPTER 15

1. Kristine Bruss, "Writing for the Ear: Strengthening Oral Style in Manuscript Speeches," *Communication Teacher* 26, no.2 (April 2012): 76–81.

2. Bourree Lam, "What It Was Like to Write Speeches for Apple Executives," *The Atlantic*, June 10, 2016, www.theatlantic.com/business/archive/2016/06 /speechwriter-poet/486329/.

3. Peggy Noonan, *Simply Speaking: How to Communicate Your Ideas with Style, Substance, and Clarity* (New York: Regan Books, 1998), 51.

4. Michelle Obama, "Remarks by the First Lady at the Democratic National Convention," delivered at the Wells Fargo Center, Philadelphia, PA. The White House Briefing Room, July 25, 2016.

5. Dan Hooley, "The Lessons of the Ring," *Vital Speeches of the Day* 70, no. 20 (2004): 660–63.

6. Sheryl Sandberg, "Why We Have Too Few Women Leaders," TED Talks, December 2010, www.ted.com/talks/sheryl_sandberg_why_we_have_too_few _women_leaders.html.

7. Susan T. Fiske and Shelley E. Taylor, "Vivid Information Is More Easily Recalled Than Dull or Pallid Stimuli," *Social Cognition*, 2nd ed. (New York:

McGraw Hill), quoted in Jennifer Jerit and Jason Barabas, "Bankrupt Rhetoric: How Misleading Information Affects Knowledge about Social Security," *Public Opinion Quarterly* 70, no. 3 (2006): 278–304.

8. Loren J. Naidoo and Robert G. Lord, "Speech Imagery and Perceptions of Charisma: The Mediating Role of Positive Affect," *Leadership Quarterly* 19, no. 3 (2008): 283–96.

9. Franklin D. Roosevelt, address delivered on July 4, 1942, Fourth of July Celebrations Database, gurukul.american.edu/heintze/Roosevelt.htm.

10. Donald J. Trump, Inaugural Address, January 20, 2017, www.whitehouse.gov/inaugural-address.

11. L. Clemetson and J. Gordon-Thomas, "Our House Is on Fire," *Newsweek,* June 11, 2001, 50.

12. Gloria Anzaldúa, "Entering into the Serpent," in *The St. Martin's Handbook,* eds. Andrea Lunsford and Robert Connors, 3rd ed. (New York: St. Martin's Press, 1995), 25.

13. P. H. Matthews, *The Concise Oxford Dictionary of Linguistics* (New York: Oxford University Press, 1997).

14. Cited in William Safire, *Lend Me Your Ears: Great Speeches in History* (New York: Norton, 1992), 22.

15. "Barack Obama's New Hampshire Primary Speech," *New York Times,* January 8, 2008, www.nytimes.com/2008/01/08/us/politics/08text-obama.html?r=0.

CHAPTER 16

1. James A. Winans, *Public Speaking* (New York: Century, 1925). Professor Winans was among the first Americans to contribute significantly to the study of rhetoric. His explanation of delivery is considered by many to be the best coverage of the topic in the English language. His perspective infuses this chapter.

CHAPTER 17

1. Kyle James Tusing and James Price Dillard, "The Sounds of Dominance: Vocal Precursors of Perceived Dominance during Interpersonal Influence," *Human Communication Research* 26 (2000): 148–71.

2. Carmine Gallo, *Talk Like TED* (New York: St Martin's Press, 2014), 97.

CHAPTER 18

1. C. F. Bond and the Global Deception Research Team, "A World of Lies," *Journal of Cross-Cultural Psychology* 37 (2006): 60–74; Timothy R. Levine, Kelli Jean K. Asada, and Hee Sun Park, "The Lying Chicken and the Gaze Avoidant Egg: Eye Contact, Deception, and Causal Order," *Southern Communication Journal* 71 (2006): 401–11.

2. Eva Krumburger, "Effects of Dynamic Attributes of Smiles in Human and Synthetic Faces: A Simulated Job Interview Setting," *Journal of Nonverbal Behavior* 33 (2009): 1–15.

3. Alissa Melinger and Willem M. Levelt, "Gesture and the Communicative Intention of the Speaker," *Gesture* 4 (2004): 119–41.

4. Virginia P. Richmond, James C. McCroskly, and Aaron D. Johnson, "Development of the Nonverbal Immediacy Scale (NIS): Measures of Self- and Other-Perceived Nonverbal Immediacy," *Communication Quarterly* 51, no. 4 (2003): 504–17.

CHAPTER 19

1. Richard E. Mayer, *The Multimedia Principle* (New York: Cambridge University Press, 2001).

2. See discussion of the redundancy effect in Richard E. Mayer, ed., *The Cambridge Handbook of Multimedia Learning* (New York: Cambridge University Press, 2005).

3. Gary Jones, "Message First: Using Films to Power the Point," *Business Communication Quarterly* 67, no. 1 (2004): 88–91.

CHAPTER 20

1. Nancy Duarte, "Avoiding the Road to PowerPoint Hell," *Wall Street Journal*, January 22, 2011, https://www.wsj.com/articles/SB10001424052748703954004 576090053995594270.

2. Nancy Duarte, *slide:ology: The Art and Science of Creating Great Presentations* (Sebastopol, CA: O'Reilly Media, 2008), 140.

3. Duarte, "Avoiding the Road to PowerPoint Hell."

4. Edward Tufte, *The Visual Display of Quantitative Information* (Cheshire, CT: Graphics Press, 2001); Edward Tufte, "PowerPoint Is Evil," *Wired* 11 (2003), www.wired.com/wired/archive/11.09/ppt2_pr.html.

5. Ronald Larson, "Slide Composition for Electronic Presentations," *Journal of Educational Computing Research*, 31, no. 1 (2004): 61–76.

CHAPTER 22

1. Katherine E. Rowan subdivides informative communication into informatory discourse, in which the primary aim is to represent reality by increasing an audience's awareness of some phenomenon; and explanatory discourse, with the aim to represent reality by deepening understanding. See Katherine E. Rowan, "Informing and Explaining Skills: Theory and Research on Informative Communication," in *Handbook of Communication and Social Interaction Skills*, eds. John O. Greene and Brant R. Burleson (Mahwah, NJ: Erlbaum, 2003), 403–38.

2. Vickie K. Sullivan, "Public Speaking: The Secret Weapon in Career Development," *USA Today* 113, no. 2720 (May 2005): 24.

3. Nick Morgan, "Two Rules for a Successful Presentation," *Harvard Business Review* Blog ("Communication"), May 14, 2010, hbr.org/2010/05/two-rules -for-a-successful-pre; Harry E. Chambers, *Effective Communication Skills for Scientific and Technical Professionals* (Cambridge, MA: Perseus Publishing, 2001).

4. United States National Archives and Record Administration, "U.S. Electoral College: About the Electors," accessed October 27, 2017, www.archives.gov /federal-register/electoral-college/electors.html.

5. Shawn M. Glynn et al., "Teaching Science with Analogies: A Resource for Teachers and Textbook Authors," *National Reading Research Center: Instructional Resource*, 7 (Fall 1994).

6. Wolfgang Porod, "Nanotechnology," *Vital Speeches of the Day* 71, no. 4 (2004): 125–28.

7. Shawn M. Glynn et al., "Teaching Science," 19.

8. Helen Osborne, "It's Like What You Already Know: Using Analogies to Help Patients Understand," January 1, 2003, healthliteracy.com/2003/01/01/analogies/.

9. Neil D. Fleming and Colleen Mills, "Helping Students Understand How They Learn," *Teaching Professor* 7, no. 4 (1992).

CHAPTER 23

1. Carolyn W. Sherif, Muzafer Sherif, and Roger E. Nebergall, *Attitude and Attitude Change: The Social Judgment-Involvement Approach* (Philadelphia: W. B. Saunders, 1965).

2. W. Hart et al., "Feeling Validated versus Being Correct: A Meta-Analysis of Selective Exposure to Information," *Psychological Bulletin* 135 (2009): 555–88.

3. Russel H. Fazio, "How Do Attitudes Guide Behavior?" in *The Handbook of Motivation and Cognition: Foundations of Social Behavior*, eds. Richard M. Sorrentino and E. Tory Higgins (New York: Guilford Press, 1986).

4. Kurt Braddock and James Price Dillard, "Meta-Analytic Evidence for the Persuasive Effect of Narratives on Beliefs, Attitudes, Intentions, and Behaviors," *Communication Monographs* 83 (2016): 1–24.

5. Winston Churchill, "We Shall Fight on the Beaches," speech delivered to the House of Commons, June 4, 1940, The Churchill Centre and Museum at the Churchill War Rooms, www.winstonchurchill.org/resources /speeches/1940-the-finest-hour/we-shall-fight-on-the-beaches.

6. John S. Nelson, "Emotions as Reasons in Public Arguments," *Poroi* 4, no. 1 (2005): 1–26, doi: 10.13008/2151-2957.1028.

7. For an extensive review of the history of the field of communication from the classical period to the present era, see Dominic A. Infante, Andrew S. Rancer, and Deanna F. Womack, *Building Communication Theory*, 4th ed. (Prospect Heights, IL: Waveland Press, 2003).

8. Ojenike Bolatito, "Linkage between Persuasion Principles and Advertising," *New Media and Mass Communication* 8 (2012): 7–11.

9. Susan T. Fiske, "Core Social Motivations: Views from the Couch, Consciousness, Classroom, Computers, and Collectives," in *Handbook of Motivation Science*, eds. James Y. Shah and Wendi L. Garner (New York: Guilford Press, 2008).

10. Abraham H. Maslow, "A Theory of Human Motivation," *Psychological Review* 50 (1943): 370–96.

11. Richard Petty and John T. Cacioppo, "The Elaboration Likelihood Model of Persuasion," in *Advances in Experimental Social Psychology*, ed. L. Berkowitz (San Diego, CA: Academic Press, 1986), vol. 19: 123–205; Richard Petty and Duane T. Wegener, "Matching versus Mismatching Attitude Functions: Implications for Scrutiny of Persuasive Messages," *Personality and Social Psychology Bulletin* 24 (1998): 227–40.

12. For good reviews of the literature on source credibility in general, see Richard M. Perloff, *The Dynamics of Persuasion* (Hillsdale, NJ: Erlbaum, 1993); and Infante, Rancer, and Womack, *Building Communication Theory*; see also Joseph R. Priester and Richard E. Petty, "Source Attributions and Persuasion: Perceived Honesty as a Determinant of Message Scrutiny," *Personality and Social Psychology Bulletin* 21 (1995): 637–54.

13. Priester and Petty, "Source Attributions and Persuasion."

14. James A. McCroskey, *An Introduction to Rhetorical Communication*, 9th ed. (Boston, MA: Allyn and Bacon, 2006), 84–97.

CHAPTER 24

1. The model of argument presented here follows Stephen Toulmin, *The Uses of Argument* (New York: Cambridge University Press, 1958), as described in James C. McCroskey, *An Introduction to Rhetorical Communication*, 6th ed. (Englewood Cliffs, NJ: Prentice Hall, 1993).

2. Annette T. Rottenberg and Donna Haisty Winchell, *Elements of Argument*, 10th ed. (New York: Bedford/St. Martin's, 2012), 24–25.

3. Mike Allen, "Comparing the Persuasive Effectiveness of One- and Two-Sided Messages," in *Persuasion: Advances through Meta-Analysis*, eds. Mike Allen and Raymond W. Preiss (Cresskill, NJ: Hampton Press, 1998), 87–98.

4. James C. McCroskey, *An Introduction to Rhetorical Communication*, 9th ed. (Englewood Cliffs, NJ: Prentice Hall, 2005).

5. Herbert W. Simons, *Persuasion in Society*, 2nd ed. (New York: Routledge, 2011).

6. S. Morris Engel, *With Good Reason: An Introduction to Informal Fallacies*, 6th ed. (Boston: Bedford/St. Martin's, 2000), 191.

7. Elizabeth Sheld, "A Gun Control Analogy," *Breitbart*, January 11, 2013, www.breitbart.com/blog/2013/01/11/a-gun-control-analogy/.

8. Alan H. Monroe, *Principles and Types of Speeches* (Chicago: Scott, Foresman, 1935).

9. C. Ilie, "Strategies of Refutation by Definition: A Pragma-Rhetorical Approach to Refutations in a Public Speech," in *Pondering on Problems of Argumentation: Twenty Essays on Theoretical Issues*, eds. F. H. van Eemeren and B. Garssen (New York: Springer Science+Business Media, 2009), doi: 10.1007/978-1-4020-9165-0_4.

CHAPTER 25

1. Roger E. Axtell, *Do's and Taboos of Public Speaking: How to Get Those Butterflies Flying in Formation* (New York: Wiley, 1992), 150.

2. "Obama, Cecily Strong Joke Around at White House Correspondents' Dinner," NBC News Online, April 26, 2015, www.nbcnews.com/storyline/white-house-correspondents-dinner/watch-live-white-house-correspondents-dinner-n348366.

CHAPTER 26

1. Sheri Jeavons, "Webinars That Wow: How to Deliver a Dynamic Webinar," Webinar hosted by Citrix GoToMeeting, December 12, 2011.
2. Kami Griffiths and Chris Peters, "10 Steps for Planning a Successful Webinar," TechSoup, January 27, 2009, www.techsoup.org/learningcenter/training /page/1252.cfm; Chris Peters and Kami Griffiths, "10 Steps for Planning a Successful Webinar," TechSoup, January 31, 2012, www.techsoup.org/support/articles -and-how-tos/10-steps-for-planning-a-successful-webinar.
3. Ken Molay, "Best Practices for Webinars," Adobe Connect, www.images.adobe .com/www.adobe.com/content/dam/Adobe/en/products/adobeconnect/pdfs /web-conferencing/best-practices-webinars-wp.pdf.
4. Patricia Fripp, "15 Tips for Webinars: How to Add Impact When You Present Online," eLearn Magazine, July 7, 2009, elearnmag.acm.org/featured .cfm?aid=1595445.
5. Fripp, "15 Tips for Webinars."

CHAPTER 27

1. Discussion of group roles based on Dan O'Hair and Mary Wiemann, *Real Communication,* 4th ed. (New York: Bedford/St. Martin's, 2018), 265; C. M. Anderson, B. L. Riddle, and M. M. Martin, "Socialization in Groups," in *Handbook of Group Communication Theory and Research,* ed. Lawrence R. Frey, Dennis S. Gouran, and Marshall Scott Poole (Thousand Oaks, CA: Sage, 1999), 139–63; A. J. Salazar, "An Analysis of the Development and Evolution of Roles in the Small Group," *Small Group Research* 27 (1996): 475–503; K. D. Benne and P. Sheats, "Functional Roles of Group Members," *Journal of Social Issues* 4 (1948): 41–49.
2. W. Park, "A Comprehensive Empirical Investigation of the Relationships among Variables of the Groupthink Model," *Journal of Organizational Behavior* 21 (2000): 874–87; D. T. Miller and K. R. Morrison, "Expressing Deviant Opinions: Believing You Are in the Majority Helps," *Journal of Experimental Social Psychology* 45, no. 4 (2009): 740–47.
3. Irving Lester Janis, *Groupthink: Psychological Studies of Policy Decisions and Fiascoes* (Berkeley: University of California Press, 1982).
4. C. Pavitt, "Theorizing about the Group Communication-Leadership Relationship," in *Handbook of Group Communication Theory and Research,* ed. Frey, Gouran, and Poole, 313–34; D. S. Gouran, "Communication Skills for Group Decision Making," in *Handbook of Communication and Social Interaction Skills,* ed. J. O. Greene and B. R. Burleson (Mahwah, NJ: Erlbaum, 2003), 835–70.
5. Pavitt, "Theorizing about the Group Communication-Leadership Relationship"; Gouran, "Communication Skills for Group Decision Making."
6. Charles R. Schwenk, *Organizational Behavior and Human Decision Processes* 47, no. 1 (October 1990): 161–76.
7. L. Richard Hoffman and Norman R. F. Maier, "Valence in the Adoption of Solutions by Problem-Solving Groups: Concept, Method, and Results," *Journal of Abnormal and Social Psychology* 69 (1964): 264–71.
8. John Dewey, *How We Think* (Boston: D.C. Heath, 1950).

CHAPTER 28

1. Lin Kroeger, *The Complete Idiot's Guide to Successful Business Presentations* (New York: Alpha Books, 1997), 113.

CHAPTER 29

1. For a review, see Priscilla S. Rogers, "Distinguishing Public and Presentational Speaking," *Management Communication Quarterly* 2 (1988): 102–15; Frank E. X. Dance, "What Do You Mean 'Presentational' Speaking?" *Management Communication Quarterly* 1 (1987): 270–81.
2. Stephen Shiffman, "Ten Tips Guaranteed to Improve Sales," *American Salesman* 55 (2010): 28–30.
3. Shiffman, "Ten Tips Guaranteed to Improve Sales."
4. Sharon Cunningham, "Progress Reports," *Best's Review* (November 2010): 54.

CHAPTER 30

1. Several points are derived from Robert Anholt, *Dazzle 'Em with Style: The Art of Oral Scientific Presentation*, 2nd ed. (New York: Academic Press, 2005).
2. Office of Naval Research, "Tips for Preparing and Delivering Scientific Talks and Using Visual Aids," modified January 1, 2001, www.au.af.mil /au/awc/awcgate/navy/onr_navyspeakingtips.pdf.

CHAPTER 31

1. With thanks to Professor Calvin Young, Fullerton College, for his input.
2. Robert Anholt, *Dazzle 'Em with Style: The Art of Oral Scientific Presentation*, 2nd ed. (New York: Academic Press, 2005).

CHAPTER 32

1. Deanna P. Daniels, "Communicating across the Curriculum and in the Disciplines: Speaking in Engineering," *Communication Education* 51 (July 2002): 3.
2. Deanna P. Dannels, "Features of Success in Engineering Design Presentations: A Call for Relational Genre Knowledge," *Journal of Business and Technical Communication* 23, no. 4 (2009): 399–427, doi: 10.1177/1050651909338790.
3. H. J. Scheiber, "The Nature of Oral Presentations: A Survey of Scientific, Technical, and Managerial Presentations," *IPCC 92 Santa Fe. Crossing Frontiers. Conference Record* (September 29–October 3, 1992): 95–98, doi: 10.1109/ IPCC.1992.672998.

CHAPTER 33

1. James M. Henslin, *Sociology: A Down-to-Earth Approach*, 12th ed. (Boston: Pearson, 2013).
2. Peter Redman and Wendy Maples, *Good Essay Writing: A Social Sciences Guide*, 4th ed. (Thousand Oaks, CA: Sage, 2011).

CHAPTER 35

1. Richard L. Sullivan and Noel McIntosh, "Delivering Effective Lectures," U.S. Agency for International Development, December 1996, http://citeseerx.ist. psu.edu/viewdoc/download?doi=10.1.1.168.184&rep=rep1&type=pdf.

CHAPTER 36

1. With thanks to Patricia Gowland, RN, MSN, OCN, CCRC, Executive Director of Cancer Research and Patient Navigation, Vanguard Health, Chicago, and Associate Director of Clinical Research, University of Illinois at Chicago Cancer Center, for her expert counsel and review of presentation types.
2. J. M. Brown and N. A. Schmidt, "Strategies for Making Oral Presentations about Clinical Issues: Part I. At the Workplace," *Journal of Continuing Education in Nursing* 40, no. 4 (2009): 152–53, EBSCOhost.

APPENDIX B

1. Patricia Nelson, "Handling Questions and Answers," Toastmasters International, Edmonton and Area, revised November 3, 1999, www.ecn.ab.ca/toast /qa.html.
2. Diane DiResta, *Knockout Presentations: How to Deliver Your Message with Power, Punch, and Pizzazz* (Worcester, MA: Chandler House Press, 1998), 236.
3. DiResta, *Knockout Presentations*, 237.
4. Lillian Wilder, *Talk Your Way to Success* (New York: Eastside Publishing, 1986), 279.

APPENDIX C

1. Patricia Nelson, "Handling Questions and Answers," Toastmasters International, Edmonton and Area, revised November 3, 1999, www.ecn.ab.ca/toast/qa.html.
2. Daria Price Bowman, *Presentations: Proven Techniques for Creating Presentations that Get Results* (Holbrook, MA: Adams Media, 1998), 177.
3. Oklahoma Society of CPAs (OSCPA), "Tips for Successful Media Interviewing," accessed June 10, 2006, www.oscpa.com/Content/page757.

APPENDIX D

1. Erin Meyer, "Tailor Your Presentation to Fit the Culture," *Harvard Business Review,* October 29, 2014, hbr.org/2014/10/tailor-your-presentation-to -fit-different-cultures.
2. MaryAnn Cunningham Florez, "Improving Adult ESL Learners' Pronunciation Skills," *National Center for ESL Literacy Education,* December 1998, http://citeseerx.ist.psu.edu/viewdoc/download?doi=10.1.1.455.7982&rep =rep1&type=pdf.
3. Florez, "Improving Adult ESL Learners' Pronunciation Skills."
4. Robert Anholt, *Dazzle 'Em with Style: The Art of Oral Scientific Presentation* (New York: W. H. Freeman, 1994), 156.

Index

QUICK TIPS

SAMPLE SPEECHES

VISUAL GUIDES

CHECKLISTS

Speech Videos ●●●●

LaunchPad
macmillan learning

Go to LaunchPad: **launchpadworks.com** to find over 120 video clips, including model speech clips and "needs improvement" clips, on a variety of speech topics that show you how to improve your technique and deliver a strong, effective speech.

Here is a list of topics and the number of videos available for each one:

- ▶ Ethics (2)
- ▶ Audience Analysis (3)
- ▶ Supporting Material (14)
- ▶ Choosing a Topic (2)
- ▶ Organization (17)
- ▶ Thesis Statement (4)
- ▶ Introductions (5)
- ▶ Conclusions (6)

- ▶ Language (11)
- ▶ Methods of Delivery (7)
- ▶ Body in Delivery (2)
- ▶ Vocal Delivery (7)
- ▶ Full Speeches of Introduction (2)
- ▶ Full Informative Speeches (6)
- ▶ Full Persuasive Speeches (4)
- ▶ Full Special Occasion Speeches (2)

- ▶ Argument (12)
- ▶ Presentation Aids (7)

Contents ●●●●